THE BOOK OF
WILTON

CHRIS ROUSELL

HALSGROVE

First published in Great Britain in 2006

British Library Cataloguing-in-Publication Data
A CIP record for this title is available from the British Library

ISBN 1 84114 499 1
ISBN 978 1 84114 499 3

HALSGROVE

Halsgrove House
Lower Moor Way
Tiverton, Devon EX16 6SS
Tel: 01884 243242
Fax: 01884 243325
Email: sales@halsgrove.com
Website: www.halsgrove.com

Frontispiece photograph: *Five young Wilton boys
pose by the Market Cross in the early 1900s.
The ornament on top of the cross is a sundial.*

Printed and bound in Great Britain by CPI Bath

CONTENTS

Acknowledgements

I would like to thank the following people who have given me their help in so many different ways, with items of information, by naming names on photographs, by loaning photographs and other illustrative material and sharing personal memories from their past. Without their help this book would not have been possible.

Such people include: Nancy Morland, the late Bill Cannings, Marcia Holley, Mary Blake, David Bowes, Mike Morris, Nick Griffiths, Bill Hewlett, Bill Browne, publisher of the *Salisbury Journal*, Henry Wills, John Aston and Gordon Saunders. Special thanks, also, to the Wiltshire Heritage Museum for allowing me to reproduce photographs of their collection of coins minted in Wilton.

Special thanks to Barbara at Wilton Post Office.

Staff at the Sawmills on the Wilton Estate in the 1930s.

Introduction

Although only a small market town, Wilton has a long-established history of which it is justly proud. Its roots are well documented; the first community was a tribe of Saxons, who quickly established themselves here in the late-sixth century. The foundations of the town were laid by them, evidence clearly revealing that the layout of the central area of the town remains practically the same today.

This first community, through the years, developed into an important trading centre, the status of which was later enhanced by the building, for the kings of Wessex, of a palace – a residence for their short sojourns in the area. The town later became an important religious centre with an abbey, and later still became renowned for its making of carpets, eventually gaining world-wide acclaim for the famous Wilton weave.

From those early times to the present day many changes have taken place, each community building on the achievements of its predecessors as dictated by the requirements of progress. Today, as it will in future generations, this process continues.

A knowledge of the town's early history is important to understand the development of the town through the centuries to the present day. Mistakes have almost certainly been made, as they will be in the future, but mistakes can provide valuable lessons to future generations, who hopefully will avoid making too many to their detriment.

With a history spanning almost 2,000 centuries I have been able merely to skim the surface, but in so doing have endeavoured to present information in a way that is easy to understand. Although no records exist from very early times of how the people of Wilton used their spare time, fortunately there are records of how they worked to make their town flourish. In the thirteenth century the town's fortunes suffered a setback with the growth of New Salisbury, the city taking away much trade from Wilton which, following a long period of decline, found its fortunes reborn through the weaving industry. None of this success could have been achieved, however, without that very important aspect of any city, town or village, its community.

Communities work, communities relax with many pastimes; the many forms of leisure activity available today were, in the past, more limited. The Victorians worked long hours for very little pay, but here in Wilton they certainly knew how to let their hair down when special events or celebrations were arranged for their pleasure. When the Wessex kings visited Wilton it became known as a royal town and a Capital of Wessex, and when celebrations for coronations or royal jubilees were arranged, Victorian Wiltonians certainly celebrated in fine style, such was their high regard for royalty. Even in later years such events, including carnivals, brought out the community spirit. That same community spirit also applied in times of hardship, during the world wars as well as on many other occasions. Other important aspects of community life included education, worship and the welfare of the poor. From mid-Victorian times, the people of Wilton were given greater freedom to travel with the arrival of the railway and not one station, but two.

The fact that I was born and bred in the town has been of great advantage to me in writing this book on Wilton. As Secretary of the Wilton Historical Society since its formation in November 1977, I have built up an extensive archive from many reliable sources, in particular from one founder member, the late Grahame Moody, who gave a series of talks on the town's early history, tapes of which have provided invaluable information concerning the first settlers and the Wilton mints. From 1992 until 1997 I was privileged to broadcast, on local radio, a series on the history of South Wiltshire, many items covering Wilton, the programme research notes of which have been invaluable to me in compiling this book.

Other sources I have found useful in my research have been posters, programmes and leaflets dating back to the early 1900s, some of which were actually printed in the town by William Jukes and later by his son, Leonard, at the Wilton Printing Works in North Street. One or two of the very early items printed by William were in full colour – quite an achievement for a small printer in those early times, revealing how highly skilled he was at his trade. Another of my sources was old trade directories, in particular one from 1851 listing all shops and businesses in Wilton at that time but now no longer in existence. Indeed looking at West Street and North Street today, many of these shops have been converted into dwellings, although there are still some tell-tale signs of their former use.

It is not only words that can reveal life in the past; photography also plays an important role, revealing many fascinating aspects, especially in the street scenes, of how the town looked in years gone by. Not only do they reveal features that no longer exist, they also show those people, dressed in the fashions of the day, who were caught on camera and are now preserved for future generations to see.

Naturally, with such a long history, one has to be selective, but I have made every effort to give a balanced account of the history of Wilton and its community, and of how it has evolved through the centuries, from the first band of Saxon settlers to the town it is today.

To have been commissioned to write this book has been a great privilege for me. It has given me a chance to offer something back to the town, where I was born and have lived, and to its inhabitants.

In conclusion, I wish to thank the following: Katy Charge, my commissioning editor, for her help and advice with any queries that arose at the compiling stage; the rest of the Halsgrove team who, during the preparation for publishing, have given me their full support; and finally, the most important person in my life, my wife Judy, who has patiently put up with my disappearing for hours on end in order to complete this book.

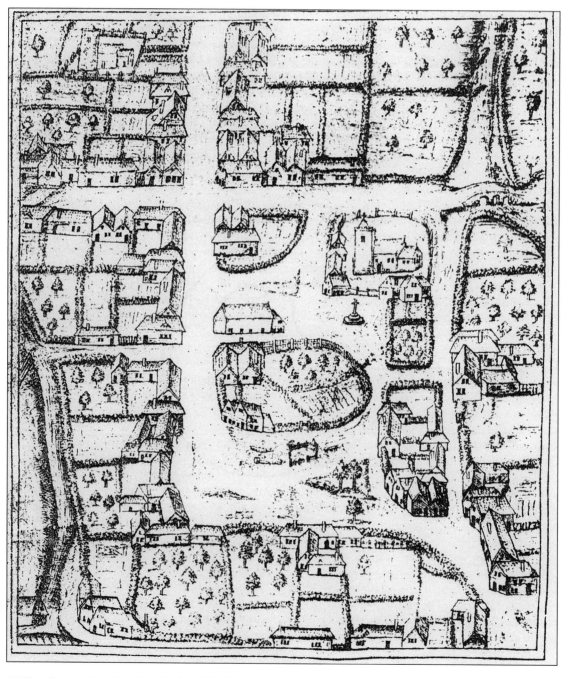

Wilton from a drawing done for Lord Pembroke, c.1568.

✦ CHAPTER 1 ✦

The Foundations of Wilton

Standing at the crossroads in the centre of Wilton known locally as 'Four Corners', at the historic core of the town, looking up West Street and the adjoining North Street and South Street, the buildings that you see can only reveal the town as it is today. Beneath their foundations, however, under the modern tarmac roads, lies the early hidden history of this ancient market town, the soil on which Wilton was founded, the soil on which the footprints of the first settlers were made, where they built their crude huts and made this area their new home. Little did these people realise how, centuries later, the site they had chosen would grow into a town which, today, has just over 4,000 inhabitants.

Who were these people? Where did they come from and what attracted them to settle here?

Prior to the arrival of these first settlers, the country was experiencing attacks from the continent. At first only hit-and-run affairs, when the invaders encountered little resistance they became bolder and increased their numbers. One band of raiders, led by Cerdric and his son Cyndric, Saxon chiefs from Germany, landed in considerable force in the year 514 on the shores which we know today as Southampton Water, the tribe then moving to a settlement at Winchester. In 519 they moved to Downton and, not long afterwards, some moved to this area. Here they found all the conditions that made it a site conducive to settlement. The two rivers, today known as the Wylye and the Nadder, would have provided plenty of fresh water, trees were in abundance and, most importantly, the soil between the rivers was extremely fertile, as it still is today.

To make the settlement habitable they had to clear the trees from the area which today lies between St John's Square and Fugglestone, then from what is now the far end of South Street and the bottom end of North Street. Thus the two rivers formed natural boundaries, while at the vulnerable western and eastern ends it is more than likely that palisades were built as extra protection. Further protection was also provided by the high downlands, which formed natural fortifications.

One interesting fact that emerges is that the Saxons continued to use the names given to the rivers by the ancient Britons. The name Nadder, which river, at the southern end of the town, winds it way through the valley like a snake, is a modern derivative of the Anglo-Saxon word *nadjra*, meaning snake. The name Wylye, the river at the northern end, appears to have been derived from the ancient British

wylig, or willow tree. The Saxons took their name from the River Wylye, becoming known as the *Wil Satees*, the latter word, meaning 'dweller of', being found all over the West of England. The tribe gave its name to the surrounding area. It is generally accepted that the county of Wiltshire derives its name from this settlement and that the town of Wilton stands on the site once occupied by these people. Reference to these early settlers was made by Bede, a monk of Jarrow who wrote a history of this period which was discovered when Alfred translated the work from Latin to English. Bede mentioned a tribe of Saxons, people of royal lineage living in an area from Winchester and to the west. This does make sense, as there are distinct links between Winchester and Wilton, proved by charters which still exist and bear out these facts. It did not take long for the Saxons to consolidate in the area, causing the settlement to grow and, reputedly, in the late-seventh century, Wilton became a royal town. This is backed by evidence from the ninth century which reveals that it was established as such. In these times Wilton was in the Kingdom of Wessex and, being a royal town, would have had a palace, enabling the king to rest here on his travels through his kingdom and to receive his subjects. The palace would most likely have been in the area known today as Kingsbury Square, Kingsbury meaning, 'the stronghold of the king'. By no means a large, ornate building, it is likely to have been built of wood rather than stone and would have been just large enough to accommodate the king and those who travelled with him.

In front of the palace and its grounds was an open market area surrounded by houses and a small minster church, the site of which is now occupied by the ruined Church of St Mary in the Market Place. The royal archives were kept here and on occasion the king would issue various documents and charters. One such occasion was in 854, when Ethelwulph granted the famous charter for the institution of titles, shown here in full:

I Ethelwulph, by the Grace of God, king of the West Saxons, by the advice of the Bishops, Earls and other persons of distinction, for the health of my soul, the good of my people and the prosperity of my kingdom, taken the prudent and serviceable resolution of granting the tenth part of my lands throughout the whole kingdom, to the Churches and ministers of religion, to be enjoyed by them with all the privileges of free tenure, and discharged from all services due to the crown, and all encumbrances incidental to lay fees.

This gift has been made by us to the church in honour of Jesus Christ the blessed Virgin and all Saints, and out of regard to the Paschal solemnity, and that of Almighty God might vouchsafe his blessing to us and our posterity.

Dated at the Palace of Wilton in the year 854, indication the second, at feast of Easter

The document, drawn up by the Great Council when they met at Winchester earlier in the year, was the result of their deliberations and only came into force when signed by the king at Wilton, as shown above. Exactly why Wilton was chosen to become a royal town is not really known. It could merely have been a convenient resting place for the king on his journeys through his Wessex kingdom or after a journey from Winchester, or perhaps, more likely, it could be due to the fact that his subjects here, as we know, were of royal lineage. Whatever the reason, being a royal town did have its drawbacks, as the presence of royalty led to many attacks from the Danes, on which occasions they sacked and burned the town.

Before the foundation of the abbey there was already an ecclesiastical presence in Wilton, the first religious establishment being recorded in about 773. This, a chantry for secular priests, was founded by Wulstan, the first recorded Earl of Wiltshire, by converting an old church, St Mary's, and dedicating it to his own soul and that of the martyr Alquimund. In his book *The Beauties of Wiltshire* (vol.1), John Britton states that in 773 Wulstan repaired an old church called St Mary's and converted it into a college or chantry for secular priests. According to a fifteenth-century chronicle, written about 600 years

later, it was founded to celebrate a victory over the King of Mercia.

When Wulstan died of wounds sustained in battle, his wife Alburga, sister of King Egbert, persuaded the king to transform the chantry into a priory for 13 nuns, which she dedicated to St Mary. Alburga assumed the mantle and the ring, and in so doing became the first Prioress of Wilton. The priory was of the Benedictine order and the nuns were dedicated to life-long celibacy. King Alfred later founded another religious establishment for women, which took two years to build and was situated near the palace in Kingsbury Square. This building was dedicated to St Mary and St Bartholomew.

In the year 871 at Wilton, between King Alfred and the Danes, a fierce battle took place on high ground, now part of the boundary of Wilton House, which at that time would have been near to the king's palace. Although Alfred succeeded in repulsing the Danes, they rallied again, sacking and burning the town. The king's initial victory, however, was not without great cost to himself, as the following story sadly relates. This version appears in the *Chronicon*, in which much of Wilton's early history is written in the form of a poem. Considered to be perhaps the most accurate account of Wilton's early history, the *Chronicon* was written many years after the event and it is possible that legend is intermingled with fact. This story, however, is well worth the telling.

During all the activity and turmoil of battle, a nurse who was bathing the king's three-year-old grandchild, became frightened and fled the palace, leaving the infant to drown in the bath. It is here that records digress, one source claiming that it was the king's grandson who died, while the *Chronicon*

On the back of this photograph is written, 'Last remains of the original Monastery, Wilton Park'. As the building has a slate roof, it is likely that the stone remains have been incorporated into the building and the wall, along with more modern bricks.

In the same envelope, given to me by an eminent local historian, was this photograph, presumably showing more of the original monastery's remains.

claims that it was his granddaughter, Princess Elfrida. When King Alfred learned of the tragedy he was so filled with remorse that he eventually had the palace pulled down and an abbey built, on the site of which, today, stands Wilton House.

The first abbess was Radegund, who founded the establishment with 12 'maydones', to which were added at later date, the prioress and 13 nuns from the priory. During the succeeding years the abbey grew in wealth and power and was highly regarded as a centre of education for the daughters of noblemen and Saxon princesses. They were taught needlework and the art of confectionery, as well as surgery, physic, writing and drawing. Surgery and physic were taught so that, there being no doctors as we know them today, some form of treatment for the sick could be provided at such religious establishments.

During the year 960 King Edgar, visiting Wilton, stayed at the abbey, where he met and seduced a beautiful young girl, Wulfrith, who was receiving her education there.

While dining at the abbey the king heard Wulfrith reading the lesson at the lectern, the sweetness of her voice attracting him. To protect herself from his amorous advances Wulfrith wore a veil, which she had not yet ceremoniously assumed. This did not deter the king, however, and not long after his visit Wulfrith retired to Kemsing in Kent, at that time in possession of the abbey, where she later gave birth to a daughter, Edith. St Dunstan made Edgar pay a penance for violating the sanctity of the cloister, despite the fact that Wulfrith had not yet taken the veil. After the death of his wife, Edgar tried to marry Wulfrith, who instead chose to take the veil, which she received from St Ethelwold, and return to Wilton with her daughter, to whom she was devoted, bringing her up with strict monastic discipline.

Edith spent the rest of her life at the abbey, where she played an important role and became skilled at singing, writing, painting, embroidery, music and sculpture. She was also meek and full of charity and

self denial. Although, according to some sources, Edith became abbess, this is most unlikely as she died before her mother, who later herself became abbess at Wilton. It is said, however, that her father, King Edgar, appointed her Abbess of Winchester and of two other monasteries, positions offered to her when she was only 15. Edith declined any position of authority, choosing to stay at Wilton with her mother.

At Wilton Edith built a wooden chapel in the abbey grounds which she dedicated to St Denis. What is reputed to be the chapel built by Edith is described as follows:

It had before it, with small entrance gates, on which were set cross-wise three crosses of right good painting of the Passion and Sepulchre of our Lord and the image of St Denis, in gold and asure and other colours. The walls were 'right royally' painted, also with gold, asure and many other colours.

Unfortunately, Edith's life was only a short one. At the tender age of 23, on 16 September 984, she died of a fever and was buried in the chapel that she had built, her early death having been foretold by St Dunstan when he had consecrated her chapel. After a period of 13 years Edith's body was removed from the chapel and placed in a tomb in the abbey, at which time she was canonised by St Dunstan and the chapel was rededicated in her name. St Edith is reputed to have had miraculous powers after her death and her tomb became a shrine for pilgrims throughout the tenth and eleventh centuries.

Soon after 986, Edith's mother, Wulfrith, became abbess, a position she held for some years. During her time as abbess two very strange incidents took place. The first occurred when she was offering hospitality to holy men who were travelling with a casket containing the bones of a Welsh saint. During their overnight stay, the casket was placed on the church altar and the next morning, when the holy men went to fetch the casket, it was so firmly fixed that they were unable to pick it up; no matter how hard they tried, no force was able to move it. There was no physical reason why the casket could not be removed, it was a complete mystery, but it is thought that Wulfrith could have been involved in the mysteries of magnetism, or that the gratuity to the holy men of 2,000s. so paralysed them that they were unable to move it.

The second strange occurrence concerns a nail. At the Abbey of Treves was preserved a nail allegedly used at the Crucifixion. Wulfrith, desirous of having a fragment of this nail, negotiated with a canon of Treves to purchase a piece for the sum of 2,000s. Her offer was accepted. After its arrival at Wilton, St Adewold, Bishop of Winchester, also requested a fragment of it, to which Wulfrith gave her consent. As they started to cut a piece off, it bled copiously, filling the chalice in which it had been placed with blood. The bishop was 'aghast' and the nuns, very frightened, fled the scene and fell into prayer. From the *Chronicon* comes the verse:

On the morrow tide at break of day,
To the Altar hied they full fast,
But the nail entire in the chalice lay,
and the blood was clean to heaven up-sent.

The abbey continued to prosper, receiving numerous gifts from benefactors in the first 200 years of its existence, eventually becoming the richest nunnery in England. It held lands over a wide area, even on the Isle of Wight, bestowed by pious Christians.

According to a charter dated AD892–1045, King Edwy, who was regarded as hostile to the Church, gave a grant more splendid than any before it. By a charter dated AD955, he granted:

... for himself and his ancestors, one hundred hides of land at Chalke, to God Almighty, St Mary and the venerable congregation in the Minster at Wilton.

He also stipulated that the land should be free of all secular burdens and strictly forbade anyone, so long as Christianity should flourish, to violate this grant. By modern standards, the amount of land he gave could not be less than 10,000 acres. Despite this magnificent grant, however, King Edwy is not recognised among the benefactors of the abbey. During its last 150 years the abbey's power and possessions dwindled, not least in later years with the influence of King Henry VIII and Cardinal Wolsey. Eventually, on 25 March 1539, the then abbess, Celia Bodenham, surrendered the abbey and its lands to the king. St Edith is remembered in Wilton to this day, as she was made the town's patron saint.

With the dissolution of the abbey, Henry VIII granted the lands to William, eldest son of Richard Herbert, whose family, of Welsh origin, was prominent in Glamorgan and Monmouth in the latter part of the fifteenth century. William's courage while fighting in France had brought him favour with Francis I who, in turn, had recommended him to King Henry VIII.

Returning to England, William had married Anne Parr, sister to Catherine Parr, the sixth wife of Henry VIII who, in 1542, granted William a coat of arms and a crest. Two years later he was granted Wilton Abbey and all its lands. Immediately he set about demolishing the abbey, using the stone to build a house for himself on the same site. This grand house was built around a courtyard, and was completed in 1550. William was made Lord Herbert of Cardiff and Earl of Pembroke in October of the following year, thus beginning the family line at Wilton.

In 1552 he entertained Edward I, the first royal visitor to the house and, after the king's death a year later, William continued to find royal favour through the subsequent reigns of Mary and Elizabeth, enabling him to wield considerable power at court. He died at Hampton Court in 1570.

William was succeeded by his eldest son, Henry, who, in the seventeenth century, made substantial alterations to the house, taking advice from the great architect and designer Inigo Jones. At this time the family became well known for its patronage of the arts through Henry's wife Mary Sidney. Many learned people of the period became regular visitors to the house, including Philip Massenger, Ben Jonson, Samuel Daniel, and Edmund Spencer. Sir Philip Sidney, Mary's brother, also spent much of his time at the house, where he is reputed to have written *Arcadia*, dictating it to his sister.

Tradition has it that Shakespeare and his company of players gave the first performance of *As You Like It* at Wilton House in 1603 in the presence of King James I. It is also thought that *Twelfth Night* was first performed there.

A disastrous fire destroyed much of the house in 1647 and it is believed Inigo Jones was involved in the rebuilding, although much of the work was probably done by his nephew, John Webb. Early in the nineteenth century the eleventh Earl employed James Wyatt in a programme of extensive rebuilding and redesign, internally and externally. Although the Wilton House we see today is the result of several periods of reconstruction, it is thought likely that the overall shape and much of the masonry correspond closely to Herbert's original design; the architectural detail, however, has been completely changed.

Naturally, the abbey dominated the religious life of the town. During its existence it has been recorded that there were 12 churches in Wilton, in addition to the churches or chapels attached to the three hospitals that were established here. However, many of these 'churches' were simply meeting or prayer houses and considered churches only in the broadest sense; churches of any importance were situated in the centre of the town. All were shown in the episcopal registers of the fifteenth century.

The sites of some churches are quite easy to establish, while the reminder can only be approximately located. In the area of the Market Place stood the Church of the Holy Trinity, probably situated opposite the Guildhall, as records reveal that this was the church of the guild merchants, established in the twelfth century. As a guild church it was important to the town, as it would have been used widely by the burgesses and for elections, particularly of the mayor. It was still in existence in the sixteenth century, when a town ordinance required the burgesses to attend at the Council House, or at the Church of the Holy Trinity, when ordered to assemble by the ringing of the greatest bell of the church. It seems that the church had a dual purpose, in that there were times when it doubled as a meeting-house. By 1568 it had simply fallen into decay and completely disappeared. Another church considered of great importance was St Michael's in South Street. This was in existence in 1200, records showing that Henry, son of Gospatrick of Wilton, was born at Wilton and baptised in this church. During the sixteenth century St Michael's fell into disrepair and disappeared, no trace of it ever having been found. There were at least three churches in West Street: St Nicholas's, St Mary's and St Andrew's, the latter thought to have been situated at what in 2006 is St Andrew's House, opposite Crow Lane. St Mary's is thought to have been higher up West Street, approximately 100 yards down from the Priory Church, near the one-time Uphill's shop and workshop. There is one strange fact concerning the Church of St Andrew. In the taxation of Pope Nicholas, it is shown as a rectory of Ditchampton, returned as being under value, although it is not in the area of the town known by that name and has only ever been known as the Church of St Andrew. St Mary's, possibly on the opposite side of the road a little further down, is recorded as an ancient rectory, of which the abbess was patron. The site of the Church of St Nicholas is recognised as having been very near, or possibly on the site of the present Parish Church of St Mary and St Nicholas. The evidence for this is very strong, remains from the former churchyard having been found when the foundations were dug for the new building. After completion of the new church, the bones were reinterred in the sarcophagus on the west wall outside the church. During the thirteenth century a community of friar preachers built a church in West Street, which was attached to meadow land known as Friar's Mead. They were here only for a short period before deciding to set up a community in Salisbury, leaving a much reduced presence behind in the town.

The Church of St Nicholas in Atrio is believed to have been situated in the Market Place, or at least very near to it, but from an early date the rectory was appropriated by the abbey and devoted to the nuns' pittances. In the year 1366, with the church in a ruinous state, parishioners were temporarily placed under the care of the rector of St Andrew's, Ditchampton. With its rebuilding looking likely, in 1435 it was united with the Church of St Michael, Kingsbury, a licence to restore it was granted ten years later and eventually it was completely restored. As it was considered to be abbey property, it passed at the Dissolution. St Michael's, in Kingsbury, under the patronage of the Crown, was in existence by 1226, though no reference to it can be found after it was united with St Nicholas in Atrio.

The Church of St Edward is the most obscure of all the town's churches, the only evidence of it being in a return of 1383, where it is described as a rectory in Wilton. Another church, known as the Conventual Church of St Edith, was governed by the abbess and situated on or very near the site where Wilton House now stands.

St Mary's, in Brede Street, situated where, in 2006, the bus stop stands in the Market Place, continued to maintain its importance. Originally a minster church it was rebuilt and by the end of the sixteenth century all remaining churches had been united with St Mary's, which then became the Parish Church.

The old Almshouse of St Giles, which stood on on the site of the ancient Hospital of St Giles.

The Priory Church of St John. This is approximately how the church and buildings would have looked not long after building. Late twelfth, early thirteenth century.

The Priory Church of St John, 2006. The area on the right is now known as St John's Square.

The Priory Church of St John from the other side. The double windows at the top still remain, the two features left of the central buttress are long gone, leaving a stone wall, while the feature on the right has also been filled in. The only other alteration is to the pitch of the roof, which is now pointed. The wall to the right is now slightly lower. Behind this wall, at the base of the building, was found a Saxon pillar, which remains visible. Late twelfth, early thirteenth century.

The Priory or Hospital of St John, at the far end of West Street, was founded by Hubert Water, Bishop of Sarum during the reign of Richard I, between the years 1189 and 1193. The original foundation was for a priory supporting two poor men and two poor women and at the time of the Reformation was considered more a charitable venture than a religious one and was therefore not dissolved. The prior, a clergyman, was nominated by the Dean of Sarum and the poor people were nominated by the prior. They were supplied with clothing every other year, their allowance being £4.10s.6d. per annum for maintenance and firing, paid at the rate of £1 to each per quarter plus 10s. in the winter quarter for firing. It is supposed that the establishment was formerly dependent to some extent on the Knights Hospitallers of Jerusalem. The small priory church still stands on the corner of Shaftesbury Road and West Street, opposite St John's Square near the Bell Inn. The houses associated with the charity still stand today and are let at a nominal rent.

The Hospital of St Giles, founded in the 1100s, is thought to have been founded by Adelicia, wife of King Henry I, and is also known as the leper hospital, having gained the name when the queen, known locally as the 'leper queen', herself caught the disease. In those times leprosy was endemic in the country, so the story has a ring of truth about it, although other skin diseases were often diagnosed as leprosy. According to John Aubrey, the queen was

The Saxon pillar of St John's Priory Church.

buried in the hospital chapel, the tomb and the inscription on it being seen there as late as 1684. It is said that an apparition of the queen can be seen walking the Fugglestone Road to this day – the leper hospital was situated just inside the park wall, opposite the small housing estate where the old Police Station once stood. When leprosy was eventually brought under control, the hospital reverted to its intended role of providing for the poor, a service which the charity still provides in its present situation, at the time of writing in the Warminster Road opposite the recreation ground.

In 1349 the Black Death swept through the town with grave consequences. The narrow streets echoed

A coin of Edward the Martyr, AD975–79. The head side (left) shows the inscription +EADPEARDREXANGLO (Edward, King of the English) while the reverse (right) reads BOIA M(oneta) o(n) Pilton (Boia, moneyer at Wilton), the name of the moneyer who minted the coin. The runic was used because there was no W in the Roman alphabet. Although looking like a P, the top part was triangular in shape. Boia is possibly an Irish name.

(COPYRIGHT WILTSHIRE HERITAGE MUSEUM)

A coin of Harold II, AD1066. That this is less clear than the coin above could be for two reasons, either it was not minted correctly, as some were circulated in this manner, or it is worn through use. The obverse is inscribed + HAROL-DREXANGL, (Harold King of the English), while on the reverse is the name of the moneyer, AELFPOLD on PILTI (Alfwold at Wilton), Pilti being short for Wiltuni. (PAX in the centre means peace). The triangular runic was still in use in 1066.

(COPYRIGHT WILTSHIRE HERITAGE MUSEUM)

to the ring of horses' hooves, the crunch of the carts' wheels on the hard dirt roads and the cry of, 'Bring out your dead'. No family was left untouched and there was no cure for this highly contagious disease. Because the houses were so close together, the disease quickly swept through the town, it later being estimated that around a third of the inhabitants had died very quickly. Wilton was hit very hard, evidenced by the discovery in later years of numerous human bones that were dug up in the centre of the town. The bodies were buried in large

pits without proper ceremony, many priests having been themselves struck down. But this was not to be the end of the plague; in the next 200 years the disease returned to the town no less than three times.

Wilton also became important in quite another way during the time of the abbey, in respect of the king holding the town. Coins were minted here from the reign of King Edgar, in about 959, continuing until the reign of Henry III when, in 1250, most of the provincial mints were closed.

It has been established that the mints were likely

Trade tokens, of which nearly 300 different designs were struck in Wiltshire at this time, three by Wilton tradesmen. Two were halfpennies, issued in 1667 by William Newman, a weaver, and by Stephen Brassier. A third, also a halfpenny, was struck in 1666 by an unidentified man with the initials G.H. Those illustrated are by Stephen Brassier, the obverse bearing his name and, in the centre, his initials with the letter, H which probably denotes his trade. On the reverse the circular inscription simply reads, 'Wilton in Wiltsheer'. Tokens were finally banned by Royal Proclamation in 1672.

(COPYRIGHT WILTSHIRE HERITAGE MUSEUM)

to have been situated in Russell Street, evidence of them having been found a number of years ago when workmen were putting in a new drainage system. Records also show that there were a number of mints working independently, all of them very close to one other. These were stone buildings, offering better security – a feature which would have been as important then as it is today. The coins were made of silver, their size, weight and quality having to conform to standards approved by the king. The penalty for making coins of an incorrect weight or of inferior quality was severe, and it was an unpardonable offence to make false declarations of the number of coins made. It is recorded that one of the penalties imposed was that the hands of the money makers be severed at the wrists. From time to time the king would collect his just dues, often referred to as 'the third penny' – a form of tax on the borough due to the king for allowing the minting to take place.

With the exception of the early coins of Edgar and one of Ethelred II, all bore the portrait of the king with his name on one side. On the other side were the names of the moneyer and the place where the coin was made. These coins show quite clearly the name 'Wiltun', which was the spelling of the period, also confirming that that coins were minted here. From time to time the king issued different sets of dies, today we would refer to them as types. This occurred on six occasions during the reign of Ethelred II and another six in the reign of King Canute. During the reign of Edward the Confessor, ten changes were made. It is interesting to note that towards the end of the reign King Ethelred and the beginning of that of King Canute, no coins were minted in Wilton. This point is covered in an Anglo-Saxon chronicle, which tells of the sacking of Wilton in reprisal for the massacre of St Brice's Day in 1002. The chronicle reports the Danes as sweeping across the country, sacking Wilton and burning it to the ground. This being in 1003, there can be no doubt that it was for this reason that minting in Wilton came to a sudden end and did not commence again until shortly after King Canute came to the throne.

With the internal trade of England developing, much of the currency made in other parts of the country, as well as at Wilton, was used to pay off the invading Danes. We know they were paid in local coinage of the day and took large quantities back with them to Scandinavia, this borne out by finds in Denmark and Sweden of many hoards containing Anglo-Saxon coins, among them a great number of Wilton coins.

An interesting document lists the officials required at the mint in 1247, when there were four moneyers, two named William, the third named Hugh and the fourth John. There were also two men to prepare the silver, another four to assist in the making of coins and one clerk to make a record of the coins made. This, of course, would have been the number of men employed at each mint, those named, being the actual moneyers. It is also surprising to find more than one moneyer working at the same time in a place the size of Wilton. However, this was in fact the case, as during the reign of Edward the Confessor no fewer than six moneyers were making coins in Wilton.

A mayoral procession on the occasion of the mayor's Civic Sunday, when, just after taking office, one of his first engagements is a special service held in the Parish Church. On this occasion, in June 1988, the mayor, Brian Henley, with the town clerk and members of the Town Council, are led by mace-bearers Chris Rousell (far left) and by Ted Williams along West Street to the service.

The mayor waiting at the Michael Herbert Hall to receive his guests for a reception following the service.

At one point during the reign of Edward the Confessor, coins bore not the profile of the king, but an image of him seated on a throne. Due to the difficulties of striking this complicated design, these coins were often distorted and grotesque in appearance and the design was eventually discontinued, reverting to that of the king's profile.

Despite the growing prosperity of Salisbury, just a few miles away, mints in Wilton continued production through the reign of Henry II and that of Henry VIII until 1250, at which time, by royal decree, nearly all the provincial mints were closed, including those at Wilton.

From its humble origins the town quickly established itself as a centre of communications. By gradually commanding a river crossing, it began to link settlements lying along the river valleys of the Nadder in the west, the Wylye in the north and others in the area of the River Avon, all of them early Saxon trade routes leading into the town. One route, from South Burcombe, entered the town over Bullbridge, 'Port Herepath' (South Street) the other from the Avon Valley, 'Theod Herewith' (North Street). Widan Street is also known to have been in existence in 988, although its location is not known. In later times of economic prosperity, a strong Jewish community was established.

Trades were later to include glovemakers, goldsmiths, skinners, dubbers, tanners and needleworkers. There is also some evidence to suggest there was a small group of linen workers. Wilton became well known for its needle making, subsequent excavations over the years leading to the discovery of needles buried in the ground. The

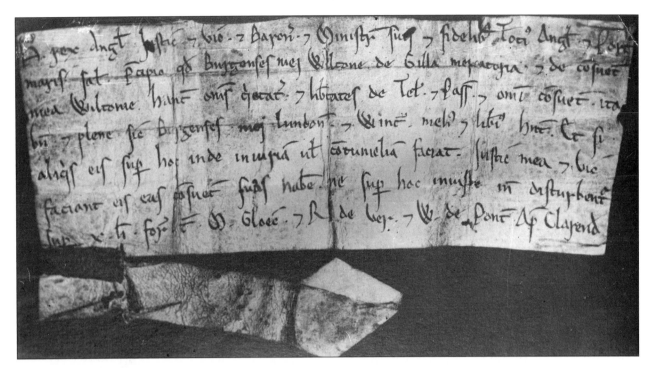

The royal charter granted to Wilton in the year 1100 by King Henry I in the first year of his reign. The translation is as follows: 'Henry King of the English to his Justiciars and his Sheriffs and his Ministers, and faithful subjects of all England, and the Ports of the sea, greeting. I command that my Burgesses at Wilton, may have all the immunities and liberties of toll and passage, and all their customs, as well, and freely as my Burgesses of London and Winchester better and more freely possess. And if anyone in this behalf cause them to have these their customs and not allow them to be unjustly interfered with in this behalf, on the penalty of ten pounds. Witnesses: Milo of Gloucester, Robert de Vere and William de Ponteach at Clarendon.'

largest groups appear to have been the glovers and the needleworkers, each having their own quarter in the town, borne out by street names of the period, Glover Street, Nedlers Street and Nedlers Bridge, all now disappeared along with all trace of their locations. There were also a number of tailors working here, their guild surviving until around the mid-fifteenth century.

Markets and fairs attracted merchants bringing fish, meat, cloth and many other items of merchandise, often including oxen, grain and iron. Many purchases made at the market, due to the presence of royalty in the area, were by appointed purveyors on behalf of the king. Traders came from nearby settlements or from places further afield, including Winchester, Dorchester, Sherborne and Bristol. With Wilton becoming a centre for the distributive trade in wine, brewing became an important activity, operating as a cottage industry in many houses. An occupation practised by all classes of society, cider and ale were produced and sold, many of the producers being women. Later in the fifteenth century, such was the output that the mayor and burgesses decided to limit the the days on which the brewers could actually brew. By the end of the thirteenth century there was an abundance of bakers, with 14 establishments in operation. Although the trade was governed by strict regulations, it seems these were often flouted by the bakers, 14 of them at

one time being heavily fined for not obeying the rules. For the one or two who did not learn their lesson, committing second and third offences, the fines were heavier for each subsequent offence.

In the early part of the thirteenth century, Salisbury was developing fast, which was to prove a bad omen for Wilton's prosperity. In 1244 Bishop Bingham had a bridge built at Harnham, on the outskirts of the city, enabling it to be accessed more directly. Realising that Wilton was about to lose a good deal of trade, Wilton merchants were in no mood to accept defeat gracefully and laid in wait on the road armed with cudgels, they also blocked the new bridge. When these tactics failed, they used blackmail, forcing the merchants to pay compensation to their counterparts at Wilton. All their efforts were in vain, however, and the town began a rapid decline. Wilton was granted exclusive rights to hold three markets a week, with an exclusion zone (which included Salisbury) on the days that they were open, but rules were soon disobeyed. Salisbury had been granted a market on only one day a week, but it was not long before it started to hold markets on the same days as Wilton. This led to a feud between the town and the city which eventually left Wilton without any markets at all. The decline had really set in by the middle of the fifteenth century; churches were falling into decay, as were the unoccupied tenement houses, and bridges were in a state of disrepair. Guild rents

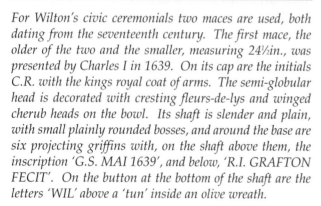

For Wilton's civic ceremonials two maces are used, both dating from the seventeenth century. The first mace, the older of the two and the smaller, measuring 24½in., was presented by Charles I in 1639. On its cap are the initials C.R. with the kings royal coat of arms. The semi-globular head is decorated with cresting fleurs-de-lys and winged cherub heads on the bowl. Its shaft is slender and plain, with small plainly rounded bosses, and around the base are six projecting griffins with, on the shaft above them, the inscription 'G.S. MAI 1639', and below, 'R.I. GRAFTON FECIT'. On the button at the bottom of the shaft are the letters 'WIL' above a 'tun' inside an olive wreath.

The second mace, known as 'The Great Mace', measures 37½in. in length, being a fine example of the ornate type of later mace. The head has the usual arched crown with the royal arms on the cap. Winged armless caryatids divide the compartments of the bowl. The bosses are chased with leafwork, and the shaft decorated with a spiral pattern of roses, fleurs-de-lys and thistles. On the foot is inscribed 'To Wilton in ye first yeare of ye reign of King James ye II. Ano Don 1685', followed by the maker's name, Oliver Nicholas Esq. The spelling is of the time.

fell and the rents of stallholders were reduced but, due to lack of trade, the stalls were abandoned. Nearly all the crafts had disappeared with the exception of the textile industry, which was growing in importance by the middle of the sixteenth century. The families of clothiers were to become the eventual saviours of the town. Although both narrowcloth and broadcloth were being made, by the early-eighteenth century broadcloth had taken over and would prove to be Wilton's salvation putting an end to the age of decline. This reversal of fortunes was further aided by experiments with special coverings for floors, known as 'drugget'. At this stage there was no pile, simply a much thicker weave than that used for cloth. The new coverings could also be coloured, as a result of which the new commodity became popular, finding its way into the homes of the monied classes. Drugget was also used for wall coverings and upholstery. Such was the success of the weaving industry in Wilton at this time that the weavers were granted a charter by William III which protected their business from unfair competition from unskilled workers cashing in with badly produced cloth. Later this protection was extended to the carpet weavers, who eventually formed their own Weavers Guild.

During the time that Wilton had borough status it was granted no less than 15 royal charters. The first, granted by King Henry I in the year 1100, is thought to be one of the oldest charters in the country. Other charters were granted by various monarchs through the years, the final one being granted by Queen Victoria in 1885.

Mayors of the town can be traced back as far as 1256, the mayor at that time being a rather dubious character. He was arrested along with one Abraham Russell, a leading figure in the Jewish community now firmly established in the town. Wilton was one of 27 centres in the country which held chests on behalf of the Jews for the registration of debts that were owed to them. Russell and the mayor, one William Isembard, were removed from the keepership of the chest for fraudulent practices. Russell managed to escape, but the mayor stood trial and, on being found guilty, was hanged in London.

Another mayor, Robert de Brudecombe, who held office from 1282 to 1299 and again in 1311, had written between his terms of office what has generally become known as *The Mayor's Common Place Book*.

A sketch of the interior of the original council chamber in the Town Hall before its move in the late 1940s. The oak chest shown was used for keeping council documents, and was secured with five padlocks, of which four keys were separately held by four aldermen with the fifth held by the mayor. This ensured that at least five persons had to be present when the chest was opened. The chest, its lid carved from half a tree trunk, stands today in the present council chamber, but no longer contains any documents.

The present council chamber, a former masonic hall, retains the original partition from the old chamber, with the mayoral chair set in the centre. The two large pictures either side of the chair are of William and Mary, while the picture in the centre above the chair is of the Wilton insignia. On the dummy (right) is the uniform of the former Wilton Free School, which has since been given to Salisbury Museum. The bust on the column is that of Sidney Herbert. The oak chest is just visible (bottom right).

An illustration from the Luttrell Psalter, c.1340. This depiction of 'The Coronation of the Virgin' perhaps helps answer the mystery, when it is compared with the early mayor's seal of 1430 (below) as it reveals the insignia is based on religious origins.

The Wilton insignia that hangs above the mayoral chair. There is doubt as to who these figures represent, one theory being that the man is King Edgar and the woman, her hands clasped in prayer, the Abbess Wulfrith. They could also be King Edward III, the other his Queen. The design of the insignia, was partly based on the design of seals of the abbesses of Wilton.

Written on fine vellum in several fourteenth-century hands, it measured a mere 8in. by 6ins. With the exception of the first four lines in early English verse, the remainder was written in Latin or Norman French, languages at the time considered necessary for an educated person. It was later translated into a type of Chaucerian English, with a Wiltshire accent, language as used by the man in the street.

The book covered many useful subjects then considered to be important, including 'matters and circumstances profitable and harmful to most organs of the body.' It also contained various prayers and meditations, lists of lucky and unlucky days, copies of documents concerning affairs of the Corporation of Wilton and various remedies and prescriptions, from a cure for fevers to assurances of success in love.

The long lists of Wilton's mayors can be divided into three sections. The first section, up to 1885, is known as the old corporation because when a new charter was granted in that year, one of the conditions was that a new corporation be elected. This new body remained in office until local government reorganisation in 1974, when Wilton lost its borough status and handed over its affairs to the new Salisbury District Council. However, Wilton retained a town council to look after its interests and, due to its ancient and historic past, was still able to retain its mayor and continue a history of which it is proud.

The Mayor of Wilton's seal, 1430.

CHAPTER 2

Trade and Industry

The Carpet Factory

A factory for making carpets was well established in Wilton by 1700. Situated in the centre of the town on the site of the Health Centre in the Market Place, it was owned by Moody & Barford. There was also a smaller carpet factory in Kingsbury Square, owned by Henry Blackmore, but it was the former partnership that was to come to the fore of carpet making in Wilton.

With the weavers protected by the charter granted by William III, the factory was, in effect, under royal patronage, and soon found a warm supporter in Thomas, eighth Earl of Pembroke, a man who was very fond of travelling. Between 1720 and 1730 he paid a visit to a factory at Savonnerie in France, where he observed that the French and Belgian carpets being made there were of a far superior quality to those made at Wilton. He decided there and then that he wanted Wilton to manufacture carpeting of this quality, which led him to ask the French authorities if he could 'borrow' some master-weavers to teach the men at Wilton their craft. When he was turned down, the Earl, a determined man, hatched a plot to enable him to get his own way.

The story goes that whilst out shopping for French wines, he made arrangements for them to be shipped home in several large barrels, two of which were to be left empty, his intention being to smuggle two French weavers into the country. Whether the story is true is open to question, but it is possible that the two men were put into the barrels and smuggled on board, then released when the ship was a safe distance from the French coast. These weavers, Pierre Jermal and Anthony Dufosee, were Huguenots who were only too glad to get out of France, where the Huguenots suffered widespread persecution. The house in which they lived on arrival at Wilton, still called Huguenot Cottage, stands on the corner of the main road at the far end of Kingsbury Square.

The two weavers joined the factory at Wilton only to discover that the looms had no facility for loops to be cut. While it was Dufosee who was instrumental in the early development of Wilton carpet, in 1741 a new loom was patented by Ignatius Couran, together with John Barford and William Moody, for making a carpeting called 'Moccadoes', from which, it is alleged, Wilton carpet derives. A year later, due mainly to Dufosee's skills, the production of hand-knotted carpeting became extremely advanced and it was eventually given the name 'Wilton cut pile', gaining a good reputation all over the world, due to the velvet-like finish of its nap. Later it became known simply as Wilton carpet.

Sadly, none of Dufosee's efforts made him a rich man, although he did marry a local girl, Mary Tanner. They lived a simple life, as did most working men of the period, and had ten children, most of whom died in infancy. Dufosee died a poor man in 1785. His descendants still live in this country today, some, it is believed, in the Weymouth area.

Business grew and at one time there were around 500 men and women workers employed, as well as a large number of children who, like the adults, worked long, hard hours. By the last decade of the eighteenth century the workforce had shrunk drastically to 168, mainly because of a shortage of child labour. This was put down to warnings published in the local press that mill overseers in and around Wilton should not apprentice children, many of whom were treated cruelly. In one instance a death had occurred as a direct result of cruelty.

Around the middle of the eighteenth century the factory was sold, a new partnership taking over in the form of Hawes & Adcock. During their partnership the factory became known as 'The Great Carpet Factory'. New lines of production were introduced, including Scotch, Persian and Turkish carpets, these being made in addition to Wilton carpet

In January 1779 Hawes & Adcock were declared bankrupt and the factory was sold. The buyer's name is not recorded, but three years later he sold up and the business was eventually bought by another partnership, Buller, Mease & Sutter who, ten years later, introduced a new line in carpets, described as mock Brussels.

During 1817 there were further changes in ownership, the Blackmore Brothers, who owned the smaller factory in Kingsbury Square, taking over the larger one from Buller, Mease & Sutter, while the Blackmores's former premises became a store and workrooms. They also took on a business partner, commencing to trade as Stevens, Blackmore Brothers. At the same time they offered top wages to the weavers who, according to experience, were paid one and a half to two guineas a week – a good deal of money in those days.

Unfortunately, two years later, with the end of the war between France and England and the ensuing peace, a depression in the industry caused work to fall off. Between 1819 and 1822 the weavers of the

Although these men remain unidentified, this Australia-bound cargo, pictured in the late 1940s was obviously of some importance. The lorry belonged to Corbin & Waghorn, who ran a haulage business in Wilton and were agents for the Southern Railway – the station no doubt being the first destination on a long journey.

Moving a carpet to the shearing shed for finishing off in the late 1940s, the tremendous weight requiring considerable manpower.

The manager of the carpet factory in the late 1940s was Mr Aston, here posing on the lawn in the old courtyard with his wife and their son John in front of the house reserved for their use.

town were offered alternative employment with the Wilton Estate, building walls, roads and bridges, the main construction being the wall which runs from Fugglestone to Netherhampton. Although weavers by trade, the men soon adapted their skills, proof of which is the wall, still standing today as a permanent tribute to their adaptability. All the work allocated to them was completed in three years, at a cost to the estate of £1,000. The names of the men engaged on on this project have fortunately been recorded, and are as follows: carpet weavers James and John Silverthorne, George Ford, William Taylor, Theo Bifs, Richard Thatcher; broadcloth weavers Thomas Routs, James Ward, Nehemiah Pomeroy, Josh Biffen, James Beams, Zachariah Hawkins, William Nash, Rab Smith, and John and James Hinton, plus a non-weaver, David Vincent, who was a shearman.

By 1830 the Blackmores were producing a much improved Wilton weave made from the wool of Southdown sheep. In the same year, when a visit was made to Salisbury by the Duchess of Kent and Princess Victoria, Wilton master-weaver James Elliot laid down a sample for them to walk on when they alighted from their carriage. The Duchess was so impressed by its quality she immediately ordered some for Kensington Palace and said that she would like it to be called the 'Kent weave'.

In 1834 the factory in the Market Place was closed, as was that in Kingsbury Square. Both of these businesses were transferred to a much larger site in King Street, occupied by Burdensball Mill, owned by Wilton Estate. There had been a mill on this site since Tudor times, originally operating as a corn and grist mill. By early 1835 the new factory was in production and, when the carpet factory in Axminster in Devon went bankrupt, the owners at Wilton were able to purchase some of the looms. The sale also meant employment for some of the redundant weavers, an outcome for which they were very grateful. With the purchase of the Axminster looms, both Axminster and Wilton carpets could be made.

By 1840 the factory was employing 30 master-weavers, and in 1844 a new partner joined the Blackmores, Alfred Lapworth, a London carpet manufacturer. Ten years later the factory was employing 100 workers, who were kept busy making Persian, Turkish, Wilton and Axminster carpets.

At the Great Exhibition, held in Hyde Park in 1851, Wilton carpets were well represented, six in all being exhibited, all of them hand woven, as carpets still were at that time. One of them was lent by Queen Victoria herself. No doubt by exhibiting at this prestigious event, the factory could well have received orders from all over the world and enjoyed another boom period of trading.

Blackmores sold their share in the factory in 1860, leaving Lapworth to carry on the business alone until his retirement 11 years later. A new partnership then took over, Yates & Wills, Samuel Pardoe Yates taking on the role of managing director, a capacity in which he spent some months of the year travelling abroad to secure orders. A teetotaller and very pious by nature, he became rather a self-important man. After his death in 1874 he was succeeded by his son,

Actor Derek de Marney signing autographs for factory workers on a visit to the carpet factory, c.1950. Bearing some resemblance to Robert Mitchum, de Marney appeared in several films, the most famous being Dangerous Moonlight, *in 1941.*

Pictured on the same day, another film star, Lana Morris, shows a keen interest in the hand-weaver's craft. This work was undertaken for the most part by young women.

Making a personal appearance at the Gaumont cinema in Salisbury, Lana Morris poses with cinema manager George Howes.

Richard Dimbleby signing autographs for some of the factory staff in 1947, when the BBC came to Wilton to record a 'Down Your Way'.

Pardoe Yates, who did not become a director until later. In May 1899 Pardoe Yates formed a new company, of which his mother, Rachel, and James Lander were company directors. Others joining the company at the same time were Charles Marshall and his wife Sarah, E.C. Rawlings and J.K. Rutter. The new company spent £53,000 on the purchase of the factory, land and stock from the Pembroke Estate, but although it appears that Wills had now completely disappeared from the scene, the name Yates & Wills was still used.

The following year saw two subsidiary factories open, Elizabeth Port, New Jersey, and Castle Street in Salisbury. Similar factories, opened in 1887 at Sugerhouse Lane, Southampton, and at Downton, only making a cheap kind of matting. All these ventures, however, were very short lived.

Pardoe Yates came to be well liked and respected in the town, appearing to be a perfect gentleman with a pious nature and liked by everyone he met. On his sudden death in September 1898, however, attitudes changed towards him when it was discovered he had been leading a double life and that his business trips had been a front for a life of riotous living, especially on his visits to Chicago. Both there and in this country he had squandered the company money and that of the shareholders, which eventually led to the factory going bankrupt.

Just after his death, there were strange happenings which have not all been explained to this day. Yates lived in a large house opposite the factory. On his death all the workers lined up and were taken over to the house to pay their respects. Ushered inside, they were asked to file past his body, which was laid out on his bed. As they did so, one factory girl touched his cheek with her hand, upon which she suddenly withdrew it and exclaimed, 'Here, he's still warm!'. She was grabbed by a supervisor and hauled out the room, those workers who had not yet filed past the body being told to return to the factory immediately. There was another strange occurrence on the eve of the funeral, when a passer-by noticed what he thought at first was a heavily veiled woman leaving the house. As the figure began to walk to a waiting carriage, he noticed that its build and walk looked more like that of a man and, moreover, seemed very closely to resemble the stature and gait of Pardoe Yates. It definitely was nothing like the build of his mother, Rachel. When the carriage drove off it passed him at a fair speed, which he thought strange given the circumstances, this supposedly being a grief-stricken women.

In this Victorian era, my great-grandfather, Josiah Jacobs, was employed as a weaver, as was my grandfather, William Lane, who eventually married Josiah's daughter. In 1884, when he became a fully fledged weaver, my grandfather was presented with a certificate by Josiah. Written in a beautiful copperplate hand, the document originally had attached to it the red seal of the Weavers Guild, which unfortunately has disintegrated over the years. The certificate reads:

Wilton Carpet Factory, 7th February, 1884.
I Josiah Jacobs, hereby certify that William Lane has this day completed his term of Service as Second Loom Weaver and having paid all demands, is now entitled to all the rights and privileges as belonging to the trade.
Signed Josiah Jacobs, Secretary to the Wilton Carpets Weavers Association.

The weavers were highly skilled and well respected by their fellow workers and, once qualified, gave long and faithful service to the factory, many serving 20 or more years. Conditions were noisy and the noise of the looms operating could be unbearable, but in the days before industrial health and safety issues, the workers' ears were unprotected which, in some cases of long service, did cause some deafness. If affected in this way, there was no procedure for compensation. One just had to put up with the conditions and the after-effects.

In 1903 the company made no profit at all; to try and resolve the situation some workers were laid off and others put on short-time working. Such was the concern for the workers that the rector, Canon Olivier, launched a special fund to help those in need. Despite the measure to save it, the following year the company went bankrupt. The fifteenth Earl of Pembroke, concerned about the situation, tried without success to interest two London companies in purchasing the factory. With this avenue now closed, the Earl himself stepped into the breach, and saved it at a cost of just over £8,000, successfully forming a company to run it.

In one respect the situation was ironic, as around this time subsidiary factories were opened in Fordingbridge, Downton, Mere and Tisbury; by 1942, however, the first three had closed down, Tisbury continuing in production until its closure in 1949.

In 1905 the factory received a very special order from King Edward VII for carpets for five rooms in Buckingham Palace, the Earl of Pembroke having used his position as Lord Steward to secure the order. The carpet for the Bow Reception Room was the largest, measuring just over 60ft in width and 50ft in length, with a pile an inch thick. With a total of 15 weavers employed in its making, it took four months to complete and weighed one ton. Two of the other carpets were made in the actual Wilton weave. This special weave, developed in Wilton rather than actually made in the town, gives a carpet its 'Wilton carpet' status. On the completion of this order, the king granted a royal warrant whereby the factory became the Wilton Royal Carpet Factory.

Prestige orders did not come from royalty alone, they came from many important establishments, both in this country and all over the world. The list is impressive and dates back for many years. In this country some of the contracts included the National Film Theatre, Heathrow Airport, the Royal Pavilion at Brighton, the *QE2*, P&O Lines and the Swedish Embassy in London. Overseas contracts included the Park Lane Hotel in New York, the Singapore Hilton, the New World Centre in Hong Kong and the Conference Palace in Riyadh. In more recent times the factory has received orders from the railway companies, including South West Trains for carpeting in their carriages. One of their biggest challenges came during the 1930s, when Dame Laura Knight, at that time well known for her paintings of circus life, asked the factory to make two carpets the designs on which were to be copies of her paintings of Pierrot and Columbine and of Neptune surrounded by water nymphs and sea creatures. This was a real challenge for the factory, but they took it on, managing to resolve many problems, the main difficulty being in estimating the scale in which to reproduce the paintings on carpets measuring 24ft square.

During the Second World War, due to the shortage of wool, the production of carpets ceased, although the factory managed to stave off bankruptcy and closure by taking on war work for the military, by washing blankets. Although starting off with a small number, such was their efficiency that this soon increased to 10,000 a week. The workload was increased further and, more importantly, extra revenue was earned, by garnishing camouflage and making kitbags and tarpaulins for the troops. When the war was over, efforts gradually turned once again to the making of carpets. Although there were still shortages of materials, the struggle to increase production eventually paid off. Unfortunately, during the 1950s, there were more changes due to increasing costs, and it was decided that the old Axminster hand looms would have to go. By 1958 all had ceased production and been sold, the last carpet to be made on one of these looms being for Guildford Cathedral. A year later output was at ten times the pre-war figure and, with the factory now owned by the Clarke family of Northern Ireland, work was plentiful and the factory in a boom period.

By then, however, a new weaving shed was in operation, designed by the company architect, which provided a floor area of 1,370 square yards, made possible by the use of a multi-paraboloid roof, the whole building being erected in just six weeks. The building housed Axminster 'gripper' looms, allowing the more cost-effective production of Axminster carpets. The plan worked, so much so, in fact, that production had vastly increased within two years. An associated company, the Solent Carpet Factory, was set up in Southampton exclusively manufacturing Axminster carpets. The Irish Youghall Group, who now owned the factory, continued with the expansion plan, creating the

The carpet of Dame Laura Knight's Pirou and Columbine, with 2.5 knots to the square inch and using 120 colours.

Hampshire Industrial Textiles Co., based at Romsey, which produced a new high-twist style of carpeting, known as the Charter range. The 1979 order for the Riyadh Conference Palace, made up of both Axminster and Wilton weaves, was, at that time, the company's biggest contract order.

In February the following year, Prime Minister Margaret Thatcher made a visit to the factory whilst on a tour of the area. During her stay at Wilton she was shown around the factory by production director David Letts and company chairman Geoffrey Wardle. She also met some of the workers, including Don Reynolds, a Tory supporter. This being the day after Valentines Day, pinned up on his loom was a sign which read 'Don loves Mrs Thatcher', which brought a smile to her face. Don thought one of his mates had put it up as a joke, but had no worries about it, as Mrs Thatcher had given him an appreciative smile. During her hour-long visit she was shown the dyeing, weaving and other processes. One carpet of special interest to her, being made in a geometrical design, was for the Orpington Conservative Club – blue in colour, naturally! The two hosts were able to point out their impressive export orders from various European and American countries, including that for carpeting for the Conference Palace in Saudi Arabia.

In the mid-1980s there was another change of ownership when Coats Viyella stepped in to take charge. There were many ups and downs in the factory's fortunes, however, and problems winning orders in turn led, on many occasions, to workers being laid off. As a result, no one was prepared for the shocking news, in January 1995, that the factory was to close, with the loss of some 110 jobs. The reason given for the closure was that the parent company, Coats Viyella, has sold its interests to Carpets International, the headquarters of which

After a private visit to the Earl of Pembroke at the end of June 1908, King Edward VII and Queen Alexandra paid a visit to the carpet factory before departing by train. Here, their majesties have just entered through the main gate, the arch of which can be seen on the right behind the lamppost.

Even in the late 1940s, the exacting process of dyeing wool for carpets was still being done at the factory. The different colours had to be dyed one batch at a time, with sufficient yarn processed in the same colour to avoid trying to match it later on. This process has since ceased and the yarn is bought in. Here, one batch is already completed and drying out, while another is being lowered into the dyeing vat.

were in Dalton, Georgia, with its main British base at Bradford, Yorkshire. A 90-day consultation period allowed discussions with the trade unions and staff, these taking place at Wilton Royal's factory and at Romsey, where 230 people were employed.

Anger and resentment were rife in the town, with good cause, many members of the same families being employed at the factory. In many cases families had been associated with the factory for generations; not only that, 110 jobs was a lot to lose in a community where carpet making was the only trade they knew. A recently retired worker, Eric Odham, aged 61, was quoted as saying, 'It's a big shock, a total surprise. Everyone is gutted.' So too was the mayor, Bob Blandford who, like many of us, was born and bred in the town and viewed the factory as an important part of the community. He quickly called a public meeting, in conjunction with fellow councillor Peter Edge, which attracted a large crowd at the Michael Herbert Hall on Tuesday 31 January. Although many of the workers who attended were still in a state of shock, the orderly meeting proved productive, with the formation of a seven-man action committee to fight for the survival of the historic factory and for the jobs of its workers. Another factor which had annoyed everyone in the town was that Carpets International had announced they would be taking the royal warrant with them, and the meeting overwhelmingly decided that the queen should be asked to remove the company's warrant if all efforts to save the factory failed. District councillor Mrs May Kiddle, herself a former worker at the factory, stated that 'The royal title belongs to Wilton and the Americans should not be allowed to take it away with them.'

Unfortunately the factory was not saved and sadly, on 3 March, the gates closed for what seemed to be the last time. The workers exited the gates with pride, carrying a banner on which was written the factory motto, 'Weave Trust With Truth'. Many were weeping. A few weeks later, however, came rumours that the factory had been saved. In early April the

Workers at the felt mill, some of whom also served as fire crew if the need arose. Left to right: *Ronald Blake, Jim Goddard, ?, Archie West, Bill Paddock.*

truth emerged and the factory reopened, thanks to a management buy-out led by former managing director Peter Le Count. A special ceremony was organised and production was soon under way. Although on a reduced scale, at least the factory was open for business once again. The former factory buildings just off the Warminster Road were eventually vacated and the site sold to Rock Eagle, who developed it into a shopping village behind which the factory buildings are now located. Since its reopening the factory has enjoyed success, and in April 2005 celebrated its tenth anniversary. There is one ironic twist to the original closure by Carpets International, however. In October 2003 it was announced that the UK's biggest carpet manufacturer had called in the administrative receivers, Pricewaterhouse Coopers, to their head office in Bradford during August. They had already cut 300 jobs, but were trying to find a buyer for the business either as a whole or in parts.

The Felt Industry

The making of felt was another major industry in Wilton, the mill manufacturing it being situated in Crow Lane in the centre of town. Originally a grist and malt mill, on occasion it was used for fulling cloth for the local weavers, thus earning extra income. The Pembrokes became involved in business in the town once again when, in the late-1600s, Lord Pembroke purchased the mill, leasing it to

The entrance to the felt mill, c.2005.

William Whitchurch in the early part of the eighteenth century. Whitchurch commenced to convert the mill's use to textiles, which proved a success, although the lease changed hands several times before 1817. During this particular year, the lease was taken over by a partnership which owned a mill in West Street, on the site of which, in 2006, stands the Community Centre (previously a school). The new partnership began manufacturing gloves, then branched out into making cheap carpeting, or drugget. Both mills remained under the control of the partnership until a slump in the industry forced the sale of the West Street mill to Lord Pembroke. Eventually, the lease of the Crow Lane mill was taken over by John Brasher.

The mill did good business and continued to do so until, in 1830, it was attacked by a group of Swing Rioters, disgruntled agricultural workers from Wiltshire and the southern counties, who broke in and smashed the machinery in protest against the loss of their jobs to mechanisation. They also argued that new machinery in the textile industry was taking work away from their wives, who traditionally wove cloth at home. As a result of the destruction of machinery at Crow Lane, 55 men, women and children were out of employment, while 12 rioters from Wilton, committed to Fisherton Gaol in Salisbury, were actually sentenced to death, though, fortunately for them, the sentences were commuted. One man, William Jacobs, was let off, while the remainder were transported to Australia.

When all had become quiet once again, Brasher continued in the textile trade, although at a much reduced capacity due to the riots, until 1835, when the lease was taken over by John Naish. A Wilton man, Naish had owned a mill at Quidhampton, a small village just outside the town on the way to Salisbury. Here he had made Bedford cord until his mill was smashed beyond repair by rioters, much reducing its capacity. In 1859 Naish was approached by James Goddard, who suggested that they get together and produce felt for the pianoforte, the instrument being all the rage in Victorian homes at that time. Both men realising that this could prove an asset to the mill, they made every effort to market their product, both in this country and abroad. With each piano requiring felt of a different quality, felt took over as the sole source of the mill's income and the production of Bedford cord was eventually phased out. Later, the range of felt products was widened further to include polishers, washers, window channelling, drumstick heads and a wide range of technical felts. Early in the 1900s the manufacture of surgical felts began. Curiously, despite the mill being in a town where carpets were manufactured, it never produced underfelts.

With part of the workforce made up of young boys, at times there was some larking about. On one particular day, when the foreman was absent, there was an accident which had tragic consequences. A boy, Samuel Leybourne, became caught in a belt on the machinery and was carried upwards, his leg becoming jammed between the belt drum and the rafters. The only way he could be freed was to cut away part of the rafter, which took some time. The leg was so badly shattered it had to be amputated and, sadly, Samuel died eight days later.

With complaints being brought that the mill was not up to standard, in 1880 an octagonal chimney was built and a coal-fired steam boiler installed to achieve greater efficiency of production, the steam engine powering a generator to supply electricity. The chimney, a feature of the town's skyline for many years, was finally demolished in 1959, when a modern oil-fired boiler was brought into use and mains electricity was installed.

Another feature of the mill in more recent times was its hooter, which could be heard all over the town, summoning the men to work at 7a.m. It was also sounded for the start and finish of the morning tea break, again at midday for the lunch period, then at 1p.m. when the lunch period was over, the final sounding of the day being at 5p.m. Such was its accuracy and reliability that many people in the town set their watches and clocks by it, claiming it to be more reliable than the Town Hall clock.

In July 2000, when the mill celebrated 200 years in the textile trade, it was not solely engaged in the production of felt. In 1975 it had formed a subsidiary company, Wallgate Ltd, to supplement its income. Wallgate began by making hand-washing machines for public toilets and by its 25th anniversary year, celebrated alongside the mill's 200th, was supplying McDonald's restaurants, hospitals and food factories and having developed its product range to include toilets, shower trays and checkout counters.

In 2006 felt is no longer manufactured at Wilton; it is brought to Wilton ready made from abroad and cut and packaged here to customers' requirements. In recent years there was a proposal to move the business to an industrial site at Amesbury, but at the time of writing this has not yet happened.

Brewer's Agricultural Merchants

Although Wilton was surrounded by agriculture, it was not until the 1860s that the needs of the workers in this industry were met by Albert Brewer. On his arrival here in 1860 he originally took up employment as a blacksmith and machinist at the felt mills, leaving soon afterwards to set up as a blacksmith in West Street. It seems rather fitting that West Street was chosen, as it has been said that for some time this wide street resembled the towns of America's Wild West, where the few buildings were functional and the blacksmith's forge the focal point. Without the blacksmith's services to horses and farm implements, neither would be able to function, making the blacksmith at that time a person of some importance.

From the first, Brewer intended his business to offer quality and good service in all departments; those who worked for him had to toe the line and make sure their jobs were done properly and to the highest standard. If they failed, they were soon told, in no uncertain terms, to improve their workmanship. Albert was a strict but fair taskmaster, as well as being a stickler for punctuality. He was certainly able to keep an eye out for late arrivals, as he lived in a house opposite the forge. Indeed, it is alleged that he had a mirror on the wall of his bedroom through which, from his bed, he could check that the workforce arrived promptly at 6a.m.

His workmanship being to such a high standard,

The original workforce of Brewer's holding the tools of their trade, c.1895, with Albert Brewer (fourth from left, back row) *and George Brewer, his son* (extreme left, back row).

Brewer's original office, demolished in 1949 to make way for the new office and showroom.

The new office and showroom. The cottage on the left was later demolished to make way for an extension to the office.

his reputation as a blacksmith spread and the farmers of the district started to bring him machinery to mend, at times asking him to make specific items. Fortunately he had an inventive mind and was able to create special tools for special needs. In those days such craftsmen had to be skilled, their living depended on it, so whatever a farmer required, Albert Brewer delivered. Business increased, a second forge was built and, when even this was not sufficient, a third was added. For six full days a week they were in constant use, and the firm quickly gained a reputation for quality and service which continued throughout its operating years. Brewer's motto, 'God Speed the Plough', was still used in more modern times.

The firm took on a number of apprentices, a surviving document revealing exactly what was required from an apprentice when he was indentured. The actual indenture was a legal document, usually drawn up by a solicitor or his clerk, which left no doubt as to the conditions of service required of the apprentice, the employer, in turn, being bound to instruct him properly in his trade.

The conditions laid down for the apprentice to abide by were strict, and certainly would not be tolerated in this day and age. The apprentice was bound:

To serve his Master faithfully, keep his secrets, will not waste any goods nor lend them unlawfully to anyone. He shall not contract Matrimony within his term of apprenticeship, or play Cards or Dice Tables or any other unlawful games whereby his Master shall have

The first Fordson tractor at Brewer's in 1917.

any loss with his own goods. He must neither buy or sell, must not haunt Taverns or Playhouses nor absent himself from this said Master's service day or night unlawfully. He must behave himself to his Master.

The document also stated exactly the wages an apprentice could expect during his term – in the first year 3s., the second year 4s., the third year 5s., the fourth year 6s. and 8s. in his final year. The parent or guardian would have to pay the employer for taking the apprentice on, the sum in the case documented being £10, a lot of money in those days.

In 1912 Albert's brother, George, the last Brewer to be associated with the firm, sold it to Mr A. Peckett, who made many changes. Although horseshoeing was gradually reduced, all three forges were kept busy making harrows, drags, etc., until as late as 1960. The business was still geared to the farming industry, making agricultural machinery and materials, but the company was diversifying, and in a 1914 catalogue of agricultural implements offered 'world-renowned machines' along with a promise that all repairs carried out would be carefully attended to. This promise of service and reliability was at the forefront throughout the firm's existence. Around this period, workers began visiting farms to

What a difference 70 decades make! With the building of tractors much larger and to higher technical specifications, a much greater degree of maintenance was required. Here Graham Hunt performs a hydraulic test in a modern workshop, c.1980.

repair machinery on site and had to continually acquire new skills, the arrival of tractors heralding a more mechanised age.

Although under new management, there was no lack of inventiveness, and an 'improved light horse hoe' was introduced. Fitted with better knives and a lever for lifting at headlands and travelling on the road, the wheels and knife stems were all adjustable. Another invention was the Andrews Patent Sack Elevator, the brainchild of Fred Andrews, a local farmer. The claim was that 'it made hard work easy' and was capable of doing the work of the three men. Unlike similar machines, sacks were lifted by endless chains, saving the carriers time in returning each sack and making things easier and quicker all round.

With large national companies starting to appear on the scene, Peckett quickly saw the potential of mechanised farming and, although already a dealer for Ransomes, took on other agencies. After the First

Brewer's trade stand at the sheep fair in September 1930, manned by (from left to right)*: Cyril Weeks* (on tractor)*, Tom Catley, Herby Emm, Ewart Lane,* (managing director)*, Reg Boon, Doug Lindsay and Bob Stacey. Behind the stand can be seen the wattle hurdles of the sheep pens, into which the sheep were put when they were off-loaded from the trains.*

Len Bryant, who spent his entire working life with the company, a period of 51 years, is shown working at one of the forges in the original blacksmith's shop.

World War crops replaced animals on Salisbury Plain, providing an opportunity to conduct experiments in mechanical cultivation. Brewer's was heavily involved in this until the outbreak of the Second World War, by which time mechanised farming had come into its own.

In 1933 the firm became a limited company, the first managing director being Ewart Lane, an uncle of mine. At the time of the change, the company was already an established sub-dealer for Fordson, a role which increased through the 1930s, and the contract was firmly established by Ewart at the time of his sudden death in 1939. He was succeeded by Frank Sherry, formerly with International Harvester, and, despite wartime restrictions, the company was able to maintain its tradition of service. Brewer's played an important role in the war. Fortunately, many of the workforce were classed as reserved occupation so that they could keep tractors and machinery working in order to grow desperately needed food.

Business soon got back to normal after the war and in 1949 the original 1860 office was demolished and a new office and showroom built. In 1950 Steve Biddle joined the company which, with his guidance and foresight, was able to branch out and expand the horticultural side of the business. Agricultural machinery was also changing, and farmers were starting to modernise with combine harvesters, balers and many other innovations. At this time it was not unusual to see a nineteenth-century binder

alongside a modern combine harvester, or a steam traction engine and thresher being repaired. It was a time of transition, old and new working together.

During the 1950s, due to the success of the business, it was thought that the company might have to move from Wilton; fortunately they were able to buy the piece of land opposite, allowing them to stay in the town. At Wilton the company serviced and sold garden machinery and, with the growth in that market, it was decided to separate this activity. In 1962 the department moved to a site in Salisbury next to the former cattle market where, subsequently, a road development in the area forced another move, to a site on the Churchfields Industrial Estate, which proved hugely successful.

Throughout its existence, Brewer's remained a family company, and who better to know this than Bill Hewlett, who served them faithfully for 51 years, retiring in 1995.

Bill started with them in 1944, after leaving the Secondary Modern School in Wilton at the age of 14. As he says, he never went to college; he got a job at Brewer's learning his trade under the supervision of Cecil Target. At the time he joined the company, he recollects, there were 35–40 employees. Bill enjoyed his job, the majority of his time being spent out in the fresh air visiting farms to repair equipment. When Bob Stacey designed the Stacey Brewer Grain Conveyor, a very successful piece of machinery, Bill installed many of these on farms all over the country, even on the Isle of Wight and in the Midlands. Later in life, he also helped install slurry systems for dairy cattle. Some of his time was spent in the workshop, but only when absolutely necessary; he enjoyed working on farms and meeting people.

By 1980 the company had increased its range of products and had introduced goods from Rover Mowers, the largest manufacturers of garden machinery in Australia, keen to establish their range in Britain. Their range of products being renowned for quality and toughness, Brewer's soon recognised it as being suitable for the British market. Negotiations continued during 1979 and that summer several machines were flown over for trials.

The product was launched in September at a reception held at the London headquarters of Quantas Airways in Piccadilly, attended by representatives of Rover Mowers and Brewer's and by members of the Australian High Commission. This resulted in the company setting up a division to run this new venture, operating from Churchfields with extensive warehousing at Amesbury. This extra warehousing was required so that the whole of the United Kingdom, including Northern Ireland, could be covered. Rover was by then established at the forefront of garden machinery in this country.

In 1980 the number of staff employed, including directors, was 60, many of them from third and fourth generation families. The same year the

Two members of the more modern-day workforce in the sundries department, c.1980. C. Weeks (left) is pictured with supervisor Mike Horner.

Bill Hewlett assembling grain dryer equipment on a farm, assisted by David Hubbard, c.1980.

Service personnel of the Wilton section of Brewer's, c.1980. Left to right, back row: B. Woodvine, I. Clark, Des Burton, N. Rouse; front row: W. Mowles (works foreman), M. Hewlett, J. Cooper, J. Paige, D. Mundy, S. Lovell, D. Burton, G. Hunt, P. Hayes, C. Steele (service manager).

A photograph of the Brewer's workforce taken outside their office and showroom in West Street to mark the coronation of Queen Elizabeth II in June 1953. In the centre of the front row is chairman and managing director W.S. Biddle.

The office staff at Wilton, c.1980, including Miss T. Postan-Easthope, Miss I. Thorne, Mrs S. White, Mr L.S. Taylor (director), Mrs K. Andrews, Mrs M. Webb, Mrs L. Roper, Miss J. Mussell and Mrs L. Buchanan.

Maurice Hewlett at work in the welding shop, c.1980.

company celebrated 125 years of trading, commemorating the event by producing a special brochure. The business continued to offer service, quality and courtesy, the principles on which Albert Brewer had founded the business. The blacksmith's shop, still in existence, had been modernised to tackle any size of machine and any job that was required.

Despite their success, in around 1985 the company went into liquidation, although the business was saved when it was bought by Pond's of Blandford. Eventually the showrooms in Wilton were taken over by a company selling cars, though the land opposite was retained. Pond's was later bought out by C.O. Cole's and the business now carries on, in a much reduced way, on the opposite side of the road. The memories of Brewer's still linger on, a firm which played such an important role in the town, all those years ago.

CHAPTER 3

Education

Of all the charitable institutions established in Wilton, there can be no doubt that the Wilton Free School is the one best remembered, not only because it remained in existence for over 200 years, but because many of the town's former businessmen and tradesmen received their education there, starting them on the road to success and prosperity.

The school was founded by Walter Dyer, a businessman of Chancery Lane, London who, in his will dated 19 July 1706, left £600, part of his personal estate, to his mother on condition that on her death or remarriage the sum was to go to the rector and churchwardens at Wilton on trust, to establish a school for 20 poor boys of the parish. He also instructed that the boys were to be taught to read and write and be grounded in the rules of common arithmetic, as well as being taught the principles and doctrines of the Church of England, as by law established. The rector and churchwardens were given the power to select boys for the school and to appoint a suitable person as schoolmaster, subject to the approval of the Bishop of Salisbury.

A large house was purchased in East Street (later North Street) in which one room was set aside for use as a schoolroom. Under the rules of the charity, the schoolmaster was to live rent free in the schoolhouse, and to receive a salary of £20 per year. The house was maintained by the charity, which also provided an allowance of £4 a year for the purchase of school stationery and for heating the schoolroom during winter months. A further £20 a year was set aside for placing four boys, at £5 each, in handicraft trades or husbandry. An allowance of £25 a year for each boy was to provide him with a new uniform every Easter, the new suit to be worn as his best for the first year and for daily wear the year following. The uniform issued for each foundationer, as new boys were known, consisted of one frock-style cutaway coat in a buff-coloured cloth which was quite thick, and a waistcoat. The coat was faced with hyacinth blue cuffs and collars which buttoned to the neck, and the buttons of both garments were made of brass, which needed constant cleaning to keep shiny. The uniform was completed with one pair of long trousers, one pair of hose, one pair of boots and a cap, this being in a buff colour with a black shiny peak, making the uniform resemble a military style of dress. Calico, buttons and cotton were supplied to parents to make two shirts for each boy.

The school, opened in 1714, was run from the outset by a board of governors consisting of the mayor, aldermen and burgesses of the borough, who worked in close harmony with the rector and churchwardens. Under the rules of the charity, this body was designated to meet at least twice a year, on Lady Day and at Michaelmas.

Naturally, the money used to set up the charity would have to be supplemented and could not rely solely on interest for its reserves. Fortunately, many other benefactors endowed gifts at various times. Richard Uphill of Wilton, for example, in a will dated 28 January 1716, donated bank stock of £1,000. In February 1733 the charity purchased Redhouse Farm at East Knoyle, which was subsequently let to a tenant farmer, the rent received being used to supplement the charity's funds. A further augmentation of £1,000, granted by Robert Sumption in 1775, enabled the salary of the master to be increased, and went towards the better education, apprenticing and clothing of the boys. By 1798 the school and the funds of the charity were on a solid footing, which led to the trustees to purchase a dwelling-house, outbuildings and a garden adjacent to the school. This was purchased for £140, with the remaining period of a 500-year lease which had been in effect since 1685. In 1801, however, the buildings were demolished, after which an addition was made to the school by building on part of the garden. Henry Ford of Burdensball Farm, just outside the town's boundary at South Newton, who had been educated at the school, endowed £100 in his will dated 1831, and from about this period further money was received from various benefactors. A report dated 1823 reveals that the farmer at Redhouse Farm was paying an annual rent of £120 a year which, coupled with £30 interest received annually from invested monies, brought in a total income of £150 a year. It was the custom, on the Sunday before Easter and on Easter Sunday, that notices were read out in the Parish Church stating that the trustees would be meeting on the Wednesday of Easter week to select boys aged eight years and upwards to fill any vacancies available. One stipulation given to applicants attending this meeting was that they bring with them a certificate of baptism. It appears that, in practice, preference was usually given to older boys and to those who had received tuition in the Church of England. Those boys not brought up in this faith, referred to as 'Dissenters', would take second place for selection to the school. Such a practice today would definitely not be allowed, but discrimination, then very much to the fore in practically every walk

WILTON FREE SCHOOL.

Please supply to Mr. _____
the undermentioned articles of clothing, at a sum *not exceeding* two pounds. The clothing will be inspected by the Governors on Good Friday.

ARTICLES OF CLOTHING.

1 Cap.
1 Dark Grey Norfolk Jacket.
1 pair Brown Corduroy Knickers.
1 pair Stockings.
1 Rubber Collar.
Calico for two white shirts.

This authority with your account must be sent to me, the undersigned, on or before Wednesday, the 16th. April, 1919.

Municipal Offices,
WILTON. Steward.
March, 1919.

Clothing docket issued by the trustees of the Wilton Free School for parents to obtain the school uniform.

Two boys of the Wilton Free School, probably in the 1900s. On the left is Lench and on the right Foyle.

Pupils of the Free School, resplendent in their military-style uniforms pose with headmaster, John Coates (left) and his wife (right) for the school's 200th anniversary celebrations.

WILTON FREE SCHOOL.

BI-CENTENARY
1714 —— 1914.

❋

THE Celebration of the 200th. Anniversary of the Foundation of the above school will be held on Sumption's Day, Tuesday, January 20th., 1914.

A Thanksgiving Service will be held at 2.30 p.m., in the Parish Church, when the Sermon will be preached by the Rector. Afterwards a Public Tea, and an Entertainment by Old Boys will take place in the Talbot & Wyvern Hall.

THE proceeds of the entertainment, and subscriptions from Old Scholars and friends of the school, will be devoted to renovating the tombs of Robert Sumption and Thomas Mease; erecting a Mural Tablet to the memory of the founder of the School—Walter Dyer, and other Benefactors; and to providing apparatus for the more efficient working of the school.

THE Committee appeals to all Old Pupils, and friends of the school, for generous contributions towards these objects, and hopes they will be present at the celebrations.

DONATIONS will be gratefully received by the Rev. Guy R. Campbell, Rector of Wilton, and Chairman of the Governors; Alderman E. Slow; and by the Hon. Secretary and Treasurer, Mr. John Coates, Master of the School.

A poster announcing the celebration of the 200th anniversary of the school, to be held on Sumption's Day at the Parish Church. Robert Sumption was one of the benefactors of the school. The rector, on 20 January each year, preached a special sermon in his memory.

of life, was blindly accepted. Examination of the boys' work was conducted by the rector on the Sunday before Easter, his reports being submitted to the trustees at their meeting a week later.

The minimum age for acceptance was eight years, with the leaving age set at 14, and although boys of the foundation were educated free of charge, they were required to pay for their school and ciphering books. Once they were able to read and write, the trustees presented each boy with a Bible and a prayer book, thereby ensuring their correct religious instruction in accordance with the Church of England and the conditions laid down by the charity. A report on the school dated 1826 shows that two boys were dismissed from the school for felony, and that some complaints were made against a former master

Wilton Free School in the 1900s. Now a private dwelling, it is known as The Moat House.

concerning his conduct. The board of governors, making this report, particularly directed their energies to both past and present management of the school, concluding that they had no reason to believe that the complaints were well founded. The report stresses that all the evidence before them tended to show that the trustees had paid great attention to the trust, that the boys, with very few exceptions, had behaved well, and that the way in which the school had been taught and managed for many years had offered satisfaction to the parish.

It is also mentioned that for the last ten years about three boys had been apprenticed, the premium to each being the sum £8.10s. Despite the regulations of the charity requiring four boys aged 14 to be indentured each year, it appears that many did not want to be apprenticed, and of those who were, none had been apprenticed to husbandry. Joel Douty, who became master of the school in 1844, found the salary too small and made the decision to take in paying boarders. The 1851 census reveals that he was sharing the school with 49 paying boarders, three male teachers, a female assistant and two maids. When he found conditions too cramped, Douty moved to the manor at Netherhampton, taking most of the pupils with him, a move which made a very noticeable difference to the census of 1871. His successor was Robert Applegate Ayres, one-time mayor of Wilton and previously a headmaster at the National School in West Street. In 1893, when the

master of the school died, the opportunity was taken to bring to the notice of the charity commissioners that, due to two deaths, the number of trustees appointed to the school had been reduced to three, of whom only two were resident in Wilton. The suggestion was made that new trustees should be appointed, this being the ideal opportunity to put this into operation, with the appointment of a new master about to take place.

The following year a new board of governors was in place, including the rector, Canon Dacres Olivier, the mayor and Alderman Edward Slow, well-known Wiltshire dialect poet and businessman, who had also been a former pupil at the school. This new body made great improvements to the classrooms, which by this time had increased to three. While one was completely rebuilt and heating, lighting and ventilation were improved in the others, increasing the height of the old rooms was found to be too expensive. Other changes were made, the most important of which was to increase both the salary of the master and the stationery allowance; the clothing allowance, which had risen out of all proportion to the original terms, was decreased. At the same time the number of apprenticeships in any one year was limited to only four. New rules for school management were laid down, especially concerning the number of foundationers, who now numbered 24, four more than stipulated, no provision having been made for the increase. Admissions were now to be

Wilton School.

NAME...FORM.........POSITION..............TERM.................................

SCHOOL RE-OPENS..........................

ATTENDANCE.	PREPARATION.	EXERCISE BOOKS.	CONDUCT.

SUBJECT.	MARK.	SUBJECT.	MARK.
1—RELIGIOUS KNOWLEDGE.		**5—MUSIC.**	
Old Testament		Singing	
New Testament		Instrument	
Catechism		**6—ART.**	
2—ENGLISH.		Freehand	
Reading		Model	
Writing		Geometry	
Spelling		Memory	
Composition		**7—DRILL.**	
Literature		Physical Exercises ...	
Grammar		Company Drill	
Geography		**8 SCIENCE.**	
History			
Shorthand			
3—MATHEMATICS.		**9—GAMES.**	
Arithmetic		Swimming	
Algebra		Cricket	
Euclid...		Football	
Mensuration		**10—OTHER WORK.**	
Book Keeping		Wood Carving	
4—LANGUAGES.			
French			

REMARKS—

SIGNED— French Teacher...

Music Teacher...

Drill Sergeant...

Assistant...

Head Master...

A blank school report form from the 1900s, showing the wide variety of subjects taught at the Free School when John Coates was headmaster.

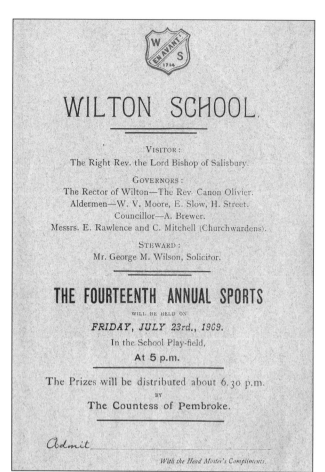

The front cover of a programme for the Free School sports day programme, Friday 23 July 1909.

limited to boys who had passed the fourth standard of examination in the National School and no boy could leave before the age of 14 or stay on after the age of 15. The curriculum was also extended to include geography, history, algebra, drawing, grammar, French, elementary science and shorthand, with German and Latin added later. Although elementary science was taught, no laboratory was provided. John Coates was appointed master on 16 May 1894 and his wife, a former teacher in a public elementary school at Sunderland, assisted by teaching elementary subjects to the juniors. An assistant master was also engaged, but for the teaching of specialised subjects visiting teachers were brought in. A sergeant drill instructor, at the master's expense, gave fee-paying pupils three drill sessions a week.

Prior to Coates's arrival, fee-paying pupils were taught separately, but this practice was changed immediately, the new master declaring that there should be no differences in the teaching of the boys. It also came to light that foundationers, on entering the school, were found to be backward in their work, this being quickly rectified once they had settled in.

Fee-paying pupils had been introduced to supplement the income of the charity. Fees were varied; term boarders paid £11.13s.4d. per term, weekly boarders £10 and day pupils 15s., with an additional

£1.15s. for tuition on the piano. A report issued in 1901 shows that there were 22 day boys paying fees and six boarders, two of whom were from Newcastle-on-Tyne, the parents of others residing in Wiltshire, Dorset and Hampshire. The report also reveals that the boys were also prepared for the Oxford and Cambridge local examinations and the South Kensington examination for drawing, modelling and geometry. Many boys were apprenticed to tradesmen including builders, plumbers, carpenters, cabinet makers, wheelwrights and coach builders. A small asphalt playgound was provided for the boys, and the master also rented a small field adjacent to his garden for their use. Coates also obtained a large field about three-quarters of a mile from the school, rent free, which was used as a playing-field, restricted to boys who joined the cricket and football club, for which privilege they paid a subscription, 2s.6d. and 1s. respectively each season.

A 1901 report notes that the intention to elect free scholars was no longer read out in church, and that there were some misgivings about the uniform. Some had complained that it had changed very little since the school was founded, and was felt to be rather drab, exposing the wearer to ridicule. The governors, however, considered it to be well known in Wilton and found no grounds for changing it. A school sports programme for July 1909 includes many familiar names of Wiltonians taking part in the various events – E. Lench, A.S. Cassey, C. White, D. Pretty, R. Cooper, W. Shepherd, S.J. Lench, H. Hibberd, A.L. West, A. Moore, W.V. Moore, R. Sutton, G.J. Sutton, E.S. Coombs, M. Whatley, and many more. It is possible that some of the names are those of girls, as the programme reveals that in the drill section there were prizes for both senior and junior girls. Other events included 100 yards, skipping, endurance, obstacle, swimming, croquet and a consolation struggle tug-of-war.

A few years ago in a Wilton shop, Collectors' Corner, which unfortunately is no longer in existence, I picked up a secondhand book which has been given to John Nash as a school prize at the Talbot and Wyvern Hall, Christmas 1919. Inside the book cover, the inscription is beautifully written in copperplate by John Coates, and glued to the binding is the programme of musical entertainment provided as part of the prize-giving, while on the back cover are the names of all the prizewinners and the titles of the books that they won. John's 351-page book cost 6s. – yes, they forgot to rub the price out! It was at about this time that girls were taken on at the school, all of them fee paying, for the sole purpose of contributing to the salary of John Coates.

When I was doing some research on the school, I talked with Wilton resident Cyril White, a former pupil who attended the school until its closure in 1923, after which he completed his final year of education at the National School. John Coates was very strict and kept discipline with frequent use of the cane. One of his favourite tricks was to stand in the doorway between two classrooms while pupils, carrying their books, were changing lessons. Should any pupil be unfortunate enough to drop something they were given a whack on the backside with the cane as they bent to pick it up and warned to be more careful in future. Every Sunday the boys would be marched in twos from the school, along Crow Lane to the Parish Church Sunday school. It appears that the uniform had changed slightly by this time, as Cyril remembered wearing a Norfolk jacket, still buttoned to the neck but with a belt around the waist. The trousers were now made of corduroy, provided free by Style & Gerrish, formerly a well-known Salisbury department store now owned by Debenhams. It seems that when the trousers were brand new they gave off a rather pungent odour. On one occasion when they wore their new trousers to Sunday school, the smell was so overpowering that the teacher was forced to send them home, instructing them to hang their trousers on the washing line as soon as they got there. Although freely admitting he was not the cleverest of pupils, with a school report to prove it, Cyril did admit that the teaching and the discipline had set him in good stead in the outside world, and he was grateful for that.

Another pupil at the school, Cecil Morris, who owned the butcher's shop that was once in West Street, appears to have done quite well at the school. Two of his school reports show that, on the whole, he received favourable comments from John Coates. At the end of the summer term of 1913, he was doing well in English subjects and in music, art, drill and religious knowledge, although mathematics was not one of his strong subjects. In his remarks, Coates wrote: 'Your English subjects are very good indeed. Work harder at your Mathematics'. In a report for the term ending Christmas 1915, concerning special classes held at the Town Hall for the Higher Education of Students, the following was written:

Your work has been very neat and much is being well done. English requires your special attention. Your spelling requires great care,and you do not express yourself clearly. You have done well in maths, which being chiefly Mensuration, should be useful to you.

At the bottom of the report a tear-off slip, which was to be signed by the parent or guardian and handed in at the commencement of the next term, reads:

I declare that there is no infectious of contagious illness in the house wherein (name of child) has resided during his (her) holidays. If illness of an infectious nature should occur in the house, I shall immediately inform the Head Master.

As was common with charitable institutions of this nature, funding was becoming a real problem. Even with fee-paying pupils, sufficient revenue could not be raised to enable the school to be run on a satisfactory basis, in accordance with the regulations stipulated by the charity. After its closure, the pupils were either transferred to the National School in West Street, or to other fee-paying schools in the district. The Board of Education devised a scheme whereby what remained of the charity's income was applied to certain specified objects, including some of the money being paid for maintenance and improvements of any public elementary school, or for any other educational purpose. Also provided for the poor children of Wilton in the early-nineteenth century were three Sunday schools. One of these was attached to the Parish Church, with 40 boys and 25 girls attending, plus another 27 children who appear to have come not just for religious instruction, but to learn to read and write. Children of Nonconformist faith had the choice of either the Congregational or Methodist Sunday schools, although the latter appears to have closed by 1835. The Congregational School, which by now had 156 children, and the Parochial School, with 100 children, were still going strong. At around this period there were also five fee-paying daily schools, catering between them for 87 children, plus two boarding-schools with 18 children. During the 1840s, the Congregational school converted to a day-school and became affiliated to the Union of British Schools. In 1858 it was teaching between 150 and 170 pupils and was praised for its high standards of teaching and equipment. Still in existence in 1871, it closed later in the century. Records show that at this period there were two dame-schools, between them teaching 50 children, though both were apparently closed by 1871.

The longest surviving school to cater for girls was Mrs Sidney Herbert's Church of England School for Girls (later known simply as Wilton Park School), which opened in 1838. This was set up in a converted baroque pavilion in the grounds of Wilton House and in 1858 between 30 to 40 girls were being taught there by a qualified mistress. The curriculum here was totally different from that of the Free School in that, while academic subjects were taught, the main emphasis was on needlework. Many of the pupils became specialists, some even becoming involved with marking and making Wilton House linen.

Such were their skills that on leaving school the girls were given a box of clothes, all home made. The box itself was of wood grown on the estate and fashioned at the Sawmills. The religious aspect of the girls' education included learning by heart passages from the Bible, singing hymns and making notes on sermons preached at Wilton Church. Whenever they went to church they would walk in single file behind the mistress, who consequently referred to them as her 'little duckies'. There was another private school at the top end of North Street, in a thatched cottage

Although faded with age, this picture, taken in 1860, shows the girls of Mrs Sidney Herbert's Wilton Park School.

The baroque pavilion in Wilton Park used as girls' school.

just over the bridge on the Wilton side of the River Wylye, behind the Wheatsheaf Inn. The school appears to have opened in about 1924, as it is listed in the rate book for that year, but it could possibly have opened two years earlier. It was run by a Miss Wright, one-time governess to Duncan McKellar, the son of the head keeper of Wilton Estate.

The school was Riverside Preparatory School, and for the first few years Miss Wright was the only teacher of a class of 14 pupils that included John Jeffrey, Alec Thatcher, Dick Broderick, Geoffrey Peevor, Desmond Hare, Mary Wallis, Betty Larkham, Olive Graham, Ruth Scott, Betty Scott, Violet Harris, Janet Corby and John Larkham. In around 1930, Miss Wright was joined by a second teacher, Evelyn Blandford.

Miss Wright was a strict Victorian disciplinarian, to such an extent that, at times, many children were in fear of her. In fact it would not be an exaggeration to say that hers was a reign of terror. As many former pupils could testify, she was also of the opinion that if a child could not absorb knowledge naturally, it could be beaten in. She saw any form of affliction, illness or inadequacy as weakness and not to be

tolerated. Some former pupils report having seen her bang someone's face so hard on the desktop that their nose bled. One small boy, who was continually having his ears boxed for failing to answer questions, was found to be deaf and simply had not heard them. Another form of discipline was a hard rap across the knuckles or fingers with the nearest available ruler.

Miss Wright certainly looked the part. With her sharp, thin face on a very thin body, and her long hair pulled back into a bun, she was described by one pupil as looking like a witch. She also had another trait, which was to spit as she spoke; worse, when her temper really rose, her spittle would get on your exercise book. I can vouch for her strictness and the terror she could instil if she thought nothing was getting through to you, as I was a pupil there from about 1942 until the school closed in the summer of 1945. Picked up from home by Jean Moore, as you can well imagine I was never very keen to go. On one occasion, when Jean was not looking, I ran for home, but she caught up with me before I made it all the way.

The schoolroom was quite small when I was there, with a long desk running down the side of the room which faced the garden, a shorter desk along the back, and another long desk on the side of the room which backed onto North Street. There was one small central window on this wall, on either side of which were hooks for hats and coats. On a rainy day the wet garments caused considerable condensation in the room, as well as giving off the special odour that only wet raincoats can produce. At the other end of the room was the gas fire, the sole form of heating, in front of which Miss Wright stood to teach. The younger pupils, of which I was one, were taught by Mrs Blandford. When she appeared, usually at ten o'clock, we were relieved to see her, as her attitude was just the opposite to that of Miss Wright. School hours were usually from 9a.m. to 12 noon and from 2p.m. to either 3.30p.m. or 4p.m. – I cannot remember which, but we were all very glad when it arrived!

We younger pupils were taught the basics of

Girls of Wilton Park School in the early 1900s, with two of the teachers. One can't help but notice the absence of smiles on the girls' faces.

arithmetic, writing and reading, which a five-year-old could take in, while the older children were taught more advanced subjects and often had to copy long poems and learn them by heart. Usually given a weekend in which to learn them, pupils would be tested on a Monday morning. Unless they had learned the poem to Miss Wright's satisfaction, they could be made to stay in at playtime to learn it prop-

erly. The catechism was another of Miss Wright's favourites for pupils to learn. There were also music lessons, held in her drawing-room, access to which was gained by a verandah which ran from the back door of the schoolroom to the French windows of the drawing-room – a quick dash if it was raining. There was also a form of PT – simple exercises, some of them performed with short canes – held on fine days

The girls of Wilton Park School look happier here, possibly celebrating an Empire Day. The boys waving their caps in the air and giving three hearty cheers are from the Free School in North Street.

Pupils from Miss Wright's Preparatory School, taken on the day the school closed down in the summer of 1945. Among those pictured are: Pamela Cooper, Ann Coombes, Hugh Moore, Diane Fullerton, Wendy Gullidge, Rachel Lewry, Anne Moody, Ann Magerison, Evelyn Lane, Elizabeth Pretty, Chris Rousell, Trevor Shepherd, Nigel Napier, Cynthia Shepherd, John Moore, Bill Major, Dick Redwood, John Aston, Leone Case, Clive Parsons and Robert Moody. The teachers are Mrs Blandford (left with dark cardigan) *and Miss Wright.*

Miss Wright's Preparatory School in North Street. The schoolroom entrance and the window at the right-hand side of the building was later demolished to make way for the building of a house.

on the lawn behind the school.

In the summer of 1945 the school closed and the pupils went their different ways. I, along with others, went to the Junior School in West Street, where the headmistress, Miss Drake, was also very strict, though thankfully nothing like Miss Wright. Despite her strict discipline, she did equip us with a good basic education which stood us in good stead in our future schooling, even if her methods were

extreme. I have often thought since that if Charles Dickens had ever met Miss Wright, she would have made an ideal character in one of his books!

In 1842 the Parochial School, situated in West Street in premises once a cloth mill, became a day-school, although it was not affiliated to the National Society until 1902.

With accommodation for 310 children, it received a Board of Education grant towards teachers' salaries and the training of apprentices. Figures for 1878 show that a certified master, assisted by two pupil teachers, was teaching 70–80 boys, while an assistant mistress was single-handedly teaching 180–190 infants seemingly with no help whatsoever, something that would definitely not be tolerated in this day and age. At this time only boys were admitted, but later in the century it was decided to admit girls. The registers for 1919 show that 102 boys, 110 girls, and 118 infants were in regular attendance.

In 1935 the Wilton Church of England Junior School was reorganised at the same time as the new Wilton Church of England Senior School was opened at the Hollows. This left the Junior School with 170 mixed pupils and 92 infants, with 177 mixed pupils on the registers of the Senior School.

The new Senior School, provided by the Church of England authorities at a cost of £9,000, was run under the jurisdiction of the rector and churchwardens

Boys of the National School with schoolmaster Mr Hibberd in 1912. Situated in West Street, the school was originally a Parochial School until it united with the National Society in 1902.

Pupils of the National School with two of the schoolmistresses, who would have taught the infants while their male colleagues taught the older children.

Some of these boys, pictured here in 1915, are wearing Scout uniform, possibly because it is Empire Day. The master in the fashhionable straw boater is Mr Long.

of the parish, assisted by the local education authority. The latter was only responsible for providing the curriculum, teachers and other factors normally supplied by this body. The Church was careful to ensure that in certain matters they had absolute power to veto any decision by the education authority that they considered to be of detriment to the school. Provision was made at the school to accommodate boys and girls from Wilton and eight surrounding parishes who were to be provided with the best basic education to prepare them, on leaving, to take up full-time employment. Children who lived outside the parish, in South Newton, Wishford

and Netherhampton, had to cycle to school each day on bicycles provided by the education authorities which, for some reason, came to be known as 'James bikes'. Children from Burcombe, Barford St Martin, Compton Chamberlayne, Dinton and Teffont, had a special bus service provided. In later years, all children were brought in by special buses. Pupils also received a third of a pint a milk a day at a cost ½d., and hot lunches, consisting of two courses, costing 3d. a day. The school in West Street reverted to catering for juniors and infants, the only other school in the town at this time being a private one owned by Miss Wright. The first headmaster of the Senior

Pupils of the National School outside the school entrance, 1907. The archway was demolished long ago and the school was converted into a community centre in 1977.

An al fresco sewing class at the Wilton and Junior Infants School in West Street, 1927. The girls in the front row, two of them holding dolls, appear not to be a part of the lesson. Left to right, back row: *Beattie Musslewhite, Joyce Furnell, Pat Jaffrey, L. Burchill, T. Pavey, W. Wilson, Grace Bryant, Molly Waterman, Edie Brow;* front row: *Pat Oakley, G. Dowell, Hilda Yates, Winnie Scott, Ruby Surman, Winnie Loveless.*

At the time this picture was taken, the National School was known as the Primary School and the girls' and boys' play-grounds were separated the toilet block. This picture was taken in the girls' playground.

Wilton Senior School, just completed, in 1935.

School was Gus Elliott, a strict disciplinarian who would stand nonsense from neither boy nor girl. As a result, it was not long before a rhyme was made up about his frequent use of the cane: 'Gus Elliott goes to church on Sunday, to pray to God to give him strength to whack the boys on Monday'. At the Junior School in West Street, Miss Drake was as strict a disciplinarian as her counterpart at the Senior School, and you certainly knew it if you got on her wrong side.

Despite wartime restrictions, both schools struggled on, maintaining their high quality of teaching as best they could and, like everyone else in those hard times, played their part in helping the country when asked to do so. They suffered shortages of exercise books, paper, pens and ink, plus many other items once taken for granted. Another problem arose when evacuees attended the school and woodwork classes were discontinued, the woodwork room being used as an extra classroom to accommodate the incomers. The woodwork classes were replaced with gardening

and nature walks. Gardening classes, listed on the timetable as rural science, were held under the supervision of Eric Ruffell, who taught gardening when I attended the school. Like everyone else at that time, pupils would have carried gas masks and the school would no doubt have organised drills at various times. Even when the war finished, it took quite a while for things to get back to normal, and some shortages of materials continued for several years

Gus Elliott remained headmaster until 1948, announcing at a school managers' meeting in April that he would be resigning his post before the Michaelmas term began in September. Although he had recovered his health after an operation, he felt it would be unwise to carry on, especially as he did not feel as robust as he once did. The rector, the Revd William Drury, spoke of how Mr Elliott had directed the work of this important Church School, which was unique in this diocese, from the very beginning, setting it on firm foundations of scholarship, of skill and of good conduct. Gus Elliot duly retired at the end of the summer term and his successor, Tom Feather, chosen from many applicants, took up his post at the start of the Michaelmas term.

Both schools were involved in activities and events in the town, and in the Parish Magazine of July 1948, the Junior School received high praise for the efforts it had made on behalf of the Bishop's Appeal Fund by organising a garden fête, at which pupils won great praise for their elaborate dances performed with wonderful precision, and for their charming plays, with gaily dressed goblins flitting in and out of the trees. Mrs Holloway, it was said, 'deserves the highest praise for her training of the

Pupils of Wilton Senior School not long after its opening, with headmaster Gus Elliott (centre back) *and deputy head Eric Ruffell* (back row, far right), *the latter a popular master who taught sports and gardening, and kept beehives at the school.*

massed choir, whose words could be heard with great distinctness.' The event raised a total of just over £61, a considerable sum of money in those days.

The following month it was announced that 13 pupils from the Junior School had passed the examination to go to Grammar School that September. The successful children were: John Brockway, David Brockway, Nigel Napier and Grahame White, who would go to Bishop Wordsworth School; Shirley Baker, Barbara Bantock, Sylvia Barnes, Tessa Collins, Glenda Garner, Jennifer Head, Margaret Roberts and Jean Switzer, who would attend South Wilts Grammar School for Girls, and Barbara Shaw, who had won a place at Gillingham Grammar School. During the summer holidays that same year the Junior School underwent extensive renovations inside and out, including the installation of electric light and a wireless, so that the children could enhance their studies by listening to the BBC schools programmes being broadcast at that time. Outside, the schoolyard and entrance were covered with asphalt, paid for with the proceeds of the Whit Monday fête and with grants made by the Wilton Educational Charities, the trustees of one of the Herbert bequests and the LEA.

The following summer a meeting took place at the Senior School involving the managers of surrounding schools who were sending, or were likely to send, pupils to the school. M. Innes, County Director of Education, announced details of plans, estimated to cost £80,000, for the enlargement and improvement of the school buildings. Although the County would fund half, the remaining half would have to be raised by voluntary effort if the school was to retain its full status as a Church Aided School. The diocese offered to contribute all but £12,000 of the latter sum, meaning that if interested parishes were prepared to contribute proportionate shares of the £12,000, Wilton's quota would be £3,000. While the offer from the diocese was fully appreciated, the demand made on the parishes was considered to be beyond their resources. As a result, it was felt that the possibility of further schemes should be explored before a final decision was made. It was in September of this year, 1949, that I moved from the Junior School in West Street to the Senior School, then known as Wilton Area Secondary Modern School, having failed to gain a place in Grammar School. Although I had passed both parts of the written examination, in those days the final decision was made at an interview. For some reason or other, that was where I failed, perhaps just as well, as I never regretted attending the Secondary Modern, where many friendships were made.

Wilton Senior School Football Team, 1947. Left to right, back row: *Peter Davis, Rex Baxter, Malcom Deacon, Jim Tutt, Tony Harris, John Case, ? Pavey, Billy Larkham;* second row: *Tom Boyce, Peter Shearman, John Trim, David Boyes, Dick Hinton, Harold Ford, Cyril Johnson;* front: *Norman Arney.*

Naturally, on the first day, everyone was nervous, all wondering what school would be like and unnerved by rumours that it was very strict and that the headmaster, Mr Feather, ruled with a rod of iron. We arrived there in good time, not wanting to be late on the first day, and all stood together in the playground. We pupils from Wilton Junior School were joined by other new pupils coming in by bus from such country areas as the Wylye and Nadder Valleys. Once they arrived we were ushered into the school for our first assembly, at which Mr Feather welcomed us. I think we were surprised at how nice he was, considering how strict we had heard he and the staff would be. He explained what would be expected of us, told us that it was no reflection of our intelligence that we had not gained entry to a grammar school, and that we could still achieve great things at Wilton. Our names were then read out for our first class at our new school and the class teacher, Miss Parsons, shepherded us from the school hall to our classroom at the end of the corridor. She then called the register and, as those from the country schools answered to their names, we sneaked a look at them. We soon settled in and by the end of the first week it seemed as though we had all been together for ages. There can be no doubt that this was due to the teachers, who made every effort to help us all make friends with one another.

Assembly, held every morning in the school hall before lessons started and usually lasting around 20 minutes, consisted of a couple of hymns, prayers and a bible reading, often by a senior pupil. The headmaster would then read out any notices he had for the school. Afterwards we all filed to our classrooms, where the register was called and lessons commenced with religious knowledge, this being a Church of England school. Some lessons were held in the same classroom, while others, such as science and woodwork, or domestic science for the girls, had rooms of their own. The art room was situated on one side of the boys' playground, along which also ran a domestic science block and another woodwork room, these prefabricated buildings being used mainly for visiting schools. There were PE and football for the boys and hockey for the girls, cricket and rounders replacing these in the summer term. As the school did not have its own swimming pool, once a week in the summer we were taken by coach to the swimming baths in Salisbury for lessons. The school was situated in an ideal position, on a hill on the edge of the town, with lovely views across Wilton to Salisbury, where the cathedral spire could be clearly seen. In the other direction, there was a lovely view up the Nadder Valley, while at the back were open fields which led to Grovely Woods. It was ideal in the summer, but you certainly knew which way the wind was blowing in the winter. One winter, after a heavy fall of snow, the buses bringing the country children to school were unable to run, while those of us who lived in the town were expected to attend

Pupils of Class One in their first year at the Wilton Senior School, September 1949. Left to right, back row: *? Foster, ?, ?, Jill Whale, Michael Skinner, Mavis Alford, Miss Parsons (form teacher), Derek Miles, Pat Furnell, Brian Burton, Anne Petty, Peter Drewett, ?;* second row: *Richard Dibble, ?, Kenneth Gibbs, Dennis Barton, ?, Chris Rousell, ? Sheldrake, ?, Derek Catlin, Caroline Samways, Alan Payne;* front row: *Pat Morrison, Ellen Martin, ?, Ann Wilmore, Edna Earley, Josephine Wilmore, Ann Walker, Pamela Webb, Doreen Stout, Jean Arney. Ann and Josephine Wilmore were twins.*

despite the slippery conditions. One consolation was that the school did close about 45 minutes early to allow us to reach home by dark. Another concession was that, with the heating not up to its usual efficiency, we were allowed to keep our coats on.

School dinners, served in the school hall, were cooked in the kitchens on the opposite side of the corridor, while those who brought sandwiches had to eat them in the classroom, which was at the back of the hall. For special events, to enlarge the hall, a folding screen between this classroom and the hall could be opened, which was especially useful at Christmas for performances of the annual school play. I was fortunate to be in the cast of two of the plays, the first of which only had a cast of five. Although I cannot remember its name, from what I can remember of the plot, a family of husband and wife, and daughter are held up in their living-room by an armed burglar. I spent most of the play behind the scenes waiting for the cue to make my entrance near the end of the play. When it came, I had to put my arm through an open window and fire a gun, in fact a loaded starting pistol, which made the audience jump, after which I entered the room via the window. However, all ended well.

The second play, in what was my final year – I was 15 and had to leave school at Christmas – was

Shakespeare's *Twelfth Night*. Learning lines for this production was not easy and there were plenty of rehearsals for which I, in my final term, and other cast members skipped lessons. I played Sir Andrew Aguecheek, a comic role in which I was quite at home. The play went very well for the two performances; we enjoyed it and so did the audience. The lighting for the school plays was always done by the science teacher, Mr Tewson who, with his knowledge of electricity, was seen as slightly lethal – more often than not a fuse would blow when he set up, making a loud bang. Naturally some wag came up with a rhyme about him: 'Live wires, Freddy pliers, bright flashes, Freddy ashes', which just about summed up his luck with electrics. He was the same at times in the science lab, health and safety not being his strong suit, though we all survived.

Our history teacher, Mr Osborne, also took us for local history, and once suggested that three of us should pick a project and take with us three other class members. As one of the three chosen, I suggested the Gaumont Cinema in Salisbury, now the Odeon, the foyer of which was once a fourteenth-century banqueting hall built by John Halle of Salisbury, a wealthy wool merchant. When the idea was given the go-ahead, I had to write a letter to the manager to arrange the visit, receiving a reply by

The cast of the Senior School production of Twelfth Night. *Left to right, back row:* John Brine, Evelyn Fryer, Brian Lovett, Derek Miles, Christopher Irish, Richard Dibble, Pat Furnell, ?, Chris Rousell; *front row:* ?, ?, Stephen Saich, Anona Toft, Dorothy Harper, Ellen Martin, Dennis Barton.

I am not sure which character Evelyn Fryer was playing, but she is shown here with me, rehearsing a sword fight we had together in the play.

return of post inviting us to come along on a Saturday morning. On the allotted day we met the manager, Mr Howes, in the foyer. As he told us the history of the banqueting hall and how it had come to be used as the foyer for the cinema, we made copious notes. Then we had a bonus; he offered to show us over the cinema, the auditorium of which was built with a mock medieval interior in keeping with the structure of the foyer. We had a whale of a time; he even took us into the projection room, where the co-chief projectionist, Ernie Hopkins, showed us around, explaining how everything worked. We really enjoyed that project.

In the summer of 1950, the school took part in an Education Week, along with other schools in the area, which included an opening service in Salisbury Cathedral, and a special sports day at Victoria Park in Salisbury, where the school distinguished itself. Our home-based contributions consisted of presenting plays and inviting parents and friends to view our many activities, which included a wonderful display of handiwork of various kinds. An exhibit which caught everyone's eye was a lectern beautifully made by Kenneth Shearman for use in school assemblies. I can still see it to this day,

The new buildings added to western end of the school to accommodate the improved facilities and additional pupils when it became a Middle School.

a really superb piece of craftmanship, and beautifully polished. I have often wondered what happened to it in later years. It is amazing how skilled many of the pupils were in those days, but we all had one thing in common, the enjoyment of making something to show our parents and friends and to show just how good our school was and how proud we were of it.

The changes that have since taken place in education and schooling are astounding. In our day we had no computers and no internet to help us with our studies. All we had were textbooks and a blackboard. When we had to copy diagrams from textbooks into our exercise books there were no photocopiers, we just drew freehand, unless we had

tracing paper, which was not very often. Somtimes we copied passages from books or off the blackboard, but anything else we wrote was from memory, so we had to pay attention or end up in trouble. If that happened we could be kept in after school, or at break-time, to catch up on our work.

Eventually the time came for us to leave school, a sad occasion in many ways, as we had all made many friends. But now it was time to say goodbye, and to make our way in the big wide world. Although there were many unanswered questions about the future, we had been well prepared and were ready to take that big bold step. Schooldays the happiest days of your life? Yes, at Wilton Secondary Modern School they were.

✦ CHAPTER 4 ✦

Churches and Religion

The ruined Church of St Mary, Brede Street, in the Market Place, stands on the site of a former minster church, which was in existence before the abbey was built in Wilton. This minster church is thought to have been of some importance in the eighth century, evidence of its close association with the royal palace being the fact that at least two of Edward the Elder's daughters, and his second wife, were buried there.

The church was altered some time in the thirteenth century, and possibly made larger, as it by then had become the Parish Church. It was rebuilt during the fifteenth century, the present ruins dating back to this period.

The most important event ever to take place at St Mary's, was the consecration on 27 May 1229 of Robert Bingham as Bishop of Salisbury. The ceremony was held at Wilton because Salisbury Cathedral was still being built and the former cathedral at Old Sarum had been abandoned.

In earlier times, the church had a small tower on the western end, while the interior consisted of a nave and chancel, each of which had side aisles. At the time of writing a model of how the church looked, complete with the tower, is on display in the chancel, which has been preserved. For some reason the model shows a clock set into the tower on the side which would have faced the original Market Place – artistic licence on the part of the modelmaker, it seem, as illustrations of the church and tower show no such clock. However, it does appear to have had a bell, as there is a record, in the steward's accounts of 1441/42, of payment for the great bell to a man in New Salisbury.

In Wilton, the parish priest is always known as a rector. Since the establishment of the church in Wilton there have been many rectors, St Mary's Church listing 32 since the year 1305. In fact in that year there were two rectors, Thomas de Boyton and Richard Corbyn, possibly because the former left during the year to take up a living elsewhere, and was succeeded by the latter.

Allowing for some artistic licence, this drawing of the former Parish Church of St Mary, Brede Street, does give a fair indication of how the building looked before it fell into a state of disrepair. Eventually the majority of the building was demolished, leaving only the ruins which stand in the centre of the town today.

St Mary's Church from Kingsbury Square around the mid-1800. The tower of the new Parish Church in West Street is just visible above the rooftops of the houses in Brede Street. Note the Market Cross next to the building on the left.

The only part of the old St Mary's Church still standing, although the pews have long since been removed. Services continued to be held in this chancel for many years. The memorials on the walls are to benefactors and worthies from the town's past. Early 1900s.

When Walter Curle left the living in 1620 he was succeeded by Walter Raleigh – not the Walter Raleigh of fame but rather his nephew, the son of Sir Carew Raleigh of Downton. Walter was born in 1586 and, on reaching the age of 16, matriculated at Magdalen College, Oxford, gaining his BA in 1605 and his MA in 1608. For a time chaplain to the Earl of Pembroke, in 1621 he accepted a living as rector of Chedzoy, in

Somerset, in addition to that at Wilton. Later in the year he gave up his living at Wilton and was succeeded by Richard Chandler. During Raleigh's tenure a carved pulpit was installed in about 1628, which was moved to Wylye when the church closed.

Richard Barford, who took up the living in 1678 and remained until his death in August 1735, was the longest serving rector – he served longer, in fact, than the famous Vicar of Bray.

Barford was born in 1652 at Wormleighton in Warwickshire, matriculated at Magdalen in 1669, became a BA in 1673 and MA in 1676. Two years later he was installed as rector of St Mary's and from 1702 was the vicar of Long Newnton.

Barford tended the parish well, devoting himself to his parishioners and involving himself in local affairs, seemingly with no interest in politics. He did, however, have a large family, although there is some confusion over their relationship to one another. It is also widely believed that he could be the same John Barford who, with William Moody, obtained a patent for carpet-weaving.

There is a black stone slab dedicated to the memory of Richard Barford which reads:

Fifty Six years a Faithful Rector of this Parish and a Generous and Kind Neighbour to his Parishioners and

Acquaintance, And of Eluzay his beloved Wife who was justly esteemed for the sweetness of her Temper and her truly Pleasant Conversation. Richard died Aug. 4, 1735, aged 82, Eluzay died Oct. 9, 1733, aged 70.

Records exist of another Eluzay Barford, grand-daughter of the rector and his wife, who died on 26 January 1733 aged 14 and who appears again in the chapter concerning the war in Wilton. The name Eluzay is possibly a derivative of Lucy.

Unfortunately, the church seems to have been constantly in need of repair over the years, which was a steady drain on its resources. In the early-nineteenth century the situation had become such that the Hon. Sidney Herbert and his mother, the Dowager Countess of Pembroke, generously offered to build an entirely new church in the town.

In 1841 Charles Amyand Harris accepted the post of rector at Wilton, having been appointed to oversee the transfer from the old church to the new. It would be up to him to persuade the congregation that the move to the new church was desirable and to ensure everything went smoothly when the time came. In 1841 he published a sermon entitled 'One Rule and One Mind', which is thought to have been based on his position as rector of the parish. Although he was to receive many honours, Harris was dogged by ill health and tragedy. His seven-year-old son, James Edward, died not long before the new church was to be consecrated and was one of the first to be buried in the churchyard of the new church.

By the time the new church was opened in West Street in 1845, the old church, then in a very bad state of repair, was partially demolished and ivy planted to render the ruins more picturesque. Only the last section of the nave and chancel were retained to use for the occasional service.

The ivy, grown out of control, gradually took its toll on the fabric of the ruin, causing serious damage to the stonework. In 1938/39 action was taken by the then rector, Revd Guy Campbell who, with Miss Edith Olivier, Wilton's first lady mayor, elected in November 1938, and with other friends of the church, transformed the churchyard into a garden of peace.

The rehallowing of the chancel of the old Church of St Mary, plus the dedication of the churchyard, which was intended as a space for quiet reflection, took place on 6 May 1939. During the ceremony, which was performed by the bishop of the diocese, a memorial tablet dedicated to Robert Bingham, Bishop of Salisbury, consecrated here in 1229, and to another Robert Bingham, a former US ambassador, was unveiled by the Rt Hon. George Charles Bingham. The US Ambassador, on a visit to Wilton, had discovered that an ancestor had been consecrated here, and had offered to restore the building in his memory. Although he died before the work was begun, members of his family honoured his wish to have the work done.

The visitors' book from that time until 1952 shows just how many people visited the church in this period, including those visiting during the Second World War, which started in September of 1939, around four months after the ceremony.

The book makes interesting reading, not least for the signatures of the dignitaries who attended on the first day, including the mayor, Edith Olivier, the rector, Guy Campbell, Neville Samson, William C. Bridges and one who simply signed himself 'Lucan', the father of Lord Lucan, who disappeared mysteriously in the 1970s. Of equal interest are the signatures of the many ordinary visitors.

The entries for August 1939 contain the names of those Wiltonians who signed as schoolchildren. These include G.M Hayter, J.L Orchard, E.M. Hayter. R.G. Noble, M.H. Hayter, F. Pearce, V. Lloyd, Brian J. Foster, B. Beck, Terry Blake, Eileen Hayter, Harold Ford and his sister Hilda, Joyce Sutton, Nancy Moore and her sister Jean, Grace Croome and Terence Lynch. Entries for September include some of the names of the first evacuees from Cosham, children whose lives were radically changed with the onset of the Second World War and who were trying to make a new life in Wilton among total strangers. It is hoped they eventually returned home safe and sound, but those of them who signed this visitors' book left their own unique mark on the town.

From the war years there are signatures of visitors from all over the country, many being those of servicemen stationed here during the hostilities. They came from such places as Norfolk, Barrow-in-Furness, Kent, Cornwall, Blackpool, Durham, Hereford, Scotland and Wales, with quite a number from London. On 13 December 1943 the first American serviceman to sign the book was Richard Q. Howell, from Jersey City, New Jersey, and in February 1944 Major Charles Damer McKenrick of Baltimore, Maryland, Major Samuel R. Turner of Washington DC, Mack Tucker of Jacksonville and Harold C. Temple of Philadelphia, Mississippi, also signed. It is quite possible that these servicemen were stationed in Wilton at the American base situated in the Avenue. A number of the Americans who visited the church during their tour of duty would have been posted abroad. Let us hope they survived the war.

One interesting and unusual was entry made by J. Vincent Ramsgate, Lieutenant RNVR, from Ruislip, Middlesex who, in July 1945, wrote the following:

Upon the walls of this church there is a notice saying 'Children are not allowed to play on this holy ground'. Will someone in the name of God, remind the Rector of who said, 'Suffer little children to come unto me'.

In June 1950 many more Wilton schoolchildren signed the visitors' book. Celia Pavey, Margaret Harris and Raymond Partridge all made their visit on

The altar and choir stalls of the new Parish Church. The altar was given by the people of Wilton.

More of the interior, showing the Italianate pulpit.

An early-Victorian likeness of the new Parish Church of St Mary and St Nicholas, soon after its opening in 1845.

This postcard was sold by Winters of Wilton, newsagents and stationers in West Street near the market.

21 June. A few days later, on the twenty- sixth, there was quite an important visitor, Robert Worth Bingham III, who described himself as 'Grandson of the restorer of this church'. Two other family members were also present, Sarah Montague Bingham and George Barry Bingham junr. On that same day, Pamela Cooper of Wilton made a visit and one wonders if she actually saw the Binghams and wondered who they were. In July some pupils from the Senior School signed the book, possibly on a local history project. Pupils from Wilton included Doreen Waters, Jean Arney, Pamela Webb and Ann Walker. The other pupils who signed, from the Chalke Valley village of Wylye, were Caroline Samways and the Wilmore twins, Josephine and Ann. It is noticeable that, with two exceptions, all these signatures are of girls. One thing is certain, their names evoke many happy memories of schooldays at Wilton.

The new church in West Street, opened on 9 October 1845, was inspired by the Lombardic churches of San Pietro and Santa Maria, which stand outside Tuscania, near Viterbo, north Rome. It was originally the intention to include some of the features of a Lombardic church; as it is, the main plan of the building follows very closely the ancient basilicas, or law-courts, of the Roman Empire.

A great many examples of early workmanship were brought in from abroad and incorporated into the interior. The marble columns used to support the arches at the south end of the aisles came from the second-century-BC Temple of Venus at Port Venere, on the Gulf of Spezia. The decorated twist columns on the pulpit are studded with mosaics from the shrine of Santa Maria Maggiore, Rome, having

formerly been in Horace Walpole's garden chapel at Strawberry Hill.

The church, though standing well back from the road, cannot be missed when one passes by, although many people, to this day, are surprised to see a building of this nature and stature standing near the centre of the town. The churchyard, large and well laid out, features broad walks either side of the church, the remainder of the ground having been planted with an abundance of evergreen shrubs at the time of consecration.

On the south side of the building is the campanile, which rises to a height of 108ft and houses six bells, possibly from the old Church of St Mary. Any doubt as to their provenance lies in the fact that, shortly before their removal, the bells were recast; at the same time, the bells from Wishford Church were also sent for recasting, resulting in a mix-up which possibly left Wilton with bells which really belonged to Wishford. If this is true, it is believed that the confusion was to Wilton's disadvantage. Separating the campanile from the main body of the church is a covered walkway, approximately 20ft in length, on either side of which is a double row of enriched columns, each in a different pattern. The ornamental work covering the interior of the cloister is described as being very beautiful and excessively elaborate.

The original organ was brought from Wilton House and placed at the south side of the chancel. To make it suitable for church use, additions were made to it including ornamental pipework to harmonise with the chancel decorations. These alterations were carried out by Mr Bevington, of Greek Street, Soho, assisted by one Mr Prangley, a local man from Salisbury. This organ was replaced in 1847 by one built by William Hill & Son, this being reconstructed in 1936 by Rusworth & Dreaper, who managed to re-use most of the old pipework. The organ is said to be one of the finest in the county, second only to that in the cathedral. Further work carried out entailed moving the whole organ to the opposite side of the chancel so that the organist could see more easily what was going on around him, particularly on special occasions.

Wilton Parish Church was a gift to the town from Lord Herbert of Lea, who was a friend of Florence Nightingale. One of the main features of the church is its stained glass, much of which is medieval and of continental origin.

It is said that, during the building of the church, the dowager duchess intended to construct a magnificent altar, which would be covered by a canopy. When the bishop heard of this, he tactfully pointed out that the Church of England only allowed a wooden table to serve as an altar. Not to be outdone, the dowager replied that if she could not have her altar, she would have an equally splendid pulpit. Although it was said that the dowager, who was of Russian descent, had the altar placed at the west end of the church because it was customary in Russia to do so, the fact is that the majority of Russian churches have their altars in the east, and that the altar at Wilton is at the west end simply because the entrance is at the east end, precluding its siting there.

At the time of the consecration of the new St Mary's it seems it was only one of many churches to be newly consecrated, reopened or rededicated. St Mary's, however, was unique in being the only church built as a result of generous individual patronage akin to that engendered by the religious zeal of the Middle Ages; also unique was the sheer magnificence of its unusual design. A report in the *Salisbury Journal* extolled the virtues of the church, describing it in such great detail that the report of the actual consecration service took second place.

On the day of the consecration, church dignitaries and clergy processed from the National School to the church, where they were joined by Bishop Denison of Salisbury for the commencement of the service at 11a.m. Led by the bishop, the procession entered the church through the western doorway, followed by the Chancellor of the Diocese, Dr Philmore, the Dean of Salisbury, the Archdeacon of Wilts and Sarum, the Revd Precentor Hamilton and the clergy. When the service of consecration was completed, the Communion service was conducted by the bishop, assisted by the rector and Precentor Hamilton.

In his sermon, the bishop noted the discrepancy which too frequently exists between the lordly mansion and the neighbouring Parish Church, the former, furnished with every luxury the skills of man can devise, contrasting with the latter's bare walls, damp, dilapidated seats and decayed furniture. He concluded by saying that no unseemly contrast between the house of man and the house of God existed in this case; here wealth had been redeemed from worldly usages, to be a testimony of God.

After leaving the church, the bishop and clergy perambulated the churchyard to perform the

Crowds gather for the unveiling of the war memorial on Sunday, 20 November 1921 by the Earl of Pembroke. The dedication was performed by the Archdeacon of Sarum.

remaining ceremonies of consecration. According to the *Salisbury Journal*, the ceremony should have taken place at an afternoon service, plans being changed at the last minute when the bishop became ill and was anxious to return to his palace in the close. The evening service was conducted by the rector, a beautiful anthem being performed on the organ by Mr C. Corfe of Salisbury, accompanied by the Salisbury Cathedral Choir.

In order that the people of the parish should not miss out on this special day, Lord Herbert made special provision for the humbler classes. Over 1,700 tickets were distributed, each entitling the holder to a liberal supply of beef, bread and strong beer. Inmates at the Union Workhouse, not forgotten by his lordship, were allocated an abundance of roast beef and plum pudding.

During the building of the church there was one unfortunate fatality. This occurred one cold, frosty morning, when the unpopular foreman of the works insisted that the men climb the scaffolding, despite their protests that it was dangerous to do so. Eventually they did climb up and commence work, but when the foreman followed them a few minutes later, he stepped on a plank which immediately gave way, causing him to fall to his death. A few years later one of the workman confessed on his deathbed to having tampered with the plank.

For the strong Nonconformist presence in the town, most of whom were Congregationalists, there was a chapel in Crow Lane. Their church was founded in 1700, when they took over a small Presbyterian meeting-house in Crow Lane, but in 1789 nine trustees of the church gave their consent for this original building, due to an increasing number of worshippers, to be demolished. An appeal launched to raise funds for a new building drew a wide response from independent ministers and congregations in the surrounding counties.

The new church, opened in 1791, remained in use on the site until its closure in the early 1980s, when its foundations were declared to be unsafe. In fact the shell of the building, at the time of writing, still

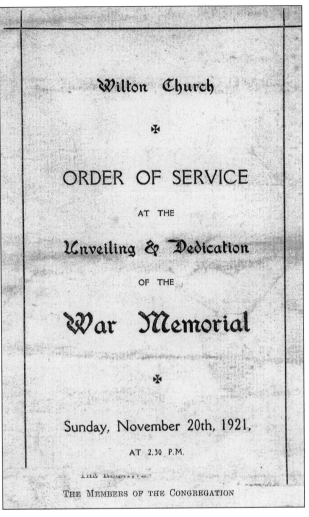

The front cover of the order of service at the dedication of the war memorial.

stands, having been converted into flats in 1987, though the Sunday school attached to the main building was demolished. That this was the original building of 1791 is evidenced by a memorial tablet from the church for a Mrs Priscilla Edwards, who died at the age of 23 on 14 December 14 1791.

Unusual for a Nonconformist church, it had an adjacent burial ground which seems to have been established before the new building was erected. Proof of this is the tombstone of Revd William Gardner, the date of his death being 11 January, 1782. A minister at the church, his tenure was the longest in its history, covering the period 1750–82. During the last two years of his ministry, when he became infirm, he engaged an assistant minister to help him. In 1781, a year before his death, the Sunday school was founded, exactly a year after a similar venture was begun in Gloucester.

As verified by the Sunday-school records of 1851, the Sunday school was eventually a huge success and was well attended on a well-nigh full-time basis, the average attendance being 110 in the mornings, 80 in the afternoons and 60 in the evenings. The church

The Congregational Church was erected in 1791 when the original chapel became too small. The building adjoining the chapel housed the Sunday school and vestry. The latter building has since been demolished, and the main body of the chapel converted into flats.

services also attracted large congregations, the average numbers being 200 in the morning, 100 in the afternoon and 250 in the evening. In 1829 it was reported that the church had 400 members. As mentioned in Chapter 3, the Congregational Church also ran a day-school courtesy of Charles Baker, the third longest serving minister and an ardent educationalist. It was through his efforts that was founded what became known as the British School.

In the late 1860s the church became disorganised, a state which was remedied in 1870 by the arrival of a new minister. It also seems that the church closed for a short period at this time, as it is recorded that extensive repairs took place and that heating was also installed at a cost of £750. When the church reopened in July 1872 it was recorded that: 'The

chapel had never been heated up to this time.'

All this effort was worthwhile, the church becoming so busy with its affairs, it had to appoint 14 persons to assist the minister in his pastoral work and administer to allotted areas in the town and neighbourhood. The church also became responsible for services at Barford and Wishford.

More repairs, carried out in the summer of 1885, appear to have been fairly extensive, as the church was closed for three weeks while work was undertaken, services being held in the Town Hall.

Though the chapel continued to thrive through the nineteenth century, during the twentieth century a gradual decline set in and in October 1945 Wilton Church was grouped with Broadchalke and Ebbesbourne Wake in the Chalke Valley. A new

The Interior of the Congregational Chapel. Note the memorial tablets on the walls.

minister, the Revd John James Haynes, was installed, his first duty being to oversee the grouping of the three churches, whereby they would share one minister between them.

The earlier grouping of Broadchalke, Ebbesbourne, Bowerchalke and Bishopstone had been attempted in the early-nineteenth century, but the arrangement had lasted only a few years.

The earliest mention of amalgamation under one minister with Broadchalke appears in the records of a Wilton church meeting held on 22 January 1929, but it seems that no further action was taken at the time. Further tentative suggestions were made at intervals, but it was not until December 1943 that the idea of joining Broadchalke and Ebbesbourne Churches with Wilton was taken up in earnest. Negotiations between the three churches, with the encouragement and support of the moderator and the county Union Executive Committee, continued through 1944. That year the Revd J.J. Haynes, of the Mid-Somerset Group of Churches, visited the district and preached at Wilton on Sunday 21 January 1945, at Broadchalke and Ebbesbourne on Sunday 18 February and at all three churches on Sunday 15 April. He was then pressed by the moderator to make available his experience in the starting of this new group, should the churches invite him to become their minister. A unanimous invitation to the Revd Haynes on 18 April was accepted by him on 7 May, and he was minister to the newly formed group from 4 October 1945 until 4 October 1956, when he took up an appointment as minister at Langley Green, near Birmingham.

During the latter part of the eighteenth century the chief evidence of religious activity derives from the returns of houses that were licensed for worship. These reveal that, although Quaker, Methodist and Independent congregations were meeting in the town, there is no record of Baptists meeting here at this time, indicating that they did not come to Wilton until the late-twentieth century.

Although two houses are shown to have been licensed for Quaker meetings in 1704, in that year and subsequently in 1761, meetings were neither well enough established nor well enough organised to be described as regular.

In 1832 a Quaker meeting-house was opened in Russell Street, this being attached to the monthly meeting of Poole and Southampton. Later in the century they moved to South Street and in 1898 the building here is described as 'Friends' Meeting House, South Street', the same building, in 2006, housing the public library. Meetings were held on the first Sunday, suggesting that they were held on a monthly basis, as they had been in Russell Street. Meetings commenced at 10a.m. with a Bible reading, followed by worship at 11a.m. with an evening Mission Meeting at 6p.m. The Quakers also ran a type of Sunday school, for adults rather than children, comprising a 'morning adult school' from 9a.m. to 10.05a.m with a women's adult school at 2.45p.m.

The years 1778, 1780 and 1794 saw major growth in Wesleyan Methodism in Wilton, with a congregation of 150 by 1829, eventually leading to a chapel being built at the top of North Street on the corner with Riverside. In 1851 the average congregations numbered 60 in the morning and afternoon, with 100 at the evening service. Despite these figures the chapel is known to have closed in the early-1930s.

At the time of writing the building, converted to residential use, is aptly named 'Chapel House', having previously been used as a warehouse.

During the third decade of the nineteenth century, the Primitive Methodists began to establish themselves, their first appearance being in 1821 at a house licensed by William Sanger, a preacher at Salisbury who had connections with 'Tent Methodists'. In 1829 there was a regular congregation of 40 Primitive Methodists and by 1837 a chapel had been established in West Street consisting of 113 free sittings, plus 50 further sittings. Records from 30 March 1851 show numbers attending as 32 in the morning, 48 in the afternoon and 69 in the evening. On the same day the Sunday school had an attendance of 16 children. In round 1880 the West Street Chapel closed and, in Kingsbury Square, a new Methodist Chapel opened in a building thought to have been intended as a temperance hall, evidence of this being that the chapel itself was upstairs, the two lower rooms being used as a Sunday school. My great-grandfather, Josiah Jacobs, became caretaker of this chapel and lived on the premises with his wife and family.

When the Primitive Methodists moved to Kingsbury Square another Methodist congregation was already established there, the Methodist Reform Church having opened a chapel in the square in 1872. In 1896, when this chapel closed, it is possible that the Methodist Reform congregation merged with that of the Primitive Methodists to become the United Methodists. In 1932 the Primitive Methodist Church became the home of the Wilton Methodist Church when the Primitive Methodists, Wesleyans and United Methodists merged.

In these early times, with a strong Methodist community, services were well attended. Not long after the end of the Second World War, however, as congregations began to dwindle, the church was taken out of use and one of the schoolrooms used in its place. The church was then used just once a year for the annual harvest festival. In 1966 the church became redundant when the local Methodists and Congregationalists merged to form the Free Church of Wilton, the Methodists moving into the Congregational Church in Crow Lane. The church in Kingsbury Square, sold to the Catholics, was then renovated and renamed St Edith's Church, Edith being Wilton's patron saint. The blessing and opening ceremonies took place on 15 November 1969. The Catholics had previously held Mass in a small chapel at Southern Command in the Avenue.

In 1984, when the church in Crow Lane was declared too dangerous for services to be held there, the Roman Catholics offered the Congregationalists a home at their church. The Catholic Church was thus renamed St Edith's Methodist and United Reformed Church and a united service was held there on Sunday, 18 November 1984.

This happy association lasted 20 years until, in January 2004, it was announced that, with falling numbers in the Methodist and URC congregation, it was no longer viable to hold services in Wilton. The final service was held on 4 January 2004, and an Epiphany supper held later was shared by both congregations. The sharing agreement was finally terminated on 31 January

It was not until Saturday, 11 April 1981 that the Baptist Church opened in the the former Town Hall, the first service, held outside the church in the Market Place, being conducted by the Revd Gwynne Edwards of the Salisbury Brown Street Baptist Church. The first service held inside was conducted by the Revd H.J. Vellacott, then minister of East Ham Baptist Church, London, who inducted his son, Revd Oliver Vellacott as minister. Since then the church has gone from strength to strength, and is today very much an active force in the town. Oliver Vellacott was succeeded by the Revd Andrew Thomson, who remains the minister in 2006.

In June 1981 a small news item appeared in the *Salisbury Journal* concerning the Christian Spiritualist Church, situated in the former church of the old Wilton Workhouse on the Warminster Road. According to the report, this interesting and often criticised group of Christian spiritualists met each Sunday to communicate with friends and relatives who, according to their beliefs, had merely passed over into another life.

❖ CHAPTER 5 ❖

Wilton's Railways

Although only a small market town, Wilton could once proudly boast that it was served by two railway stations operated by rivals the Great Western Co. and the Southern Railway Co. Although both lines still run through the town, trains no longer stop here, both stations, long since closed, being no more than a distant memory.

The eventual arrival of two railway companies was a major boost for the traders of the town, meaning the quicker arrival of goods, especially of fresh fruit, vegetables and other perishables. Industry also benefited, goods from the felt mill and the carpet factory now being sent much more quickly to customers by rail.

With frequent trains from two companies to choose from, Salisbury became much more accessible to residents, who no longer had to rely on the carrier's cart or to walk the three miles to the city. The bulk of local passenger traffic between Wilton and Salisbury was captured by the London and South Western Railway (LSWR), the station being that bit nearer to the town and with a more frequent service. The bulk of passenger traffic on the Great Western Railway (GWR) was of course to Bristol, although their revenue was mainly from freight, particularly from coal. In Wilton, coal merchants

could now collect supplies direct from both stations, making delivery to customers much easier.

There were other bonuses; it was possible to visit relatives and friends more frequently in outlying villages in the Nadder and Wylye Valleys, and later there were special excursion trains to the coast, facilities which we take for granted today. Although the world was thus opened to the people of Wilton, such luxuries were within the reach only of the well off. For the working classes such days out remained largely inaccessible.

The Great Western Railway

The railway arrived at Wilton in 1856 with the opening of the Great Western Railway station just off the Warminster Road, to goods traffic on 11 June and to passengers on 30 June. The line through the town ran between Salisbury and Bristol via the Wylye Valley, through Warminster, Trowbridge, then on through Limpley Stoke and Bradford-on-Avon, after which it joined the GWR's main Paddington to Bristol line at Bathampton. The GWR had been persuaded by influential businessmen to build the line which, forming as it did a direct link to Bristol, would be more beneficial for trade than the proposed

Steam power in the late 1940s. From Salisbury to the Avenue bridge at Wilton, the GWR and Southern lines ran side by side. This GWR Bristol-bound express is about to enter Wilton just where the two lines go their separate ways.

(PHOTOGRAPH BY BILL CANNINGS)

63

A painting by the author of the GWR Station in the early 1900s. To the left is the booking hall and entrance to the station, while on the left, behind the footbridge, is the goods shed. A siding ran from the signal-box (centre right) behind the up platform, emerging onto the main line. Note the small platelayers' hut to the right of the signal-box.

Just after its closure in 1956 the station had changed very little since the early 1900s.

GWR link with Chippenham. In fact the line only ran from Bathampton to Salisbury, the then terminus, the GWR considering it no more than a branch line, despite the services it operated. Originally a single line in broad gauge, a feature of the GWR in the pioneering days of the railway, there was only one crossing loop between Wilton and Warminster, situated at Wylye. When traffic increased, this loop became inadequate and extra loops were installed at Wilton in 1867, at Heytesbury in 1888 and at Codford and Wishford in 1898. However, due to the services operating to Bristol, it did allow Exeter and Plymouth to be reached from Salisbury in these early days, even if the journey by this roundabout route was long and tedious. In fact, at this time, although the rival Salisbury & Yeovil Railway Co. had been up and running for six months, their service only operated between Salisbury and Gillingham, the extension to Sherborne, Yeovil and beyond having not yet been completed.

According to a railway timetable dated November 1859, in the up direction to Bristol there were only three trains which stopped at Wilton. The 10.57a.m. arrived at Bristol at 1.35p.m., with a connection to Exeter and Plymouth leaving Bristol at 3p.m. Arrival times were at Exeter at 6p.m. and at Plymouth at 9p.m. The second train left Wilton at 1.50p.m. and arrived at Bristol at 4.30p.m. with a connection to Exeter and Plymouth at 6p.m., arriving at Exeter at 8.33p.m. and at Plymouth at 12.05a.m. The third train of the day left Wilton at 6.05p.m., arriving at Bristol at 8.40p.m. In the down direction to Salisbury, the first train of the day to stop at Wilton was the 6.50a.m. from Bristol, departing here at 9.25a.m. and arriving at Salisbury ten minutes later. The next two trains to arrive at Wilton were the 7.10a.m. from Exeter, arriving at 1.50p.m., followed by the 6.50a.m. from Plymouth, reaching Exeter at 9.55a.m. and Wilton at 4.16pm. The final train of the day was the 12 noon from Plymouth, reaching Exeter at 2.45p.m. and arriving at Wilton at 9.01pm. However, services from Salisbury on this route only operated on weekdays, with no service at all on Sundays. It was not until conversion to standard gauge that Sunday services came into being and then only on a limited basis; so limited that on Saturday nights, when the signalman finished his shift, the signals at small interim stations on the line were set to clear for the Sunday workings. When I was still a young boy, just after the end of the Second World War, I can remember the signals being left at clear all day on a Sunday. It was not until 18 June 1874 that the conversion to standard gauge took place, gangs of navvies moving in to slew the sleepers so that conversion could take place as quickly as possible. Three days later, with the work complete, the first standard-gauge train ran to Salisbury at walking pace. A small tank engine, No. 615, was used to haul this train, which was to open a completely new era

for the GWR in this area. The line, once a mere branch, was to become a major through route, an agreement to allow through running between Bristol and Southampton having been made with the LSWR, which had built a new station beside the GWR terminus at Salisbury. The through connection was finally opened in February 1874, trains for the journey south being hauled by locomotives of the LSWR, a practice which continued through the years of steam operation until July 1967.

After the conversion of the gauge both passenger and goods traffic greatly increased. There was certainly a great increase in mineral traffic, including coal traffic from the Forest of Dean and, with the opening of the Severn tunnel in 1886, coal from South Wales. Passenger traffic grew, especially in the summer months, with six trains each way during the week and one a day on Sundays. In order to improve efficiency, the decision was made to double the line, which was done in stages. The section between Salisbury and Wilton was doubled by 1 July 1896 and that between Wilton and Wishford by 28 April 1901.

The majority of coal trains from Wales were extremely long, up to 40 wagons, full to the brim. Because the engine was pulling such great weight on the up gradient through Wilton to Salisbury, it was important that these trains had a clear run through the station. I do remember one occasion when one of these trains was brought to a halt. On being given the all clear, it took the driver minutes to get the train moving, inching it forward by degrees until the driving wheels could get a firm grip on the rails. Due to his skill and expertise, the train was soon on its way and, by the time the last wagon had passed the end of the platform, the train had picked up speed.

The first recorded accident on the GWR was late in the afternoon of Tuesday, 5 August 1873 at Skew Bridge. Although a crossing was installed at Wilton, the line between there and Salisbury was still single track. A Bristol-bound train had arrived at Salisbury about 30 minutes late and the Wilton stationmaster, Mr Isaacs, was anxious that it leave as near to its original departure time as possible. He telegraphed to his counterpart at Salisbury what is termed a 'cross order', announcing that the line was clear, a procedure consistent with single-line working. To ensure there was no mistake, the Salisbury stationmaster took the precaution of returning the message then, when he was fully satisfied that all was correct, despatched the train. Meanwhile, the Wilton stationmaster, forgetting that he had signalled 'line clear' to Salisbury, signalled the train from Bristol, which had arrived earlier at Wilton, to proceed to Salisbury. Quickly realising his mistake, he threw off his coat and ran after the train in the hope of stopping it, but was unable to do so. The two trains were involved in a head-on collision at Skew Bridge, with seven people seriously hurt and others sustaining minor injuries. Among the seriously injured were guard

William Tucker, from Bristol, with scalp wounds in two places, both lips cut through and both large toes broken; stoker Henry Bell, from Bath, with a compound fracture of the skull and a broken leg; driver Thomas Harvey, from Bath, with a compound fracture of the skull and a broken leg; driver Thomas Atkins, from Chippenham, whose left leg was broken; and George Brandis, who sustained a scalp wound. Such was the impact that the two engines were locked together, the guard's van of the Bristol train was completely smashed, the first trucks of the Salisbury train, which was a mixed passenger and goods, were tipped up on end and the line was completely blocked for several hours. The newspaper report concluded:

We believe that Mr Issacs, the station master at Wilton, is in a state of mental distress bordering on distraction, in consequence of the occurrence.

On Saturday, 9 August, Isaacs was replaced by Mr E. Miller, who had been in charge of Heytesbury station for two and a half years. Mr Miller remained at Wilton until 1906, when he resigned his position as stationmaster. He wrote two letters on 18 August, both to the Divisional Superintendent, C. Kislingbury, at Bristol, one being a letter of resignation, the other setting out why he was disgruntled with his position at Wilton. Both make fascinating reading, giving a good insight into exactly what led to his resignation, and are transcribed exactly as he wrote them:

Traffic Wilton   *August 18 1906*
C. Kislingbury
Bristol

Resignation
Sir, I beg to tender my resignation as from August 20 to end Sept. 15, and should be glad if you would transfer my name after that date to the Pension List. I joined the Service February 2, 1864, and after two days at Bristol, was sent to Salisbury Goods two and a half years later to Passenger dept. and worked Salisbury and Wilton section by Single Needle and crossing order system. April 30, 1867 to Weymouth as Signalman, Dec. 1868 to ???????? as Signalman, January 2, 1871 to Heytesbury to take charge – afterwards August 9, 1873 to Wilton – so that I have served 25 years as Station Master, making 42 years 8 months Service, and I hope I have given satisfaction.

From Sir,
Your obedient Servant.
E.Miller.

His second letter read:

To C. Kislingbury   *August 18 1906*
Bristol.
Sir, I have this day sent you my resignation. I regret

having to do so, as my health is good and I have completed 42 years easily. My reason for doing so is the uncertainty of the staff. Men are here for a short period, and get used to the work and are got useful – are taken away and another sent of little or no use to take their place – my work here is double to what it was twenty five years ago – then I had better men – men who would help and try to keep things right – but the men we get now are but very little use – and their one aim is to do as little as possible. This worry me – and I feel to go on under such conditions would wear me out before my time. You will no doubt have seen before this have seen my application to a Lad Porter, I may say for your information, that our competitors have two Signal Porters, and one Porter, outside man, also a Clerk, and from what I can gather from some of their staff – their takings for Goods and Passenger Traffic, is less than ours – they have a good parcel traffic, viz; Milk and watercress in its season. The Station Master resides at the station and with help he have, is able to get about and see traders and keep in touch with the general public. On the other hand, I fail to find time for this work – and sometimes to the loss of traffic to the company and so the work viz; one to Station, many hours over this time keeps, and I think to resign is the best step I can take. Thanking you for your kind consideration.
I remain Your obedient Servant
E.Miller.

Reply from C. Kislingbury   *August 21, 1906*
Divisional Superintendent

Dear Sir,
Resignation
I am in receipt of your letter to me of the 18 instant, and regret the time has come for you to leave the Service. I hope you will live to enjoy a well earned rest and that you will reach a good age.
Yours sincerely
C. Kislingbury.

Among Mr Miller's correspondence concerning his resignation is a reply from a Mr Pope, who was in charge at Langford Station and who, it is obvious from this letter, has been recommended by Mr Miller as a suitable successor at Wilton. Although Mr Miller's original letter has not survived, Mr Pope replied as follows:

From Langford   *To Mr Miller*
August 24th 1906   *Wilton*
Dear Mr Miller,
Allow me to thank you for your of the 20th inst. It was very kind of you to think of me. I have had a good try but I am afraid I do not stand much chance. I hear there is a good lot in for it, no doubt older hands than myself. However one cannot do more than try. We had the notices out the same day as I got yours, so they

did not waste much time. All the applications to be in by tomorrow morning, so I suppose we shall soon hear who has got it. I have my leave start November 13, hope to see you then if not before. Where are you going for your annual leave. Any chance of you paying a visit to Langford while you are out, should like to see you if you could come down for a day, supposing I do not get to Wilton. In any case, hope to be in Wilton in November. Hope you will spend a pleasant and joyful time, and that you will feel the better for your hard earned rest. Mrs P. joins with me in sending best wishes and I hope you will long enjoy good health and so be able to enjoy the full benefit of your long holiday.
Yours sincerely
M.G. Pope.

The station at Wilton, typical of GWR designs for small country towns, consisted of two platforms. On the platform of the up Bristol line was a red brick building which housed the the small entrance hall and ticket office, the stationmaster's office and a small waiting room. The platform on the opposite side, the down line to Salisbury, was reached by the traditional GWR covered footbridge. On this platform the only shelter for passengers was a small wooden hut, inside which a wooden seat ran the length of the back wall. The front had two square-

Also in March 1982, an HST passes through the former station. Although these trains did not usually run on this line, on this occasion it was had been diverted due to continuing line works on consecutive Sundays on its usual route from Exeter.

A 33 class diesel hauling a four-carriage passenger train from Bristol. With these diesels mostly used on small freight trains, this was a most unusual sight.

At dusk on the last day of March 1982 this double-headed train of empty stone-carrying trucks passes through the former GWR Station on its way to Westbury. Note the former booking hall, then used as an office on a small industrial site in the former station yard.

paned glass side panels but no door, so that passengers, though dry, would have been freezing cold in winter. At the Bristol end of this platform was the signal-box, while behind it a siding ran from near the signal-box to just beyond the end of the platform at the Salisbury end, where it joined the main line just before the bridge which carries the Kingsway Road over the railway.

From a point just past the end of the platform a line ran into the goods shed, which was situated about 50 yards from the end of the Bristol line platform. There was another set of points here, which allowed connection to the line running to Salisbury. The line running into the goods shed originally continued right through and reconnected with the main line just before the bridge over the Warminster Road. The majority of trains on the line were expresses, running to Bristol and Cardiff in one direction and to Southampton and Portsmouth in the other. In 1901, it was reported, two trains a day ran from Portsmouth to Cardiff and two to Bristol, with the same amount running in the opposite direction. In 1922 a service with through carriages commenced from Brighton to Cardiff, with an equal number of trains running in the opposite direction. The express services were supplemented with local slow services, stopping at all stations to Bristol. This could possibly have had a knock-on effect on passenger ticket sales, figures for 1923 showing the number issued as 4,956, while ten years later there was a drastic drop to only 865. With reference to parcels forwarded, 1923 shows a figure of 4,646 with an increase in 1933 to 5,016.

Most GWR standard-class locomotives were able to work the line, the only real exceptions being the very large King class. Most workings were done by the Hall, Grange or Manor classes. From the early 1930s there were regular workings of Southern Region steam locomotives between Salisbury and Bristol until, in 1963, diesels took over completely

Until just after the Second World War, both goods and passenger traffic remained steady, but in the early 1950s the motor car was becoming more popular and more affordable, while bus services into Salisbury were more frequent and easier to access, and fares were cheaper. As a result, passenger traffic slowly declined and, on 19 September 1955, was discontinued. Goods traffic continued for a further ten years, until its inevitable decline was followed by complete closure of all goods services on 6 September 1965. A single siding, retained for private use for a number of years, eventually fell into disuse and was finally removed.

With the exception of the building which housed the ticket office and the goods shed, which was used for other purposes by a private firm, the whole station was demolished. The former ticket office building was used by an agricultural firm as offices until 1987, after which they were demolished. Since then the former station site has changed completely, the only building still standing being the former goods shed, while opposite, an earth bank marks the site of the former down platform to Salisbury.

Services still run on the line between Brighton, Portsmouth and Cardiff, operated by the Wessex Line with two- and three-carriage units.

The Southern Railway

The Southern Region line, which ran through Wilton and was originally built by the Salisbury & Yeovil Railway Co. between Salisbury and Yeovil, was eventually to connect with the London and South Western line planned to run between Yeovil and Exeter. The building of this line through Wilton brought about the end of the GWR monopoly in the town.

On 3 April 1856, the day of the 'turning the first sod' ceremony at Gillingham, the weather did its worst. High winds and driving rain persisted throughout the ceremony, throwing the words of the speakers back into their teeth. The opening was performed by Miss Seymour, sister of the company chairman, Henry Danby Seymour. The balance held in the company's bank account at this time amounted to only £4.2s.4d. After the ceremony, even the huge marquees did not afford much protection from the weather, as the rain penetrated the canvas, even getting into the wine and champagne. One of the party was heard to comment, 'We have had so much cold water thrown upon us before, that a bucket or two extra now can make no difference.'

Although originally a single-track line, eyes were set firmly on the future, and all the earthworks, stations and bridges were built to accommodate double track, thus cutting down on any future expenditure. In fact, by 1870, the doubling of the line had taken place.

The first section of line to be opened, on 2 May 1859, was between Salisbury and Gillingham, the Gillingham to Sherborne section opening on 7 May 1860. A few weeks later, on 1 June, the Sherborne to Yeovil section was opened, followed on 19 July by the opening of the LSWR line from Yeovil to Exeter.

The station at Wilton opened to passengers on 2 May 1859 and to goods traffic on 1 September of that year. On weekdays trains running between Salisbury and Gillingham left Wilton at 7.44a.m., 11.21a.m., 2.04p.m., 6.21p.m. and 8.11p.m. Trains from Wilton to Salisbury left at 7.44a.m., 11.09a.m., 2.04p.m. and 6.04p.m. These running times show that there was a passing loop installed at Wilton, departures at 7.44a.m. and 2.04p.m. leaving the station in both directions at the same time.

The trains were operated by the LSWR, which made matters easier all round. In 1872, when the LSWR made a takeover bid for the Salisbury & Yeovil Railway, the offer was firmly rejected. In 1877, when the chairman of the Salisbury & Yeovil Railway died, the LSWR made another, successful, bid and in January 1878 the takeover was completed.

The Southern Station at Wilton consisted of two platforms, the up platform, towards Salisbury, being the main one. The buildings on this platform consisted of the stationmaster's house, an outside covered waiting area, a small inside waiting-room, a booking-office and the signal-box. Beyond this platform at the Salisbury end, there were three sidings and a goods shed. The sidings were connected to the main line just before the Avenue road bridge which passes over the line.

On the downside platform there was just a red-brick shelter, the two platforms being connected by a footbridge. Until after the Second World War the bridge was covered, except for a section which

Mr Ricketts a porter at the LSWR station, talks to some of the passengers involved in the crash in August 1915. This photograph was taken by my grandfather, at the time a local community reporter for the Salisbury Journal.

passed over the sidings behind the down platform. This section accessed a footpath which led down to the Warminster Road, saving passengers the longer walk up the Kingsway Road, where the main station entrance was situated. The sidings were much larger than those of the GWR, and through the years freight handling was a major source of revenue, hundreds of boxes of watercress being handled when it was in season. Access to the sidings was gained just beyond the end of the down platform, where a single siding doubled just beyond the footbridge. The siding nearest the platform was the shortest, finishing just beyond the platform at the Salisbury end. The longer siding ran back as far as the Avenue bridge and served the earth-built, brick-faced platform used for loading and unloading sheep on sheep fair days. The field in which the fair was held was adjacent to this platform. In its heyday this was a very busy area of the station, most sheep being brought in by rail, and an engine was kept here all day, busy with shunting operations. To save the engine having to run back to Salisbury for coal and water, special arrangements were made to provide these facilities on site. In 1915, with the First World War in progress, two sidings in addition to those serving the Fairfield were installed to accommodate extra troop traffic. Not only had a small Army camp been built at the bottom corner of the Fairfield but there were Army camps springing up in villages all

along the Wylye Valley. On Saturday 7 August 1915 there was a tremendous crash at the station when an Exeter express ran into three trucks left on the main line after shunting operations at a point between the down platform and the Avenue bridge, where the line curves to the left, continuing on through the station. The down signal was set to clear for the express, driven by Mr J. Coombes of Exeter who, carefully observing the signal, was under the impression that the line was clear. As the train rounded the curve, driver Coombes saw the trucks on the line ahead of him and instantly applied the brakes. As the train was a full ten coaches long and travelling at 50mph, it was not possible to stop it in so short a distance. On striking the trucks, the train ploughed through them as if they were matchwood, finally coming to a halt at the end of the down platform. By some miracle, neither the engine (a Drummond T9) nor any of the coaches was derailed, or the accident could well have been much more serious. The sound of the engine hitting the trucks was so loud that people living a fair way from the station heard it and, fearing there had been a terrible accident, flocked to the station to see what had happened.

One truck, hurled into the air, fell onto the platform and destroyed 14–15 yards of masonry, tearing a gap in the fencing at the rear. Not completely thrown clear of the train, one corner of the truck sheared off coach door handles, splintered wood-

The engine involved in the accident, streaks of tar running down its boiler. This Drummond T9310 suffered damage to its front but was soon repaired and back in service. The driver, J. Coombs of Exeter, was praised by the passengers for his skill in averting a much worse disaster.

work and smashed windows. Strangely, the first coach, occupied by soldiers, escaped damage, with not even a window broken. A second truck was lifted into the air, crashing down, wheels uppermost, on the right-hand side of the train, while the third truck, wedged in the broken part of the engine, was dragged along by the train, tearing up great chunks of the permanent way for about 200 yards. Adding to the horror of the moment, barrels of tar being carried on the trucks burst open, scattering their contents in all directions, over the engine as well as the track and platform. It is said that the permanent way at one point looked like a river of tar. Fortunately, only four soldiers and a Mrs Lane of London required any

The LSWR station in the early 1900s, when it was extremely busy. The train on the left is departing for Exeter, while that on the right has arrived from Salisbury.

A Merchant Navy Class hauling an express from Exeter has just passed through the Southern Station and is about to pass under the Avenue bridge, from which this photograph was taken in 1949.

A Drummond T9, on shunting operations at Wilton in 1949, about to enter the siding on the up line. These engines were used in the early 1900s for hauling express trains on the Southern Railway.

A painting by the author showing the station in the days of British Rail, when it was renamed Wilton South. Note that the protective cover over the bridge has been removed.

medical treatment, chiefly for cuts. They were treated in the stationmaster's house by the local medic, Dr Stratton. The most severe injury was sustained by Gunner Hayman of Minehead who, as the train rounded the bend, was looking out of the window and, realising a collision would occur, jumped from the train and was cut about the head.

One person to escape serious injury, even possible death, was the station porter, Ricketts, who had been posting bills on railings at the Salisbury end of the platform. Hearing the noise of the impact and seeing the train and the wrecked trucks hurtling towards him, he jumped from the platform in front of the engine and crossed to the other platform. As he jumped, he saw a barrel with jets of tar bursting from it fly through the air and land on the spot where he

had been working. At 4p.m. a relief train arrived to move the passengers, who had been stranded at the station since 11a.m. During this time it had been possible to pass trains through the station with single-line working. With the passengers gone, workman began to clear the tracks and, later that night, the line was completely cleared and normal traffic restored.

A few years ago I was talking about the accident with Ken Foyle, once in business in Wilton as a corn and seed merchant. It seems that, as a small boy, he had actually witnessed the accident happen. He had been on the footbridge at the Exeter end, watching the shunting operations, which had suddenly ceased. The engine backed into the siding and the signals cleared for the Exeter express from Salisbury to run through the station. Seconds later he heard the express approaching but, because of the curve of the line, was unable to see the far end of the line. Suddenly there was an almighty bang as the engine smashed into the trucks, and he could see them being thrown into the air, followed by loud bangs as they crashed onto the platform. There were grinding and cracking noises as the engine ploughed through the station, pushing debris before it. At this point Ken ran from the bridge and down the steps to the safety of the footpath, only venturing back when all went quiet. He did not remain there long, as he was spotted and told to go home, but he did notice that, apart from the sound of steam escaping from the engine, there was complete silence; not a sound came from the passengers, many of whom were, even then, being led from the train in an orderly fashion.

Resplendent in her Southern livery, Merchant Navy Class No. 2164, Cunard White Star, waits in the siding, complete with name plate attached, waiting to take the 'up' Devon Belle to Waterloo.

With the new engine waiting in the adjacent siding, the 'down' Belle arrives, c.1948, at Wilton. The London engine would be detached and returned to Salisbury in reverse while the new engine took the train on to Exeter.

An unidentified Merchant Navy Class eases the Devon Belle out of Wilton, having just taken over the train for the remainder of its journey to Waterloo. The train is about to pass under the Avenue bridge, which takes the road over the line.

The Devon Belle all-Pullman Service on its way non-stop to Waterloo. Both this and the photograph on the left were taken by the late Bill Cannings of Wilton. The Nissen huts were by built by the Americans during the Second World War.

The observation car at the rear of the Devon Belle was another great feature of this train, affording passengers a view of the tracks they had just travelled. This train, just approaching Wilton from Exeter, was photographed from the Hollows Road. Just visible in the background is the chimney of the felt mills rising above the treetops.

(PHOTOGRAPH BY BILL CANNINGS)

Not long after the end of the First World War, Parliament ruled that the railways should be divided into four major companies, the LSWR becoming the Southern Railway. At Wilton the daily routine continued much as before. Figures for 1928 show the number of passenger tickets issued for the year as 2,480, with 3,051 tickets collected, but in 1936 there was a drastic drop, only 917 being issued and 1,687 collected. Similarly, in 1928, 1,949 parcels were forwarded and 4,621 received, while in 1936 the number of parcels received had increased to 4,760, with a drop in parcels forwarded to 1,643.

During the Second World War, the Southern Railway saw an upturn in both passenger and goods traffic, the station having become important to the military, the headquarters of Southern Command being at Wilton House. Later in the war, with the arrival of the Americans at a camp in the Avenue, the station was used for many different purposes. One familiar sight, as the war progressed, was that of ambulance trains being laid up overnight in the sheep fair sidings. The postwar period of the late 1940s and early 1950s is firmly implanted in my mind. These were busy periods for the Southern, with fast, semi-fast and slow trains passing through the station on a daily basis, especially on summer Saturdays during the peak holiday season. This was a dream come true for such nine-year-old boys as myself, who were interested in trains at that time. From midday onwards was absolute paradise.

The first train through to the West Country was the Atlantic Coast Express, or ACE, as it was affectionately known in railway circles. Its origins go back to the LSWR days, when a West of England express left London's Waterloo Station at 11a.m., but it was not until 1926 that it was given its famous title. This train served many destinations in the West Country, its different sections being split off at various points in its journey, so that one had to be in the right part of the train at the right time in order to reach one's destination. Although the train would have made only one stop, for a change of engine at Salisbury, by the time it reached Wilton it would have achieved a fair speed, making a magnificent sight as it rounded the curve to run through the station, pulling its rake of up to 14 green carriages.

Because this line carried traffic to many holiday destinations in the West Country, it came to be known as 'the holiday line'. In 1947 the Southern Railway introduced a new luxury service for the holiday traffic, the all-Pullman Devon Belle, complete with its Pullman coaches of brown and cream livery with a special observation car attached to the rear. This train was introduced in an attempt to attract more holiday traffic to the West of England via this route.

In theory, the Devon Belle ran non-stop between Waterloo and Exeter, but as there were no water troughs on this route and the tenders could not carry sufficient water for the 159 miles, it meant a change of engine was required. Salisbury, although the normal place for this operation, was not an official stop, and it was decided to change engines at Wilton, thereby avoiding confusion for passengers at Salisbury. News soon got around the town that the Devon Belle was to change engines here, much of the excitement being due to the fact that a Pullman train was actually to pass through Wilton. When the great day arrived, Saturday 16 June, it seemed the whole town took to several vantage points to see this new train pass down the line to Exeter, and as it went by, at about 2p.m., many gave it a hearty cheer. The down train, timed to arrive at Wilton at 1.47p.m., was given six minutes for the change of engine, the same amount of time being allocated to the up train on its arrival at Wilton at 3.30p.m. The train first ran at weekends only, but during the peak of its popularity it ran from Thursday to Tuesday inclusive. Those at Southern Railway were proud of this train, every effort being made to attract passengers.

In this postwar period, both the Devon Belle and the Atlantic Coast Express were hauled by the Merchant Navy class Bulleid Pacifics, as were many expresses on this route, their lighter sister engines of the West Country and Battle of Britain classes working the semi-fast services, and the familiar Maunsell 2–6–0s the stopping services. Express services ran at regular two-hourly intervals during the day, interwoven with the slower stopping services. Between Salisbury and Yeovil the typical routine was for a slow train to precede a fast to Salisbury, whilst in the down direction the slow followed the fast, a system of working which enabled passengers travelling from intermediate stations to travel to London reasonably quickly with only one change of train. On Saturday afternoons, at around 3.45p.m., the all-stations train to Exeter would arrive at Wilton bringing with it the evening newspapers from London, in those days the *Star*, the *Evening Standard* and the *Evening News*. These were collected from the train by Mr Trowbridge, from the newsagent B. & M. Winters. He would take the papers into a small shelter on the platform, where he sorted them. He would then put them into a bag and take them to his bike – a trade bike with a huge basket and a tiny front wheel – then ride into town, delivering some of the papers and taking the rest to the shop for sale.

Soon after the slow train to Exeter had left, the pick-up goods would arrive from Salisbury, spending about half an hour on shunting operations before continuing its journey westwards. One very chilly spring day still stands out in my mind. On this occasion, after the engine had been uncoupled from its trucks on the main line to run through the station, it stopped at the platform and the driver invited me onto the footplate for a ride while the shunting took place. I had seen this shunting operation many times before, so I knew what I was in for. I needed no second invitation! It was an enjoyable experience for a nine-year-old boy and has remained in my memory ever since. Being lifted up by the fireman to pull the whistle cord and informing the signalman that we were ready for the points to be changed was a great thrill. In January 1949 the Southern pulled out all the stops to help some local workers get to Salisbury. Heavy overnight snow having prevented the early morning buses from running, about a dozen men walked to the station to see if they could catch a train. The depth of snow was such that it took them longer than anticipated and they arrived at the station only to be informed that they had just missed the train. With the next stopping train not for three hours, the workers had three options – wait for the train, walk to Salisbury or return home. The signalman, who was in the booking hall, asked the men to wait while he made a telephone call. On his return he informed the workers that a late-running express was due in about 15 minutes and that he had permission from the management at Salisbury to stop the train at Wilton to pick them up and take them to Salisbury. It seems the driver, who was running late, was rather surprised to be halted, but his unexpected passengers were soon aboard and on their way to work.

With the nationalisation of the railways British Railways renamed the two stations at Wilton to avoid confusion for passengers. The GWR Station was named Wilton North and the Southern Railway station, Wilton South.

Much remained the same at the Southern Station, but in 1954 the Devon Belle service, by then losing money, ceased. Although people still travelled by train to their summer holiday destinations, they were no longer prepared to pay luxury prices, even for the extra touches offered by the Devon Belle. In the ensuing years a gradual decline set in and at Wilton

North, in 1955, passenger services were withdrawn, although they continued at Wilton South. In June 1964 all goods traffic ceased, passenger traffic surviving for a further two years until March 1966.

At this time the area was taken over by Western Region, which had control of the line between Wilton and Exeter. They immediately introduced single-line working from Wilton in the down direction, causing a huge outcry from those who saw this as the first step in a plan to close the line and switch passenger traffic to Western Region's own Paddington to Exeter route. Although Western Region hotly denied these allegations, it was many years before people were finally convinced this would not happen. Not long after the closure, demolition gangs moved in, tearing up the sidings, removing the footbridge and completely demolishing the down platform. This left only the up platform intact, including all the buildings. The former stationmaster's house was still lived in by Bob Blandford, a signalman at Salisbury, and his parents, his father also having once worked for the railway.

The signal-box remained in use until November 1981, when its duties were taken on by a new panel box in Salisbury. The former signal-box was not left to rot, however. It was purchased and preserved by the members of the Mid Hants Railway, who removed it the following year and installed it on their railway at Medstead and Four Marks.

At the time of writing more changes have taken place. The site of the former sidings on the up side has been built on, the new industrial units being completed in 2005. The stationmaster's house is no longer lived in, Bob's father having died several years ago and his mother in October 2003. Sadly, her death was followed that same November by that of Bob, who had suffered a terminal illness for some years.

An early Sunday morning HST running through what was left of the Wilton South Station in March 1982. Due to fairly extensive line works, many HSTs took this route to accommodate the Paddington to Exeter service.

CHAPTER 6

Special Events and Celebrations

The people of Wilton have always known how to let their hair down and celebrate, supporting such events as coronations, the granting of a new charter and those organised by the various societies and organisations of the town. Whatever the occasion, Wiltonians have turned out in force to enjoy themselves and give their whole-hearted support. Many of these events have traditionally taken place in Wilton Park, the grounds of Wilton House and part of the estate of the Earl of Pembroke, and succeeding Earls have carried on this tradition to the present day.

Without doubt, one of the most successful events to take place in Wilton Park in the early days was on 4 August 1873, a bank holiday, when a fête organised by the Foresters' Friendly Society attracted 20,000 people, each of whom paid a shilling (5p) to watch performances by the famous tightrope walker Blondin, a Frenchman whose main claim to fame was his numerous crossings of the Niagara Falls, each renowned for its theatricality, including his sitting down midway to make and eat an omelette.

The event at Wilton was described in great detail by Edward Slow, the dialect poet, who wrote:

Well, thick hallerdy in August last,
Beat everything as wur gone past;
Zich a day wur never zeed avore,
An spoose ther never will no mwore.
Tha Voresters zich lucky elves,
Had got tha day ael to therzelves;
An they mead up ther minds outrite,
The hood get up a tidy zite,
An zummit that should tract tha voke,
An wich they did wiout a joke;
Var we a man neamed Blondin thay,
Did gree ta com here on thick day;
Ta wak upon a rope za high,
That he hood nearly touch the sky.

The Foresters agreed a fee of £100, and to make sure that word got around, posters were put up both in the town and in villages and towns for miles around. The only thing left to chance was the weather and, fortunately, when the day dawned, it was bright and sunny, remaining so for the whole day.

By as early as ten o'clock the streets of Wilton were alive with people; vans, brakes and wagons choked the roads and West Street was a mass of hats and bonnets. Outside the park the scene resembled that of a country fair, with numerous stalls and booths, the one selling ginger beer doing a roaring

trade. Amid the rows of carriages and horses, the crowd shouted and and bawled to be let quickly into the park so as they could get a good view. Such were the numbers of people that the gates opened at 10.30a.m. to ensure no one would be disappointed.

Soon there was not a blade of grass to be seen, with people walking about in every fashion imaginable – Slow described it as being even better than Rotten Row. There were shawls and gowns in every colour, bonnets of every hue trimmed with green or blue. The ladies' hats, all of different shapes and sizes, attracted much attention:

Wich they did car on top their hair
Wie velvet, ribbon, tule, an leace,
An bows and ends aroun ther feace;
An veathers, too, stuck up za high,
Vrim every bird that wings the sky.
An lor ta zee zom on ems hair,
Like girt bee pots a hanging there.

For years Edward Slow was thought to be the only Wiltonian to have put into verse the story of this great event, but a few years ago, whilst browsing in a junk shop, I discovered a small book of poems by Fred Robinson, who owned a drapery business in North Street, and who had also written a short poem on Blondin's visit. He mentions some facts not covered by Slow. It appears that a procession from the Bell Inn, in which the Foresters, dressed all in green, marched behind their banner, travelled through the town to the LSWR station to meet Blondin, who was to arrive from London by train. The large crowd which greeted him, along with the Royal Marine Artillery Band, then accompanied him to Wilton Park. Fred also mentions that the Byzantine Church was also open on this day, as was the Wilton Carpet Factory, tours of which were apparently free of charge. As Fred put it in his poem:

Beautiful carpets are there for you to see,
As you may see on the Foresters' bills,
By kind permission of Messrs Yates and Wills.

On arriving at the park, Fred and his friends walked around admiring the flowers and watched a performance of Shakespeare, after which they strolled along the edge of the river before the start of Blondin's performance at 3.30p.m.

Blondin certainly kept the crowd on edge and biting their nails at the feats he performed. He

For the celebration, on 24 June 1897, of the diamond jubilee of Queen Victoria the weather could not have been more perfect. Here the people of Wilton enjoy a free dinner in the Market Place, many of them with black umbrellas raised against the sun. Note the group on the right, seated on a long plank supported by piles of bricks. The gentleman at the end of that table, wearing a bowler hat, is my grandfather, William Lane, the lady in white wearing a white straw hat is my great aunt and the lady behind her wearing a black dress and bonnet is my great-grandmother.

The same event, showing just how huge the crowd was – no doubt a bit of a headache for the caterers. The square was attractively decorated for the occasion and it appears that when darkness fell, fairy lights were hung among the trees in the churchyard. Next to the Town Hall (on the left) is the Fire Station, the word 'Fire' being clearly visible on the open door. Later in the day the children were given a free tea at these same tables.

started normally enough, walking the rope with a balancing pole, standing first on one leg, then on his head, then balancing on chair, all 60ft in the air. What came next truly amazed everyone. An iron cooking range was raised up to the Frenchman, followed by bellows to blow the fire. Next came eggs, fat and flour, which he mixed together in a large tin and proceeded to cook, lowering the food down for people to try. The crowd were amazed at the ease with which Blondin carried out the task. He then lay on his back, blindfolded and with a sack over his head; he then slowly walked the length of the rope, turned and ran back again. Next, an assistant climbed up and sat on Blondin's shoulders. Still blindfolded, the Frenchman again ran across the rope, turned and ran back again. Each time he reached the middle of the rope Blondin stopped, the man on his back shouted, 'hooray' and the crowd echoed the cry. Finally he rode a velocipede, an early form of bicycle, along the rope. When he finally came down it was to tumultuous applause.

The day ended with dancing to the music of the Royal Artillery Band and amusements of every sort. One attraction popular with the men was archery, while some of the younger girls set up a kissing ring and made plenty of noise chasing the boys before brazenly kissing their quarry. Such was the fun of the day, however, that no one seemed to mind this outrageous behaviour. Refreshments for those staying late were provided by Henry Small of the Wheatsheaf Inn, and festivities finally ended with a grand firework display at 9p.m., after which the band played the people out of the park. The townspeople had seen nothing like this before, and the feats that Blondin performed at the Foresters' Fête in Wilton Park were talked about for years afterwards.

For the Victorian working classes, who worked long and arduous hours over a six-day week, bank holidays were a bonus. Sundays were usually set aside for attending church and wearing one's Sunday best. After lunch, there being none of the leisure activities available today, it was not unusual for a family to go walking, favourite destinations being the meadows or Grovely Woods. A bank holiday at the end of the working week meant two whole days off, and various activities would be arranged in the town. With the arrival of the railway in the late 1850s, it became popular for those who could afford it to take an excursion train to the seaside for the day.

The next big celebration at Wilton occurred on 9 September 1885, the town having been granted a charter by Queen Victoria empowering a new corporation to run the town and extending the town boundary to incorporate parts of the parishes of Fugglestone St Peter, South Newton and Burcombe. The process of incorporation complete, the *Wilton Magazine* reported, in September 1885:

In the course of the last week in July, the new Charter

of Incorporation for the borough of Wilton was received from the Town Clerk to the satisfaction of many of our townsfolk. Wilton will not now disappear from the list of English Boroughs, but will remain within it with a rather extended area.

The day of was certainly a lavish affair, celebrated amidst much jollification by the people of the town.

Lore wurden there a start las week,
In thesase yer leetle town;
Dang if the voke an pleace did'n zeem,
Agean turn'd upzide down.

Var one an ael, bouth girt an small,
Jin'd in tha jollification,
Ta zelebrate the grantin o'
A bran new Carperation.

There was an early start to the day, the young men of the town out and about at four o'clock in the morning, waking the residents to the sounds of pipe and drum. To make sure everyone was up, cannons were fired, the whole town resounding to their noise. Now thoroughly awake, people began to decorate their houses with flags and flowers and, in many instances, garlands of flowers were stretched across the streets. Here and there were small banners bearing the words, 'Success to our new New Charter'. By midday, everything was in place and the festivities began with a procession in which all the town's clubs and societies took part.

At the appointed hour the grand procession moved off behind a huge banner bearing the names of the kings who had previously granted charters to the town, the first in 1100. Then came the Wilton Band, playing for all they were worth, followed by the oldest club in Wilton, the Weavers, formed in the 1600s. Behind them came the Good Samaritans with a donkey ridden by one Gargy Bindun, proud as a king until the donkey decided to kick his heels and fling poor Gargy off. Although the hearty laughter of the crowd did nothing to soothe his wounded dignity, Gargy got up, gave his pants a rub, remounted and carried on.

Next came the Oddfellows, all wearing the sash and star and carrying their banner before them, followed by the Foresters, dressed as Robin Hood's merry men, Little John, Will Scarlet and Friar Tuck making a grand sight. Following on were the two fire brigades, their engines gleaming, followed by Sam pulling the water cart. Bringing up the rear were the schools, marching to pipe and drum.

On reaching the Town Hall they were met by the mayor and, after a short respite, the procession moved on through the streets of the town, bands playing, bells ringing, people shouting and boys and girls singing. The procession broke up with three hearty cheers for the queen and the corporation, and everyone made their way to a large tent where, at 2p.m., they sang grace and tucked into a free meal. There were large joints of beef, piles of bread and barrels of ale and stout, and by 4p.m. around 500 adults had been fed. No sooner had the meal finished than hundreds of children began their special tea of bread and butter and plum cake. Rich or poor, the townsfolk made the most of this opportunity to eat as much as they wanted.

Afterwards all sorts of diversions were provided, including Punch and Judy, children's races and battledore and shuttlecock. Following this was a tug o' war across the River Wylye between the Foresters and the Oddfellows. A bugler sounded the start of the contest, which lasted just over two minutes. With one mighty heave, the Oddfellows, pulled the Foresters head over heels into the river, at which the crowd roared with laughter. The greasy pole contest, in which people were invited to try and win the leg of mutton on top of the pole, was won by one Vincent who had rubbed his hands in sawdust to secure a better grip and was given a hearty cheer when he cut the leg of lamb free. There was also a concert performed by blackface minstrels who sang, danced and told jokes.

As darkness fell Chinese lanterns were lit and there was a firework display, with catherine wheels, rockets zooming into the sky and squibs and crackers making loud bangs. After this the band played and people danced until festivities stopped at 10p.m. Hearty cheers were given for the new corporation, for the committee who had arranged the celebrations and for the house of Pembroke, after which the National Anthem was sung.

Thus closed thease memerable day,
Tha girt big Zelebration;
On tha grantin of a Charter var
A lected Carperation.

Of course, not all social events were on such a grand scale. Smaller, but just as important, were the many fêtes, bazaars, sports events and concerts held by clubs and societies to raise funds for their individual causes or for some special community project. Indeed, this practice continues today and, although the causes may differ, the common factor remains community spirit. Today the most popular method of raising funds is the coffee morning, many being held in Wilton each year, bringing people together not just to buy items, but to have a quiet cup of coffee and a chat with friends.

In 1907, on Wednesday 5 June, the Wilton United Football Club held their annual dinner at the Talbot and Wyvern Hall, at which the chairman for the evening was the Mayor of Wilton. It seems the club was enjoying some success, as on the front of the evening's programme they were described as, 'Winners of the Salisbury and District Junior League

Celebrating the coronation of King George V in 1911. These being the days of Empire, nearly all processions, even into the 1950s, were staunchly patriotic, the British characters of Britannia and John Bull, with his Union Jack waistcoat, featuring large at such events.

A prize-winning float at the coronation celebrations.

– 1905–6–7.' After dinner there were various toasts and an evening of songs and pianoforte solos, rounded off with the singing of 'Auld Lang Syne'.

One of the biggest celebrations in the early 1900s took place on Thursday, 22 June 1911 for the coronation of King George V and Queen Mary, which Wiltonians celebrated in grand style. At 10.30a.m. the mayor and corporation, accompanied by the various friendly societies and headed by the South of

Crowds celebrate the coronation in the old Market Place. Here, at the end of the Edwardian era, on what seems to be a sunny day, umbrellas are again used as protection from the sun.

Coronation coin presented to Cecil Morris.

The reverse of the coronation coin with the insignia of the Town Council and name of the mayor.

England Band, processed to the Parish Church for Divine Service. The procession then reformed and returned to the Market Place, where a free dinner was provided for all persons of 14 years and over, as long as they had subscribed to the fund and were in possession of dinner tickets.

For those under 14 years of age there was a free tea, which commenced quite early, at 2.45p.m. Before attended the tea, the children were asked to assemble at the school playground, where they would receive their coronation medals from the mayor. Then, on entering the Market Place, each child was presented with a coronation mug by the mayoress. The reason

for the early tea that Wilton Park, opened at 4p.m., was to be the venue for Old English sports and pastimes, with dancing arranged for 5.30p.m.

The day's celebrations were rounded off with a torchlight procession starting at 8.30p.m. from the Pembroke Arms Hotel, where prizes were also given for the best fancy dress. The procession then moved off via the Market Place, Silver Street, along West Street, up Grovely Hill to Grovely Down for the lighting by the mayoress, at 9.45p.m., of a huge bonfire. In fact, torchlight processions were quite a feature of Wilton celebrations, and it was said at one

The huge bonfire on Grovely Down, lit to celebrate the silver jubilee of King George V in 1935. This field became known as Jubilee Field, an oak tree, the Jubilee Oak, being planted as a more permanent reminder of the event. A commemorative tablet was later added.

time that the town would invent an occasion just as an excuse to have a torchlight procession

The torches, made at the felt mills, were of felt soaked with especially thick oil to make them burn well. Although there were times when burning felt flew off the torch and landed in the crowd, no one complained. It was just accepted that such a thing was bound to occur and, as far as is known, no one was ever burned as a result. Standing in West Street and looking up to the entrance of Grovely, the torches made a lovely sight as they were carried up the hill by the torch bearer.

On Wednesday, 2 August 1911, the Wilton House branch of the Children's Union held a fête and sale of work in the gardens of the house. Among the attractions were stalls offering plain work, fancy work, dolls and toys, plus many other items. Teas and ices were also served, and during the afternoon a band had been engaged to play. There was also boating on the river, plus the added attractions of the Great Doll's House being exhibited, and the miniature garden also being open to the public.

At this time there was a thriving Wilton Horticultural Society, and on August bank holiday Monday of 1912, they held their nineteenth annual show in the grounds of Wilton House, the opening ceremony being performed by the Countess of Pembroke. Although prizes were given for vegetables, fruit, flowers, honey and eggs, the event was not restricted to things horticultural; athletic sports and an open bowls match were added attractions, with, to round off the day's activities, dancing to the music of the South of England Band. This society certainly varied the entertainment in their shows, as in 1910

the two supplementary attractions had been completely different, with a cricket match between Wilton and Sarum Casuals and a military display. The latter included vaulting horse, sword feats, bayonet fighting, fencing, foil fencing, boxing and blindfold boxing, described as 'very amusing', finishing with a grand display on the parallel bars. The band of the fourth Batt. Wilts Regt played by kind permission of Lt Col The Earl of Radnor.

Sunday, 11 August 1912 was the date of the annual event known as Hospital Sunday, at which money was raised to help supply extra comforts for hospital patients in Salisbury Infirmary. Many other towns and villages in Wiltshire also held this event. The words printed at the top of the poster read:

Be merciful after thy power. If thou hast much, give plentiously: if thou hast little do thy diligence gladly to give of that little: for so gathered thou thyself good reward in the day of necessity.

In the Market Place formed a procession which, at 2.30p.m., marched to the Parish Church for a special service conducted by the Revd Canon Bourne, DCL. The procession consisted of organisations including the Weavers Guild, the Good Samaritans, the Wilts Friendly Society, the Oddfellows, the Foresters, the Rechabites, the Slate Clubs and the Pig Assurance. Also included were the mayor and corporation, B Coy 4 Battalion Wilts Regt and the United Services Veterans Club, the whole procession headed by the Bishopstone Band. The money collected was divided between Salisbury Infirmary and the Herbert Convalescent Home, Bournemouth.

In an effort to raise money to purchase a roller and seats for the recreation ground, under the patronage of the mayor and mayoress the Wilton Minstrels gave an entertainment at the Talbot and Wyvern Hall, on Wednesday, 26 March 1913. The poster advertising the event invited the public to come along and 'see their Old Favourites in their Comic Songs, Ballads, Choruses, Jokes.' Although perfectly acceptable at the time, in these days of political correctness what appeared next on the poster would cause an outcry. The minstrels, it stated, could be seen in the Nigger Absurdity Sketch 'Lodgings to Let', and in the wide scarlet border were caricatures of minstrels with blacked-up faces and black curly wigs. At the foot of the poster were the words 'Carriages at 10p.m.'

On 18 November 1914 the auction took place at the Pembroke Arms Hotel, held by Woolley & Wallace, of some brick cottages in Crow Lane, the will of Samuel Moore giving instructions for the sale of the following;

The Four substantially erected cottages (brick and slate), being numbers 4,5,6,7, in Crow lane, each containing 4 rooms: brick and slated Outhouse containing Wash House with Copper and W.C. Water laid on. Now in the respective occupations on weekly tenancies of, Mrs Hill, Mrs Smith, Mr Oakley, and Mrs Bowns, at rents amounting to £36.8shillings per annum. Also Landlord paying all outgoings.

The YMCA held a Whit Monday fête on 28 May 1917 in the grounds of Wilton House, in aid of war work. The programme of events was varied, commencing with the arrival of two Australian bands which entertained the crowds during the afternoon. A grand cricket match was held in the Deer Park between an English Army 11 and an Australian 11, and there was maypole dancing by children of the National School. In the evening a grand concert in the Riding School was performed by Miss Lena Ashwell's London Concert Party. The Australian bands taking part were stationed on Salisbury Plain, training for front-line action in France.

In December of that year, a special concert held in the Talbot and Wyvern Hall, in the presence of the mayor and corporation, was performed by the Official Concert Party Third Brigade HQ (AIF), who were touring the district with their highly acclaimed revue 'A Night on the Austral'. The various acts included a conjuror, a mimic, a ventriloquist, a character comedian, a monologuist, a sketchographist and three singers. The evening was a complete success, the considerable proceeds being donated to the Wiltshire Prisoners of War.

On Monday, 6 May 1935 the town celebrated the silver jubilee of King George V and Queen Mary, with a day of events for everyone to enjoy, as the official programme shows. On the back page is this short poem about Wilton, written by A.G. Street, local farmer, broadcaster and author:

From Wishford Bridge to Fugglestone the Wylye wanders down,
And just before it greets the park, why there lies Wilton Town.
Although it isn't very big, it ain't exactly small;
But you wouldn't have altered it, for it's Wilton after all.

You've hated it, you've scorned it, you left it for abroad;
But when you did return again, 'twas of your own accord.
You can't precisely say where lies the power of its call;
You only know you love it, and it's Wilton after all.

Miss Edith Olivier who, in 1939, would be Wilton's first lady mayor, also contributed a short poem.

Wilton gave (The Minstrels sing),
In the past, this realm, a king.
Later, as was only fair,
The king gave the town a Mayor,
Our respect and love are due
Now as ever to the two.

Celebrations started at 8a.m. with a salute of guns and a peal of bells, followed later in the morning by a thanksgiving service in the Parish Church attended by the mayor and corporation and other dignitaries. The official ceremonies now out of the way, the people of the town were ready to enjoy themselves, commencing in the afternoon with sports for children and adults at Wilton Park, with a free tea for everyone in the town.

In the evening there was a grand carnival procession, which attracted a huge number of entries – it seems that almost the entire population took part. There were certainly plenty of children, from six to 16, competing for a prize as the best-dressed girl or boy, characters including Margaret Coombes as 'Washing Day', Pamela Todd as 'Basket of Flowers', Brenda Cook as 'Child's Bottle of Milk', Sybil Jay as 'Wood Nymph' and Marcia Jukes as 'Chinese Girl'. In the boys' classes, Phillip Coombes dressed as 'Toy Soldier', John Rumbold as 'Dutch Boy', Roy Golding as 'Sandwich Man', Leonard West as 'Rival Blues' and Peter Croome as 'Jubilee Souvenirs'.

The best-decorated trade vehicle attracted 11 entries, four of which were entered by Wilton Sidney Herbert Co-operative Society. Other entries included Barrett & Brown, grocers, International Stores, Maffey & Lewry, drapers, their entry being listed as 'Pompadour Tea Cosy'. The entry from Brewer's in West Street was very aptly named 'The Village Blacksmith'. The procession also included an entry described as, 'Historic Pageant of former Kings and Queens of England' – 51 individuals, including the six queens of Henry VIII – no doubt an impressive sight. This section was arranged by Miss Edith Olivier, chairman of a carnival committee consisting of Mr V.H. Moore, Chief Marshall, Secretary and Organiser, and Mr R.J. Lewry, with committee members including the mayor and mayoress, Councillor and Mrs A. Marks, Mr F. Cooper, Mr C. Ayres, Mrs S. Shergold and Mr W. Jukes.

Pageants

Today pageants are no longer held in Wilton, but until the mid-1950s such events were very popular in the town, drawing huge crowds to witness the playing out of episodes of the town's history. One such pageant took place in the grounds of Wilton House on 7 and 8 June 1933, to commemorate the tercentenary of the death of George Herbert, rector of Bemerton, a suburb on the western border of Salisbury. Herbert also preached at Fugglestone Church which, standing near the roundabout at Wilton on the Salisbury Road, was once part of the Parish of Bemerton. In fact, Fugglestone was then a small settlement just outside the Wilton borough boundary, and became part of Wilton when the new charter was granted by Queen Victoria in 1882.

Before his ordination, George Herbert, a poet and orator, was a courtier to King James I until the king's death in 1625. In his early life, George Herbert had been torn between a political career at court and a desire to take orders in the Church of England. On advice from kinsmen, including Lord Pembroke, George Herbert was eventually ordained in September 1630 and offered the rectory of Fugglestone, with the Chapelry of Bemerton at St Andrew's Church. In the short time he had left to him – he only lived until 1633 – he attained all that he had wished, he was loved by his flock and was admired and imitated by a remarkable group of poetic friends and followers.

The pageant, in four episodes, the first consisting of three scenes, the remainder of either one or two scenes, was performed in the grounds of Wilton House and traced the life of George Herbert, including his time as a courtier with James I, when the king paid a visit to Wilton House for the knighting of Henry Herbert, George's brother.

This episode, with its subsequent scenes, contained no less than 37 characters, of which nine were the main characters, the remainder being court ladies, hunting courtiers, hunting ladies and huntsmen, plus two grooms and two hunt servants. One Major Ellison played the part of James I, William Earl of Pembroke being played by the then Earl of Pembroke and Montgomery, while Lady Juliet Duff played the Countess of Pembroke and Mr Eden Hawkins played George Herbert. The Marquis of Hamilton was played by Captain Siegfried Sassoon, who achieved fame as a war poet in the First World War and who was a frequent visitor to Wilton House.

In order that the spectators could distinguish the various characters, each wore a costume of a different colour. James I wore blue and red, William Earl of Pembroke wore purple and gold and George Herbert wore a green and grey cloak.

In episode III was depicted the visit of King Charles I to Wilton with his chaplain, Bishop Laud, the then Bishop of London, during which he presented the living of Fugglestone (then Foulestone) to George Herbert. After the presentation of the living, in the final episode, George Herbert was shown at work amongst his people in what were to be the last three years of his life.

The final scene, entitled 'Merrymakers on the Green', consisted mainly of inhabitants of Bemerton, Quidhampton and Fugglestone. The programme informs us that for the greater part, all the costumes for this episode were made by the players themselves or by an excellent working party under the supervision of a Mrs Squarey, of Bemerton. This episode also included country dancing and maypole dancing by children from Bemerton School, gypsies, Puritans, morris dancers and mummers.

Coupled with the pageant was the re-enactment of a seventh-century fair, held just inside the main entrance of Wilton House and presented in the form of street theatre. The fair was set out with booths selling wares similar to those that would have been sold at such an event in the seventeenth century. These included sweets, cordials, toys, herbs, vegetables and flowers, dairy produce, tobacco and ale. Street scenes were also depicted, with boys playing marbles, children playing 'jingling match' and Merry Andrews, a type of jester, in the stocks.

Another historical pageant took place in the grounds of Wilton House on 30 June and 1 July in 1937, under the direction of Miss Edith Olivier, the theme of which was the last 1,000 years of the history of Wilton and its neighbouring district of South Wiltshire. A far as possible, the production involved those people connected with the actual parish or locality to which the scene in question related.

The ten scenes depicted the main historical events, commencing in the year AD860 and finishing in AD1854, seem mainly to have concentrated on Wilton, five of them being presented by Wilton residents, the remaining five being from Harnham, Redlynch, Britford, Steeple Langford and Shrewton. The pageant was organised by the Salisbury Division Constitutional Association. This excellent pageant, although not on the scale of that four years earlier, attracted large numbers of spectators on both days.

In May that same year, Wilton, together with South Newton, celebrated the coronation of King George VI and Queen Elizabeth with a peal of bells at 7a.m. followed later that morning by a special service in the Parish Church. Once again, Lord Pembroke opened Wilton Park to the public for a day of sports which, besides the more usual events, included a bicycle obstacle race, veterans' races for both ladies and men, tilt the bucket and a ladies' and gents' wheelbarrow race. A public tea was held for children aged from four to 16 with another for the adults.

In the evening there was a carnival procession which, after judging had taken place in the Daisy Field at the top of the Shaftesbury Road, moved down through the town via West Street, North Street, King Street and Kingsbury Square to the Market Place, where special tableaux, arranged by the Misses Rawlence, Miss Edith Olivier and Mrs Parker, depicted scenes from Wilton's history. In the opening scene, the character of St Edith was played by Pamela Street, daughter of A.G. Street, who was later to become an author. Classes for each section of the procession were much the same as in 1935 and again attracted a large number of entries. Two young girls taking part in the procession, Phyllis Turner as Puck and Mary Shergold as Little Bow Peep, would later become carnival queens themselves. As an additional feature of this carnival, prizes were presented for the best-decorated home in two classes, according to the size of your house, plus a prize for the best decorated business premises.

At 8p.m. the king's speech was broadcast from the

The float of the 1950 Carnival Queen inside the gates of Wilton House. Horace Uphill, who created the swans stands next to them in the light suit. On the float, left to right, back row: Hazel Shearman, Eileen Hooker (carnival queen), Mary Shergold; front row: Trevor Ford (page), Olive Sutton, Phyllis Turner (retiring carnival queen), and Barbara Beck.

During the Festival of Great Britain Celebrations in 1951, the carnival that year reflected the theme. The tableau on the right represents Wilton Abbey and nuns, while that on the float at the front represents the visit by Queen Elizabeth I to Wilton House. In the role of the queen is Mary Shergold, now Mary Hawley, who was to play the same role at the celebrations held for the coronation of Queen Elizabeth II.

A scene from the 1951 pageant, showing Queen Elizabeth I presenting a lock of her hair to Sir Walter Raleigh. The original lock of hair is on display at Wilton House.

Having been selected for the 1951 carnival, the successful candidates pose for the local press. From left to right: Hazel Shearman, Barbara Beck, Olive Sutton (wearing the sash of the carnival queen), Eileen Hooker and Mary Partridge.

The judges in the background compare notes while the 1951 procession waits to move off down the Wishford Road, led by the carnival queen and her attendants. Olive Sutton (the carnival queen) is flanked by Eileen Hooker (back left) and Barbara Beck, with Mary Partridge (front left) and Hazel Shearman. The page boy is Gerald Harper.

At the carnival concert, the queen and her attendants are joined by guests Grahame Moody (with glasses) who was mayor, and Dick Best, one of the main organisers of the carnivals.

Wilton carnival, 1952. From left to right: Phyllis Turner, Mary Partridge, page boy John Davis, Peggy Lovett *(carnival queen),* Olive Sutton, Wendy Osbourne, *with Richard Marks as the jester.*

The procession en route. Page boy John Davis stands behind Peggy Lovett, the carnival queen, while Olive Sutton (left) and Mary Partridge take the driver's seat. Walking beside the carriage are, from left to right: Margaret Horrill, John Waters, Gillian Hogger and ? Wilson.

Peggy Lovett waves to the crowd as the her carriage arrives in the Market Place, having been pulled there by Guides and Scouts. The two Girl Guides at the front are sisters Mary (left) and Jill Whale. The name of the tall Scout is not known, but he is thought to have lived at Quidhampton.

Led by jester Richard Marks and one of the bands, the carnival queen and attendants head down South Street towards the Sawmills entrance to Wilton Park.

Town Hall, and at 9p.m. there was a torchlight procession from the Market Place to Grovely Down for a huge bonfire and firework display. The bonfire was donated by Lord Pembroke, and the fireworks, an all-aerial display, were promised to be bigger and better than ever. The events of the day were rounded off with a floodlit open-air dance in the Market Place, where a varied programme of the newest and oldest dance music had been arranged.

The idea of a whole carnival week, thought up by the Town Council, came into vogue after the Second World War, commencing in 1949. At the time looking for ways to improve recreational facilities in the town, the council came with the idea of holding a carnival as an ideal way of raising funds, having already entered into negotiations to purchase Castle Meadow in North Street for use as a playing-field. Although the main intention was to use it for sports, they also saw that it could be used for other events which would draw the crowds.

Wiltonians responded with great enthusiasm, raiding attics, cupboards and garden sheds for flags and bunting which had been stored since the celebration of the ending of the war. The decorations transformed the town into a mass of colour, leaving no one in any doubt that Wilton was in carnival mood and that it was going to be fun.

On the first Saturday of carnival week, just over 2,000 people crowded into the Market Place where, on a special dais erected in front of the Town Hall, Wilton's first carnival queen, Phyllis Turner, was crowned to loud cheering and a burst of applause from the crowd. Her crown, specially commissioned, was made by Horace Uphill. By trade a cabinet maker, he was renowned for the making of miniature antique furniture, and had a small shop in West Street. Extremely skilled and inventive, he designed the crown in a single week as an exact replica of those worn by Wessex kings. Fashioned from wood and aluminium and trimmed with ermine, the crown is embellished with rock crystals and imitation pearls, emeralds and turquoise, finished with a lining of red velvet. Still worn by Wilton's carnival queens, the crown stands as testimony to the craftsmanship of a remarkable man.

The carnival was a huge success, setting the standard for those that were to follow. Processions held on the last Saturday attracted vast crowds which, flocking in from Salisbury and the surrounding villages, made it impossible to walk along the pavements. Large numbers of entries were also attracted, processions averaging around 50 floats and, together with the walkers and eight or nine bands, measuring up to a mile in length. It took quite a while for the procession to pass through the town, but the crowd and the participants enjoyed every minute. In 1952 records were broken when it was reliably estimated that there were 6,000 people lining the three-mile route through the town. Wilton really came alive on these nights.

The 1950 programme gives a flavour of these early carnival weeks, this being the year when 16-year-old Eileen Hooker was carnival queen. With attendants Barbara Beck, Olive Sutton, Phyllis Turner, Hazel Shearman and Mary Shergold, and her page, Trevor Ford, she rode through the street in fine style on a trailer, its base disguised as a giant flower petal, drawn by a tractor cleverly hidden between two huge cut-outs, so that the group appeared to be drawn along by swans – once again the work of genius Horace Uphill.

The carnival had opened the previous Saturday with sports and a fête in Wilton Park which included sideshows featuring a miniature passenger railway, a model aeroplane stunt flying display, a dog display, bowling for a rug, a bazaar and a treasure hunt. Music was supplied by the band of the Wilton branch of the British Legion, with supplementary music on gramophone records. The carnival queen was crowned early in the evening by the Mayoress, Mrs Stokes and the day was rounded off with a carnival ball at the Michael Herbert Hall.

Other events of the week included a Wilton Industries exhibition held at the Town Hall, where various tradesmen of the town exhibited their wares. There was a table-tennis tournament, an old-time ball and dancing to Freddie Cooper and his Orchestra, from Bournemouth, while on the following evening an open darts knockout tournament was held. On the Friday evening, David Redway and John Batt presented a programme of variety acts, one of the guest artists being Douglas Horner, a dialect comedian. In fact Douglas was well known on the radio at that time, playing the character of Jonas in the Children's Hour production of 'Cowleaze Farm', written by local farmer and author Ralph Whitlock. Also appearing in the variety show was Wilton man Bob Sutton who, complete with blacked-up face, mimed to Al Jolson records. His act won praise from the *Salisbury Journal* reporter, who wrote that: 'His acquired timing and expression was excellent'.

On the opening day in 1952 an historical pageant in 19 acts was presented entitled, 'A Wiltonian Saga', written by the rector, the Revd William Drury, and produced by Mrs Philip Moore. Another first was the introduction of a United Service on the Sunday, held in the open air in the Market Place, with the combined choirs of the Congregational Church and Wilton Parish Church. The Southsea Entertainers provided entertainment for the variety show in this particular year. The last Saturday of the carnival, which took place in September, coincided with the arrival of Cole & Sons' funfair, an added bonus as it also drew the crowds.

Other events were gradually brought in, including fancy dress and talent competitions, whist drives, comic football matches and a schools' six-a-side football tournament. The Wilton Dramatic

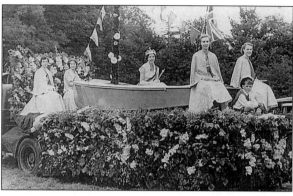

A patriotic float in the 1953 cornation carnival, with Mary Partridge as Britannia riding up West Street, escorted by Sea Cadets.

For the 1954 procession, carnival queen Eileen Bryant rode round town in a boat. Her attendants on this occasion were, from left to right: *Pamela Bevins, Mavis Alford, Elizabeth Pretty, page Raymond Partridge and Peggy Lovett.*

Although undated, this float entered by the Wilton Women's Institute, depicting women's dress of former years, could well have been entered in an early 1950s carnival, possibly the Festival of Great Britain carnival in 1951. The young boy on the float is dressed in the uniform of Wilton Free School.

Members of the Congregational Church and Sunday school combined to enter the Wilton Carnival with the tableau 'Happy Families', based on the card game. Leonard Jukes (in the top hat) was Sunday-school superintendent in the early 1950s, when this picture was taken. His wife (fourth left, second row) was also a teacher at the Sunday school. Their daughter Marcia, is in the front row (fourth from the right).

Mrs Bessie Partridge, in patriotic mode, with her daughter Mary, in a procession to celebrate the coronation of King George VI in 1937.

Society put on several plays including, in 1954, the farce *The Happiest Days of Your Life*, which included in its cast many well-known Wiltonians, including David Brockway, Tony Ford, Cyril Bryant, Christopher Moore, Elizabeth Pretty, Leonard Jukes, Rosa Harper, Richard Blake and Jean Ford.

The carnival programmes of this early period reveal that the majority of classes were for children, including 'Best Dressed Boy or Girl in Character', 'Couples of School Children' and 'Decorated Bicycles or Trolleys', the entries to which are full of the names of Wilton children. An interesting note printed in the carnival programme for 1954 lists the nine bands taking part in the procession and at the bottom reads, 'All Bands are very kindly giving their services free.' The programme for the opening carnival gala the previous Saturday reveals that the main attraction was to be amateur radio demonstrations by the Salisbury and District Short Wave Club, who would be trying to make contact with other amateur stations across the world. There were also demonstrations of a mobile transmitter, a tape recorder and other home-constructed equipment.

In 1953, coronation year, the carnival was brought forward to the end of May, on the week commencing Whit Monday. As a prelude to the festivities, on the last three days of the previous week, a huge Elizabethan pageant was presented in Wilton Deer Park, attracting large crowds. There were 39 main characters portrayed, all by residents of the town, and many extras playing the parts of messengers,

soldiers, knights, lords and ladies.

During the following week the usual events opened with a dance for which the music was provided, as usual, by Charles S. Hart and his Orchestra, who played at many of these early carnivals. Other events included a coronation carnival party and a comic football match between the 'Nifty Shooters' and the 'Dabbling Drips', which was kicked off by the mayor, Councillor V.H. Moore. Entered into the spirit of things, on arrival at the centre circle, he rolled up his trouser legs to just above the knee before kicking off to huge applause from the crowd. At a special coronation variety show, Horace Uphill presented his hilarious 'Taxi' sketch, with a full size, specially adapted and fully working car, from which doors fell off amid loud bangs and clouds of smoke; there being no roof, the back seat also tipped backwards. During the act, Horace actually cranked the starting handle and started the engine. The week's events concluded with a procession through the town, once again attracting large crowds.

Coronation day itself followed more or less the usual pattern, starting with a peal of bells from the Parish Church. There was a public lunch for residents over 65, and the usual children's tea, at which they were presented with special coronation mugs. After dancing in the Market Place and a broadcast of the Queen's speech, the day ended with a torchlight procession, bonfire and firework display.

A crisis developed in 1955 when there was a

Coronation day, 1953. Here the children of Wilton enjoy a free tea at the Michael Herbert Hall. Note the coronation mugs, presented to them earlier in the day.

The Sidney Herbert Memorial in the Market Place was completely covered with this decoration, designed by Horace Uphill. The crown at the top was made in his workshop and illuminated with coloured lights at night, would slowly revolve, adding to its impact.

shortage of entrants in the carnival queen competition. Fortunately the committee took swift action and the day was saved. The first and only entrants were Mavis Alford and Pamela Bevins, Mavis winning the competition.

Efforts were always being made to present fresh items and, with Castle Meadow now available, more spectacular displays could be mounted. One such event was 'Hells Angels', at the time Britain's foremost motorcycle show, their speciality being to ride through a ring a fire. Other attractions included a ten-mile road race and a veteran and vintage car and steam traction rally.

By the 1960s, although the carnivals were still doing well, interest was on the wane and they eventually ceased. Tastes were changing and, while people still wanted entertainment, the age of making one's own entertainment was passing. With the increasing ownership of private cars, people were able to travel further afield more easily, looking for new things to do and see. The growth of television was also having a big impact on people's lives. In

1977 a carnival was held to celebrate the Queen's silver jubilee, though an attempt to hold another in March of 1988 failed, due mainly to lack of interest.

In September 1992 the carnival was revived and proved a huge success, despite some initial controversy. The following year it reverted to July and now takes place annually at the beginning of this month. In 2004 response to the carnival was less enthusiastic, but there was a bigger and even more colourful procession in 2005.

Glossary of some of the dialect words used in this chapter: *avore* before; *arroun* around; *agean* again; *ael* all; *car* carry; *carperation* corporation; *feace* face; *girt* great big; *hallerady* holiday; *hood* could; *leetle* little; *lected* elected; *leace* lace; *pleace* place; *spoose* suppose; *tha* the; *thease* this; *tract* attract; *therezelves* themselves; *thic* that; *ta* to; *upzide* upside; *vrim* from; *voresters* foresters; *voke* folk; *var* for; *wur or wuz* was or were; *wich* which; *wiout* without; *wak* walk; *wie* with; *wurden* wouldn't; *zee* see; *zaa* saw; *zeem* seem; *zite* sight; *zummit* something; *zom* some; *zich* such.

CHAPTER 7

Changes Over the Years

When one looks back over the history of a town, it is amazing just how many changes have taken place. Wilton, like any other village, town or city, has changed considerably, even in the comparatively short period of around 150 years.

The Wilton of 1851 was a thriving and prosperous community, busy and vibrant with the hustle and bustle of the its inhabitants, housewives, workers and businessmen, going about their daily toil. The only transport on its dirt roads, dusty in summer, muddy when it rained and treacherous in snowy winters, were commercial horse-drawn carts and the ponies and traps of the upper classes, while the working classes simply walked.

The town was able to supply most of the goods and services that Salisbury offered, albeit in a much smaller way. It had to because, although the city is within easy reach today, in those days there were only two ways of getting there, by walking or, if there was room for you to ride, by carrier's cart. Wilton had a choice of carrier, three in fact, James Hopkins, Sarah Ware and Isaac Wingrove, each leaving Wilton for Salisbury at 11a.m. six days a week. These carriers were a vital asset to the community, the local carriers, as well as those who carried goods further afield, being very much in demand. For a shopkeeper or factory owner, items that were not obtainable locally could take days to arrive.

Today it is hard to imagine that in the area

An advertisement from the 1898 Wilton Directory. The firm of F.W. Marks, which took over Edward Slow's carriage-building business, remained under that name until the early part of the twenty-first century. First carriage builders and wheelwrights, they became a garage, later with a car sales showroom. When they closed, the site was sold off for the development of housing.

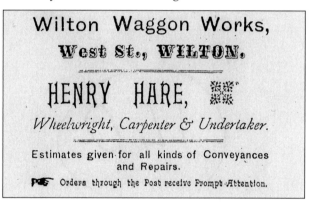

There being no separate funeral directors in these times, such business was taken on by the likes of Henry Hare, who offered this service alongside his wheelwright's and carpentry business in 1898. His son, Percy, ran the business well into the 1960s, after which his assistant, Reg Boon, took it over.

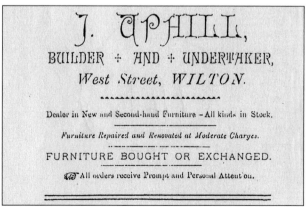

Joseph Uphill, in competition with Percy Hare, also offered undertaking alongside his business as builder and cabinetmaker. Joseph was the father of Horace Uphill, who made miniature antique furniture and lent his skills in the early years of Wilton's carnival after the Second World War.

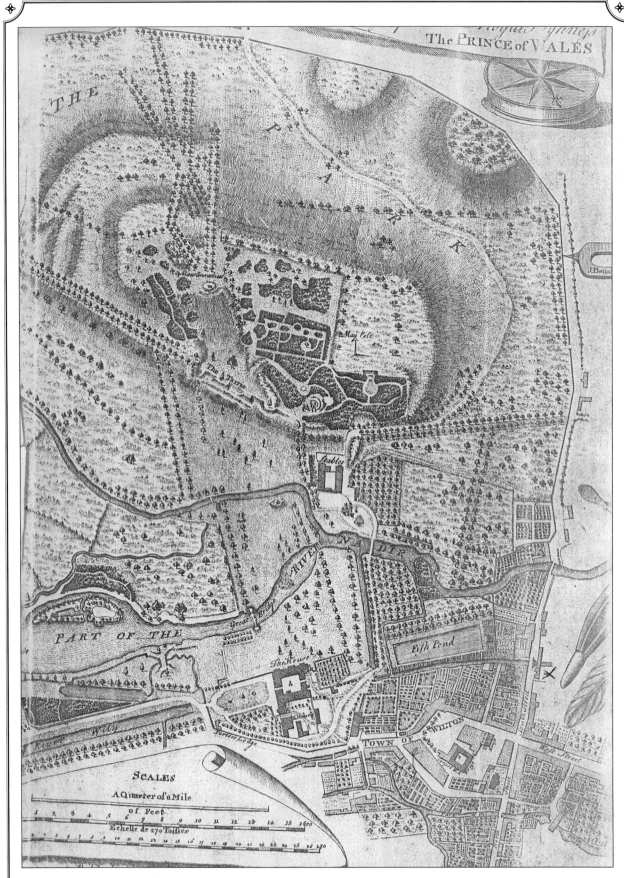

A map dated 1754, showing the part of the Earl of Pembroke's estate known as Wilton Park. To the bottom right is the town centre, showing the Market Place and the carpet factory that was there at the time. The narrow road leading from the market to Kingsbury Square is clearly shown as Carpet Walk.

covering West Street, the Market Place – which was laid out differently – and North Street, there were 89 businesses, including small shops and the local blacksmith, serving a local population of approximately 2,000. The inhabitants were certainly spoilt for choice, having access to a variety of retail outlets which are simply not available today.

Nearly every trade imaginable was represented in Wilton at this time, each owned by a familiar Wilton name, including basket maker Alfred Chalk, cheese dealer George Howell, straw hat maker Susan Roots, hardwareman William Moore and brewer John Rogers. There were eight boot- and shoemakers, two blacksmiths, ten grocers and three linen drapers, the shop of Joseph Ward in North Street, was Barclays Bank, being at one time the Greydawn Café, owned by the Perry family. Another of Wilton's banks, Lloyds TSB, was also a retail outlet at this time, owned by James Nightingale, a wine and spirit merchant. Other trades included plumbers, painters, glaziers, carpenters, builders, bricklayers, milliners and dressmakers, a chemist, saddle and harness makers and tailors. There were also four solicitors and even a local doctor, William John French, called a surgeon, as many doctors were in those days. The rector at this time was the Revd Richard Chermside who, presented with the living in Wilton in 1848, held it until the time of his death on 30 July 1867.

Beneath this veneer of prosperity the poor of the town, of which there were many, had to rely on

Joseph Ward's draper's shop in North Street, where he lived with his two daughters, who assisted in shop. The shop on the right became Keith's, a ladies' hairdressers.

regular handouts from the poor relief fund. This relief was administered by the Wilton Charities, set up by the many generous benefactors who had genuine

The New Inn West Street, c.1890. Proprietor Henry Street, in 1912, made a third successful application for a billiard licence at Salisbury Licensing Sessions. His family had owned the premises since about 1842, Henry being born there not long after. Henry took over the house in 1877 and was still listed as owner in the 1916 Street Directory. Not content just to run a pub, he also ran from the premises a bakery and a grocery business.

This photograph, taken c.1875, is thought to be the oldest picture to survive of West Street, looking towards the western end of the town. The house standing almost in the centre is the former Gatehouse, which once marked the old boundary of the town. The toll gate, partially visible to the right of the Gatehouse, was demolished in 1963, as were the cottages on the right and the thatched house a little further down. In the early 1990s retirement flats known as Pembroke Court were built on the site of the cottages on the right. The left-hand side looks much the same today.

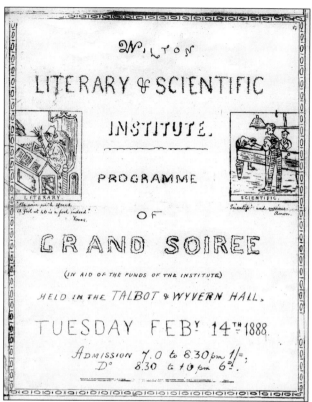

A reproduction of the front cover of a programme for a Grand Soirée, held by the Wilton Literary & Scientific Institute.

concern for the welfare of these unfortunate people. Two of the main benefactors were Robert Sumption and Thomas Mease, who between them provided relief from the cradle to the grave, including the payment of maternity benefit to poor married women. After the birth of a child, these women were provided by a shopkeeper in the town with baby clothes to the value of £1.5s. When the child could walk and talk, it was educated and clothed, and when the boys left school provision was made for them to be apprenticed.

For poor young women marriage portions were provided, and for the elderly (the five poor men and five poor women, who were natives of Wilton and over the age of 50) there was a form of old-age pension. In later years the age limit was raised to 60, it being agreed at the same time that recipients of this charity should receive additional relief during sickness or other emergencies. Thus the poor of Wilton managed to survive, further aided, in the spirit of community which existed then, by those townspeople who were wealthier than themselves. As an example of this, on Sundays, at around midday, ladies would visit the homes of the poor, carrying baskets containing basins of sliced of meat with vegetables and gravy. Thanks to the efforts of one particular lady, the local drunkards also benefited. Because all the public houses were closed on the Sabbath, she visited their homes with jugs of strong coffee and other drinks, a subtle attempt to wean them off beer, perhaps. At around the turn of the century, the poorest woman in Wilton was, reputedly, a Mrs Jeffry. She lived entirely on payments given to her by the guardians amounting to 2s.6d. per week, of which she paid 2s. a week in rent. She also received one loaf of bread a week, the underpart of

which she cut off and sold to a neighbour for 2d., leaving her the princely sum of 8d. for the rest of the week. Somehow she managed to eke out a living by working part-time on a farm, mainly hoeing and weeding, toiling many long hours in the fields in order to earn a few extra pennies. She would even work with her baby, which she was still nursing, slung across her shoulders. A highlight of her life, it is said, was when she was invited to tea at the farm one day, and had real butter on her bread. On 1 May 1851 the Great Exhibition opened in Hyde Park, and such was its success and importance that, over the summer, those people of Wilton over the age of 12 were given the once-in-a-lifetime opportunity to travel to London to see this event. They were able to do so thanks to the generosity of the Rt Hon. Sydney Herbert, who chartered a special train from Salisbury. The trip, which was a great success, demonstrated that the aristocrats at Wilton House did involve themselves in the affairs of ordinary people and were good benefactors to the town in many different ways, earning the respect of the working classes.

In mid-September 1854 cholera broke out in Wilton, causing great alarm among the population, especially in parishes around the town. It was at first thought to have been brought by the navvies laying the Great Western Railway line, but these fears were unfounded. The parish of Wilton generously subscribed to the building of a temporary hospital on a site adjoining the garden of the workhouse,

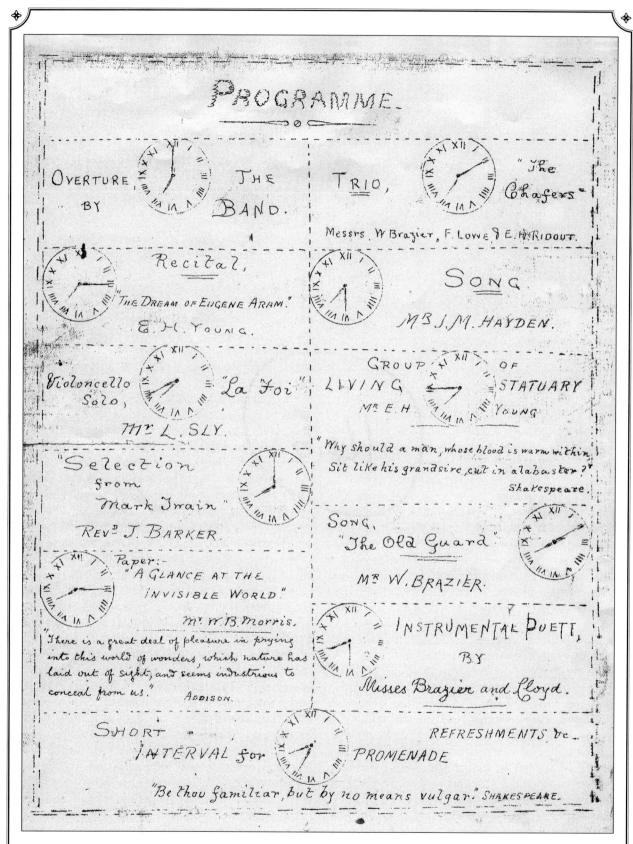

A section of the programme showing some of the entertainment in the first half of the soirée. Note the novel use of clock dials with hands to show the times of the various acts. The programme, despite being over 100 years old, is still in fairly good condition, though the pages have yellowed with age.

Edward Slow.

district then being supplied from Salisbury.

In 1855 a 14-year-old boy left the Free School in North Street to take up an apprenticeship with a coachbuilder and wheelwright in Salisbury, walking to work each day – a round trip of approximately eight miles. That boy was Edward Slow, briefly mentioned in Chapter 6. Born in August 1841, he was the youngest child to survive in a family of one elder brother and two sisters. Seven years later his father died in a cholera epidemic, leaving the family in poverty. Although his brother and sisters went out to work, Edward being too young, was sent to the Wilton Free School to be educated.

He worked long hours so during what little leisure time he had, he devoted to reading and writing. He joined the Wilton Literary Society and by the time he was 21 had read nearly all the works of Scott and Dickens. On completion of his apprenticeship, with a half sovereign given to him by his master, Slow hired a small shed to use as a workshop and set up business on his own. As his business prospered and orders increased, he obtained new premises and entered into partnership with another businessman, although this was unsuccessful and, by 1875, Slow was back on his own.

During this time he continued to read and write in his spare time. On making his first visit to London in 1860, he recorded his impressions in a dialect piece entitled, 'Janny Brown in Lunnon'. In it he spoke of the countryman's surprise at all the wonderful things he had seen there.

In 1865 he married a Miss Batten and two years later, with his by now ample resources, had printed his 'Poems in the Wiltshire Dialect', published by Wilton bookseller Alfred Chalke, and also by E.W. Allen of London. The book was well received, the most popular poem being one entitled 'Harvest Home At Wilton'. In the *Salisbury Journal* it was described as 'a faithful picture of that annual agreeable festivity', the writer concluding that, 'were the good old custom to die out, which we hope it never will, the poem before us would truthfully portray to posterity.' Unfortunately the custom did die out, and Slow's poem remains a memorial to this once annual event.

Slow now began to busy himself with the affairs of Wilton, becoming keenly interested in all that was going on. As a hobby he took great delight in researching the charters and old records of the Wilton corporation. Hundreds of visitors to the town inspected these valuable documents under his guidance, and were charmed by his enthusiasm in responding to their interest. He was a staunch supporter of Lord Pembroke, the town's Member of Parliament, and was also a keen churchman, glorifying the beautiful Parish Church and revering the old church in the Market Place, jealous of anything that was likely to spoil its amenities.

He became associated with a group of Wiltonians

although, when the outbreak was arrested by February the following year, the hospital was not used again. Possibly as a result of this outbreak, in October of 1854 a government enquiry, lasting four days, was held at the Town Hall into the sewerage, drainage and water supply of Wilton. Soon afterwards, the provisions of the Public Health Act were put into force, resulting in the election of a local Board of Health. This in turn led to a drainage and waterworks being established, to which the Earl of Pembroke contributed £500, granting free use of the land through Wilton Park. Eventually a waterworks was built at Ditchampton, off the Wishford Road, complete with a pumping station and an underground reservoir at the entrance to Grovely Woods, at the top of the Hollows.

Later in 1854, a proposal to light the town with gas was met with approval. The Wilton Gas Co. purchased land at the back of the workhouse garden, which at that time was just outside the borough boundary. Although gas was available to private houses near the carpet factory and the Warminster Road, there was no public lighting. Proposals were made by the Town Council in 1887 that they should purchase all assets of the gas company, and the Wilton Gas Order of 1888 was evoked after a loan had been secured. When everything was set up, the corporation was authorised to make the purchase and supply gas to the parishes of Wilton, Burcombe, Fugglestone and South Newton. This arrangement remained in force until 1935, when the gasworks was closed, all the gas in the

Wilton Town Council members, 1898. Left to right, front row: *William Vincent Moore junr, ?, William Vincent Moore senr, Joseph W. Ward (mayor), John White, Edward Slow and John Moore. The other men have not been identified.*

who, after some years of effort, established a new charter for the borough, granted in 1885. As a result he was elected councillor at the first municipal election of the new corporation, on which he remained until his retirement due to ill health in 1924, when he was the oldest member of the corporation. During his time he served as mayor in 1892 and again in 1902, and was elected alderman in 1893.

Retiring from work in 1895, he went to live in Shaftesbury Road, in a house which he had built for the occasion. Here he continued to read and collect books on local history and in 1903 wrote his famed *Wilton Chronology*, which lists important dates and events in the town's history. He died in 1925.

On the day of the Foresters' Fete, in August 1873, the foundation stone for the new Temperance Hall was laid by Sir Edmund Antrobus, MP for Wilton. The Temperance Society, formed in the town in 1858, had previously leased a hall, the cost of which had put them in debt. Lord Pembroke, sympathetic to their cause, allowed members to hold a demonstration in Wilton Park which proved highly successful, clearing the debt with sufficient funds remaining to purchase land to build a hall.

The new building was to provide a large room for public meetings, open to all without distinction of sect or party, with a coffee room, a reading room and a room for what were described as 'innocent games'. The building was intended as a public house free of the evil drink; at the time of the laying of the foundation stone, one-sixth of the town's population were

teetotal. Situated in Silver Street and built in the Doric style, the grandly named Talbot and Wyvern Hall soon became known, to many residents, as the 'Coffee Tavern'.

At that time Wilton had its own Parliamentary Borough, and in January 1877 Sir Edmund Antrobus retired as the town's MP, having served in that position for over 20 years without opposition. At the election, held in February, the Hon. Sidney Herbert was elected as the town's Conservative MP, securing 751 votes, which gained him a large majority over his opponent, J.S. Norris. Until 1832 Wilton had always returned two members to Parliament, but some anomalies came to light which were reported to the parliamentary surveyors in 1832. They concluded that quite a number of practices needed to be corrected, Wilton then being made into a single constituency. Further changes were made in 1885 when, under the new Distribution of Seats Act, Wilton was made head of the Parliamentary Division of South Wilts, extending the borders to cover a much larger area. At the first election under the new Bill, sitting member the Hon. Sidney Herbert was defeated by Sir Thomas Grove.

On the night of 22 January 1884, a severe gale swept through the district, causing a tragedy in the town near the Pembroke Arms Hotel. A tree standing opposite the hotel was blown down in the high winds, one of its branches striking both William Spackman, second coachman to the Earl of Pembroke, and Samuel Jenkins, a night watchman employed on the Wilton Estate. While Spackman was killed outright, Jenkins was more fortunate, sustaining a broken arm and a serious injury to his ankle. He was taken to Salisbury Infirmary for treatment. At the inquest on Spackman, held a few days later by Mr H.A. Wilson, evidence was heard from two gentlemen who had pulled Spackman's body from under the tree. It appeared that the body was not crushed, death evidently having been caused by a severe blow to the head. There was also a severe cut over the left eye. The verdict returned was of accidental death.

A Wilton Guide of 1898 reveals many fascinating facts about the town and shows just how well the community was catered for. Certainly many activities and services were concerned with the welfare of the residents. The town even had its own tax inspector, Mr F. Tutt, and an assessor, Mr J. Corby. There was even a tax office, situated in the Pembroke Arms Hotel, its position evidenced, at the time of writing, by some faded writing still just visible on part of the wall.

The postmistress, Mrs F. Pretty, ran the Post Office in Kingsbury Square – a private house adapted for the purpose. Its location in the square is marked by a painted sign on the wall, still clearly visible. Through the front door was a small lobby, into one wall of which was set a frosted glass window on which one would knock. Miss Pretty would then open the window and attend to one's requirements. It was certainly open long hours, from 8a.m. to 8p.m., Monday to Saturday. It was closed on Sundays, Good Friday and Christmas Day, but telegrams could be sent on those days on application to the Postmistress at her private door from 8a.m. to 10a.m., or in the evening from 5p.m. to 6p.m. for an extra fee of 1s. The town postman was J. Lawrence, with deliveries to such outlying districts such as Winterbourne Stoke, Shrewton, Wishford, Netherhampton and Quidhampton made by auxiliary and rural postmen based at Wilton.

There were certainly many clubs and societies, including the Constitutional Association, a Liberal Club, Wilton United Football Club, with Mr F. Macey as captain and Mr J. Goulden junr as sub-captain, while caption of the cricket club was Mr S. Taunton, with Mr G.J. Carse as sub-captain. The Literary Institute was very popular and, for those of an artistic nature, there was a school of art. For the not so well off there were slate clubs, doctors' and clothing clubs, a coal club and loan and blanket societies. One of the busiest men in the town seems to have been Mr J. Goulden, who was surveyor to the District Council as well as being the Inspector of Nuisances, School Attendance Officer and Secretary to the Weavers Association and to the doctors' and clothing clubs. Among the numerous Wilton shops, in North Street there was W.E. Burrough, a family baker and confectioner noted for his farmhouse bread, which he delivered to all parts daily. He also stocked assort-

ments of sweets and chocolates, along with a varied selection of cakes. In addition he sold home-cured bacon and hams, best selected Canterbury mutton and the celebrated Lammermoor beef.

There were two coal merchants, F. Whately in the Market Place, and Read & Son, whose depot was at the Great Western Railway yard. The business of Henry Hare of West Street, a wheelwright, carpenter and undertaker, was later taken over by his son Percy, who remained in business well into the the late 1950s. George Bell was the saddler and harness maker, also repairing portmanteaux, trunks and bags, while at the Fancy Repository in North Street, Mrs L. Grant sold sweets, toys, tobacco, cigars, cigarettes, pipes and pouches, as well as being a newsagent and an agent for Lipton's teas and coffees. Another business in North Street was that of H. Carew, who ran a women's tailoring business, making jackets and costumes in all the latest styles. For those who wished to make their own clothes, the shop sold the latest up-to-date sewing machines for up to 20s. less than anywhere else. Haberdashery, fancy goods, yarns and wools, hosiery, corsets, and flannelettes could be bought at Miss Chalke's shop at No. 41 West Street, which also offered ladies' and children's outfitting and dressmaking, with good work guaranteed. For Christmas, New Year and birthday cards in new and artistic designs, plus stationery of all kinds, there was the Wilton Printing Works in North Street.

Around the turn of the century, one Mr Thresher, a miser, owned a small shop in West Street. He sold all manner of assorted items, although in truth the shop was actually run by his wife and a relation. Thin of build and gaunt of face, with a straggly beard, Thresher lived up to his miserly reputation, being of a sinister nature with no charm whatsoever.

A familiar sight in the town, he bustled here and there, clutching a black cloth sack, containing stock for the shop, tightly in his hand. It is said that Thresher was so mean that he would never buy goods wholesale, preferring to walk to Salisbury, being too mean to travel by rail, and spend his money buying goods at retail prices. He would never pay a carrier to bring stock back to Wilton, but three times a week would walk to Salisbury, his empty sack under his arm, later walking home with a sack so heavy, he was positively staggering under its weight.

Although he paid retail prices for his goods, he made his money by selling them in his shop at twice the price, sometimes even more. Amazingly, people still came into his shop and paid these inflated prices, even though they could see that Thresher was making his fortune at their expense. Much of his profit was invested in buying derelict properties in the town and renting them to people too poor to complain about the bad conditions or to move elsewhere. On the days he was not walking between Wilton and Salisbury, he would be collecting rent.

CHAPTER 8

Wilton 1900–1939

In 1900 Wilton entered the new century with, on 19 September, a grand celebration of the first charter granted to the borough by King Henry I, 800 years earlier in 1100. These festivities included a grand choral service at the Parish Church attended by the mayor and corporation, a free dinner for all males over 17, a free tea for women and children and sports and pastimes in Wilton Park. The day's festivities concluded with a grand firework display and the traditional torchlight procession. Many people from Salisbury and district also attended the event.

Who could have predicted what would take place in this new century? Along with two world wars, the atomic bomb and men landing on the moon, came the invention of television, computers and jet aircraft.

In September 1901 Edward Slow wrote in his *Wilton Chronology* that the largest sheep fair for many years had taken place at Wilton, between 58,000 and 60,000 sheep being penned. Sheep fairs have been an institution in Wilton for hundreds of years, but the

present site, known as the Fairfield, only came into use in 1775. Up until this time, sheep fairs were usually held in the Market Place. Unfortunately, with the building of the railway in the 1850s, approximately four acres of the Fairfield were appropriated and sidings and a platform built, the owners of the land being given the opportunity to purchase a field next to them, lower down.

In the early years, most of the sheep were brought to Wilton fairs along what were known as ox droves, which often became very crowded near the town as the fair approached. It has been recorded that one shepherd, from Exeter, took three months to bring his sheep to Wilton, although on such long journeys penning fields would have been provided where sheep could be rested and grazed for just a few pence. This practice ceased at about the time of the Second World War, Teffont farmer Bill Fisher Crouch being the last to drive his sheep any distance to Wilton. Since the closure of the railway station, all

The power of advertising! Buckeridge's advertisement from 1903.

Another of Buckeridge's advertisement, 1908.

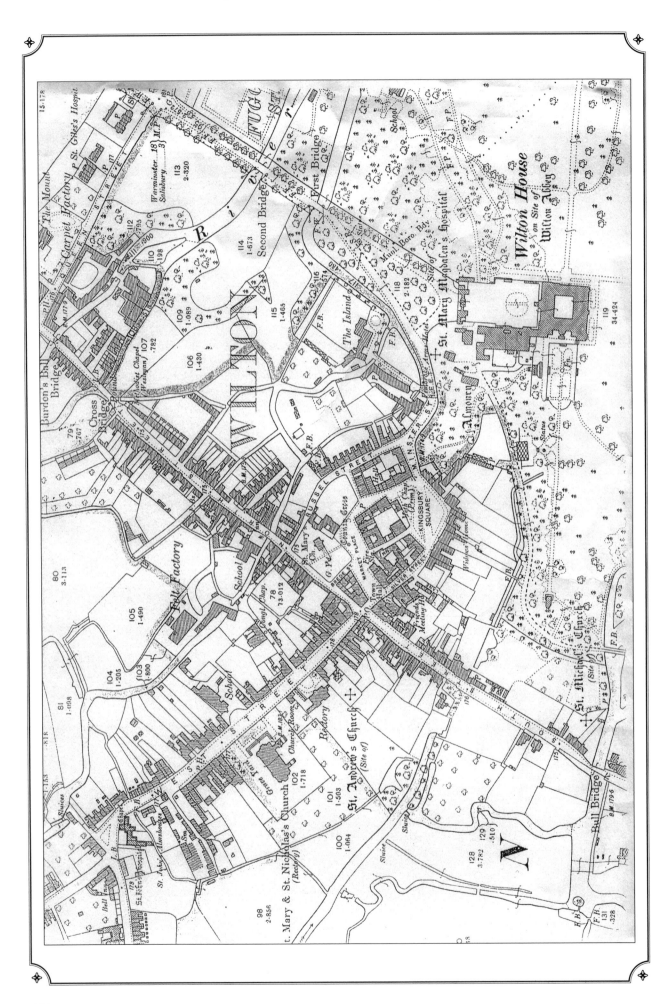

The mayor and members of the corporation, waiting patiently at the Crossroads, to formally greet King Edward VII and Queen Alexandra, who were to arrive by carriage from Salisbury Station on a private visit to the Earl and Countess of Pembroke at Wilton House.

On arrival at Wilton, King Edward VII is presented with the Loyal Address on behalf of the corporation and townspeople of Wilton.

Opposite page: *Ordnance Survey Map of Wilton, 1900. Long since disappeared are West Street School, the Congregational Church, Crow Lane; the Free School, North Street; the houses and Wool Loft adjoining Brede Street in the Market Place; the Primitive Methodist Chapel, Kingsbury Square; the Wesleyan Methodist Chapel, North Street; and The Mount, Queen Street, which in 2006 is King's Gate, a small housing development.*

Crowds gather at the railings of the Parish Church to watch the arrival of dignitaries at the Sunday service attended by King Edward VII and Queen Alexandra.

sheep are now brought to Wilton by road. The main sheep fairs are held on the second Thursdays of August, September and October and, in the past, a clearance fair was held in November. The practice of penning sheep in the traditional wattle hurdles ceased in the late 1980s and early 1990s.

In the spring of 1903 Buckeridge's, calling themselves 'The People's Draper' held a spring sale, offering all kinds of bargains bought in from Edwin Jones of Southampton. Buckeridge's was a cash only shop, and would not 'Book for anyone, Rich or Poor'. The proprietors were adamant on this point, the following statement being released:

What we are aiming at is to do all the READY MONEY TRADE in the District. We do not want credit trade. We would rather lose the trade than enter for anyone.

They informed the public that their profits were too small to allow losses arising from bad debts or the expense of book-keeping. However, their prices were cheap, with lace and embroidery, 2–4ins wide, ranging from ¾d. to 1¾d.; ladies' chemises from 1s.6¾d. to 1s.11¾d. and white Turkish towels from 1¾d. to 1s.11¾d. In fact the catalogue listing their bargains revealed that, with six exceptions, all the bargains on offer had ¾d. attached to the sale price – perhaps representing their actual profit margin.

On the weekend of 27 June 1908 King Edward VII and Queen Alexandra made a private visit to Wilton House. The royal party drove in an open carriage from Salisbury Station to Wilton, where they were greeted by the mayor, John Montague Swayne and, with the loud cheers of Wilton inhabitants ringing in their ears, were presented with a loyal address, designed in a seventeenth-century style.

The next day being a Sunday, the royal visitors attended the morning service at the Parish Church, driving through streets lined with hundreds of cheering people. In the evening a visit was made to Longford Castle, and the following day their majesties returned to London by royal train from the LSWR station at Wilton.

There was a touching moment during their departure when, as the queen walked past the blind daughter of the stationmaster, the Countess of Pembroke (who had a keen interest in the welfare of ordinary people) asked the stationmaster's wife to bring her daughter forward, informing the queen that the girl, inflicted with blindness since March of that year, was sadly diagnosed as incurable. The queen, touched by what she had been told, took the girl's hand, kissed her and said, 'My poor dear child, God Bless You'. Then, turning to the daughter of Lady Beatrice Wilkinson, she joined the two children's hands, saying to the other child, 'Take care of this poor little girl', before speaking some words of sympathy to the stationmaster's wife.

The town has had its share of flooding over the years, the inhabitants of the Waterditchampton area suffering a miserable Christmas in 1910. The

Wilton Crossroads, c.1900. The almshouses still survive today, but the crossroads themselves have been replaced by a roundabout at this busy junction of the A30 and A36.

flooding was the result of heavy rain which caused a torrent of water to rush into the area from the downs, affecting an area from the railway bridge, past the Bell Inn, almost to the church in West Street. The water lay in the area over Christmas and in places was sufficiently deep to float a small boat. Despite the inconvenience, residents were determined not to be put off celebrating Christmas, despite many of them being forced to live upstairs. One very ingenious resident fitted a platform in the kitchen so that food could be prepared without having to stand in icy water. Another resident, claiming to be better off than most, with only eight to ten inches of water in the house, lit a fire and sat by it with her relatives,

A photograph by William Jukes, taken from the railway bridge looking towards the town, of the flooding at Ditchampton, December 1910. The water reached almost to the Parish Church, which can be seen in the distance.

West Street during the 1910 floods.

Children walking in West Street as the water starts to recede.

In January 1915 the town again suffered serious flooding, not only in Ditchampton but in North Street and Russell Street, shown here. The water stretched from North Street to the junction with the main road, from where this picture was taken. Reportedly, an eel was seen in the water.

North Street in the 1915 floods. The makeshift boat (on the left) is positioned at what is, in 2006, the entrance road to Castle Meadow.

Floods at Ditchampton in February 1937.

their feet up on a plank to keep them out of the water. However, as if water in their homes was not enough to contend with, conditions were made even worse, due to the front and back doors having to be left open day and night, as the entrances had been banked up with boards and turves in an effort to keep the water out.

One strange effect of the flooding was that it virtually cut the town in half from east to west, with staging erected over pathways to allow pedestrians to get from one side of town to the other. To try to ease the situation, the Town Council hired a wagonette in which the public could be conveyed through the floodwater completely free of charge. Although the flooding lasted just over four days, it caused a lot of damage to the homes affected. Even

A flood-free Ditchampton, seen from the railway bridge.

South Street in the early 1900s, the former Wool Loft allowing only a very narrow entrance to North Street, which is to its left. The loft was demolished just after the First World War, the military having used it for storage. The tall Post Office building on the left is, at the time of writing, a bookmakers. The small shop next door has been used by a number of different retail outlets and has hardly changed in its outward appearance. The building on the right is, in 2006, the premises of Lloyds TSB.

A view along South Street towards the Market Place and the Wool Loft, taken from near where the Michael Herbert Hall stands today. The street, seen here in the early 1900s, remains almost the same today.

A bird's-eye view of Wilton Market Place in 1913, with the Wool Loft at the far end and, just across the road, a wine shop which in 2006 is Lloyds TSB, the frontage being almost the same. Also seen, opposite the churchyard of St Mary's Church, are the houses in Brede Street and the small shop on the corner of the Market Place. Note the three boys on the corner of the churchyard. The picture is taken from the roof of the former Co-op building which stood on the site occupied in 2006 by Wilton Health Centre.

with all the surplus water mopped up, homes took a long time to dry out in the winter temperatures. Five years later, in 1915, more serious flooding affected the town, this time in the North Street and Russell Street areas, the water, again, being deep enough in some places for a small boat.

In a report issued in 1911 by the Medical Officer of Health for Wilton, he estimated that, by the midsummer of the previous year, there had been an increase in the population of the town and urban district to 2,371 by natural increment. This led him to estimate that the census to be taken later in the year would reveal the population to be in excess of this number. He based his estimate on the fact that, as the census of 1901 had recorded a population of 2,371, the figure would now be much higher, with 168 more births than deaths registered. As it turned out, he was proved totally wrong, the actual census figures revealing that, since 1901, the population, standing at 2,124, had decreased by 79.

It was around this time that Wilton first experienced problems with traffic passing through the town, pedestrians complaining to the council that they were being covered in dust when cars travelled through the town centre. The mayor noted that outlying areas had already asphalted their roads, and that Wilton was lagging behind in the matter. As far as he could see, there was no reason why Wilton roads should not be asphalted, especially as the cost of the work could be cut considerably by the fact that

the gasworks had an abundant supply of tar.

Attempts were also made to impose a speed limit of 10mph on cars passing through the town, some vehicles having been reported as travelling at speeds estimated to be as much as 40mph in the Shaftesbury Road, posing a positive danger to children.

In January 1911, Thomas Challis, head gardener at Wilton House, completed 50 years of faithful service to the Herbert family, during which time he was responsible for many of the improvements to the gardens. Every glasshouse in the kitchen gardens had been designed to his specifications, almost every fruit tree had been planted by him and for the unique fruit arcades, entirely his own invention, he was presented with the Vetch Memorial Medal. Mr Challis also extended the famous lawns, arranged the planting of specimen and memorial trees planted by various royal personages, and also reared large numbers of cedar trees from the cones of the original cedars brought from the Holy Land in 1640. Among his other achievements as head gardener, he was responsible for the rearrangement of the Italian gardens, for laying out two islands in the park and for designing and arranging the rock garden and the lily garden. Mr Challis was presented with a solid 18ct gold watchchain, with a locket attached containing portraits of himself and Mrs Challis and the inscription: 'To Mr T. Challis, V.M.H., on completing 50 years at Wilton Park, from his friends and assistants, January 1911.'

The drinking fountain erected in 1901 as a memorial to the Earl of Pembroke, who had died six years earlier. The picture shows the fountain soon after its official opening by the succeeding Earl of Pembroke. Originally at the bottom of the Avenue at its junction with the Crossroads, the fountain now stands at the entrance to the recreation ground, near the river. The inscription around the bowl reads: 'This fountain is given by Gertrude Countess of Pembroke in memory of happy days at Wilton. Trusting that it will be a comfort to all passers-by and thirsty animals. 1901AD.'

Horses drinking at the fountain not long after its opening. This approach to the Avenue was excavated in the 1840s, a period when many people had fallen on hard times. The Pembroke family are thought to have instigated the making of the road and the planting of trees as a means of providing employment to those in need.

James Henry Sanger at the award ceremony held in his honour, after the opening of the recreation ground, May 1912.

In October of 1911 it was announced in the local press that, for the past six weeks, electricians of the Westinghouse company had been busy installing electric plant at the Royal Carpet Factory and in the manager's house, the first private house in Wilton to be so supplied. The carpet factory was the second business to have electricity, the first being the felt mills in Crow Lane.

During November of 1911 a public meeting was called at the Talbot and Wyvern Hall to inform parents and boys about the Boy Scout movement, many of the boys attending being very enthusiastic. Lady Muriel Herbert, presiding, introduced Mr C.K. Hubert, who had been engaged to explain the movement to the people of Wilton. Although Wilton already had a scout room and boasted a small troop of eight boys who had commenced training, more were required to bring the troop up to strength. It was emphasised that slackers would not be tolerated. The meeting had the desired effect, and in May 1912 a report appeared in the *Salisbury Journal* concerning a parade of Wilton Boy Scouts through the town to Wilton House, where they were inspected and addressed by the Hon. George Herbert. The boys, it was reported, looked very smart in their uniforms, and their marching was excellent. In his address, Mr Herbert said that he hoped the boys would, in friendly rivalry, do their best to beat one another in their work, and strive to become full scouts.

In that same month, the girls of the National School in West Street presented a special entertainment for about 400 parents and friends in Wilton Park. The event, described as a 'pretty entertainment', was under the direction of Mrs Stone, headmistress of the school. The songs were sung to perfection, and the dances and maypole twining faultlessly performed. Dorothy Hibberd was chosen by her schoolfriends as Queen of the May and, accompanied by her attendants, took her seat on the throne, from which she presided over the festivities. After expenses, the event made a profit of £2.12s., the greater part of which was to form the nucleus of a fund for the purchase of a piano for the school.

Practically all of Wilton turned out for the opening of the recreation ground, which had been developed on a piece of waste ground known as the Hop Gardens, situated at the entrance to the town from Salisbury and owned by the Wilton Estate. As the site was rather an eyesore, the Town Council approached Lord Pembroke and suggested that the council would be prepared to lease the land from him for the purpose of turning the area into a playground for children, as well as an area for peace and quiet for the elderly. Lord Pembroke agreed and steps were taken to develop the area as a memorial to King Edward VII.

To be paid for by public subscription, the scheme was not popular with the people of the town, and in the early days money was very slow in coming – so slow that the committee overseeing the project got into debt and a new committee was formed. Despite lingering resentment and apathy, with the help of the council the project eventually came to fruition. The ground was laid out both by men from Lord Pembroke's Estate and by council workmen, all under the direction of head gardener Mr Challis.

The opening day was favoured with splendid weather, and a procession formed in the Market Place headed by Mr G. Bell, who had originally instigated the scheme when he was mayor, and the Bishopstone Band. They were followed by the mayor and corporation, members of the fire brigade, the Boy Scouts and children from all the town's schools. They marched by way of North Street to the ground where, soon after their arrival, the memorial seat was unveiled by Lady Pembroke and the ground officially opened by the Earl of Pembroke. In his speech he paid tribute to all those connected with the scheme, and hoped the inhabitants of Wilton would take pride in it.

Lord Pembroke then performed a second ceremony which, for the sake of convenience, had been combined with this event, presenting a certificate and medal, together with a watch and a cup, to Wilton resident James Henry Sanger. Mr Sanger was being honoured in recognition of his brave attempt to save the life of a friend who, one midnight in the previous December, had fallen over the low parapet of a bridge into a swollen river. Despite his gallant efforts, with no thought for his own safety, Mr Sanger had failed in his attempt to save the man.

Lord Pembroke first handed him the Royal Humane Society bronze medal, obtained on the representation of the Chief Constable of the county. Next came a heavy, double-cased silver watch, presented by the trustees of the Carnegie Hero Fund, on the representation of the editor of the *Salisbury Times* and bearing the inscription, 'He serves God best who most nobly serves Humanity.' Inside the cover were the words:

Presented by the Trustees of the Carnegie Hero Fund to James Harry Sanger, of Wilton, for heroic endeavour to save human life, 27 December, 1911.

Finally presented was a beautiful silver cup from the master and members of Mr Courtenay Tracey's otter hunt, of which Mr Sanger was an employee.

As with the rest of the country, the First World War, commencing in August 1914, was to profoundly touch the lives of every resident of the town by the time it ended four years later. Many would lose husbands, fathers and sons in a conflict which proved to be pure carnage for those young men and women fighting for their country's freedom.

Very quickly, large numbers of troops descended on the surrounding area, and camps to house them were quickly built in the Wylye Valley at such places as Sutton Veney and Hurdcott, and in the Nadder Valley at Fovant. Some new camps were built on Salisbury Plain and others enlarged, all to train troops who would be mobilised and sent to the front. In Wilton a small camp was built on a site at the bottom of the Avenue, at the edge of the Fairfield. Soon after the commencement of war, training took place in Grovely Woods on the edge of town, and in other areas of the surrounding downlands. Wilton LSWR station became extremely busy, handling extra goods traffic for the war effort, and two extra sidings were eventually added on the Fairfield side

Corporal Sid Cannings, one of many Wilton men to volunteer for service in the First World War.

Sid Cannings in what appears to be a family group. The girl on his right was to become his wife.

Training on Salisbury Plain.

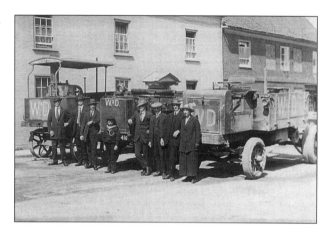

Civilians with War Department vehicles outside the Town Hall in the Market Place.

of the station. In the town centre, the Army requisitioned the Wool Loft, which had ample storage space. They also took over some of the empty houses in Brede Street, converting them to offices. As the war progressed there were shortages, particularly in some food commodities. Rationing was brought in but proved neither successful nor reliable, causing much frustration and aggravation.

As the war progressed there was a friendly invasion of troops from Australia which, as part of the Commonwealth, had come to the assistance of the British. Here for training prior to being sent to the front in France, many of them were stationed at Hurdcott Camp in the Wylye Valley. In their off-duty hours they took advantage of the many local places of interest, visiting the surrounding countryside and taking a keen interest in the historic lore of ancient ecclesiastical buildings. In their quest for knowledge, they were helped by a Wilton woman, Miss B.L. Uphill who, in a ten-month association with these soldiers, came to know them extremely well, discovering their true emotions and thoughts.

These rugged fighting men so impressed her that

she wrote to the Brisbane *Daily Mail* paying them tribute. She spoke of the privilege of having known thousands of them, showing them over the church at Amesbury, in which they had shown a keen interest. She was amazed at their love of nature, particularly of flowers, many pressing them between the pages of their notebooks. Outside one village blacksmith's, she wrote, was a tree which, in the height of summer, was almost devoid of leaves as a result of the soldiers' enthusiasm.

It appears, however, that they were not as keen on our fruit. To one lady renowned locally for the quality of her grapes, the Australians remarked they could get better ones at home for ½d. a pound. Afterwards, in all humility, the lady referred to her grapes as blackcurrants.

Children played a great part in the soldiers' affections, Miss Uphill recalling that on many occasions she witnessed some burly fellow holding a tiny child, its arms draped round his neck. She also remarked that these men, for all their rough exteriors, had the manners more of a court than of a camp, noting they were most courteous, never scrambling into a car until the ladies were seated.

Such was the trust these soldiers had in her that many asked if she would write to their loved ones on their behalf. One such soldier asked:

Lady, will you write to my dear old mother, she is breaking her heart away in Australia. My father and younger brother were killed. I'm off to France next week and my remaining brother is on his way over.

A sergeant asked, with tears in his eyes:

I hear you write to many Australian mothers. My mother is never a moment out of pain. I am her only child. Will you write to her?

Miss Uphill did all she could for the troops, even

Standing proudly beside his 36in. cucumber in the summer of 1914 is Mr Scamell, gardener to Mr Kendell of South Street. The cucumber was grown for a bet of £5.

Water carts damping down the dirt road in North Street during the First World War. Note the uniformed soldiers just visible on the right.

opening up a room in South Street where all troops, Australian and British, could relax in a quiet atmosphere away from their duties. Her room, which soon earned the name of 'Miss Uphill's Dugout', is used, at the time of writing, as the town's library.

Local families, including my maternal grandparents, also offered hospitality to the Australians. I have in my possession my mother's autograph book which, in 1917, some of these soldiers signed and illustrated with beautiful pen and ink drawings, as fresh in 2005 as the day they were made.

There was great relief when the war ended, the

Crowds gather in the Market Place in May 1924 for the unveiling of the Sidney Herbert Memorial, paid for by public subscription. Later demolished to make way for car parking facilities, the memorial is said to be stored in pieces in a council shed at the Fairfield.

A Salisbury & District Motor Services bus at Wilton in 1920. In the following year the Wilts & Dorset Co. acquired the firm, and eventually became the main company operating between Wilton and Salisbury.

joy of the occasion marked by the ringing of the bells of the Parish Church. The townspeople, after decorating their houses with flags and bunting, went to the Market Place to hear the mayor declare that an armistice had been signed and hostilities had ceased. He paid tribute to the Army and the Navy, to women workers and to all those who, in varying ways, had played a part in attaining this happy result. A short thanksgiving service was held in the Parish Church that evening, followed on Sunday by a much larger one. Amidst all the celebrations there was sadness for those Wilton men who would not be returning, having given their lives on battlefields across the sea. For their families there was no homecoming, though their names, along with the names of those who gave their lives in the Second World War and other conflicts, are inscribed on the war memorial, which was dedicated at a special service held on Sunday 20 November 1921. The names of all the Wilton men who gave their lives are read out at the annual Remembrance Service in the Parish Church.

After the initial relief at the ending of the war, the townspeople started to concentrate on peacetime pursuits. With the military no longer requiring use of the Wool Loft or the empty houses in Brede Street, during 1919 they were demolished, a decision which had been discussed before the war, the increasing road traffic through the town necessitating the demolition of the building, which took up too much room and made the road too narrow for cars to negotiate. Also proposed, as the area had become run down,

was a scheme to extend the Market Place, erecting at its centre a memorial to Sidney, fourteenth Earl of Pembroke, a former mayor of the borough and one-time MP for Wilton. The rents paid by the military during the war had provided an appreciable amount of additional funding for the memorial and the enhancement scheme. Completed in May 1924, the unveiling of the Sidney Herbert memorial took place on what appears to have been a showery day. The unveiling ceremony was performed by Lord Radnor in the presence of the mayor and corporation, who had been recommended to attend by a special committee, as the memorial was to be handed over to the corporation in perpetuity.

Other changes were taking place locally on the travel front, offering competition to the railway, in particular on the journey to Salisbury. In 1920 the first bus service was operated by Wilts & Dorset Motor Services between Wilton and Salisbury via Harnham Bridge, from the start using open-topped double-decker buses. The buses were well patronised, even if the ride was rather bumpy at times, and there was a choice of companies, the buses of Salisbury & District Motor Services also running to Salisbury before being bought out by the Wilts & Dorset in 1921. The following year another company, Victory Motor Services, started a rival service and held out until 1933, when Wilts & Dorset took them over, thus winning back their monopoly. It is a monopoly they still enjoy in 2006, although in the late 1980s a rival company, Badger Line, operated for a

A Wilts & Dorset bus waits in Wilton Market Place in the late 1930s before heading back to Salisbury, the crew resplendent in their summer uniform of long white coats and white topped caps. The identity of the other gentleman is not known. The site of the cottages on the right is, in 2006, occupied by Wilton Health Centre.

A Bristol L6B ECW single decker on the No. 54 service for Wincanton and Yeovil, approaching the Wilton Crossroads before the roundabout was built, possibly in the late 1940s or early 1950s. The bus following is a Leyland Lion, a relief bus for the first one.

A Wilts & Dorset Bristol Saloon, waiting at the entrance to Wilton Senior School to take pupils from the country areas home at the end of the school day.

A bus waits in the Market Place for passengers to Salisbury while the crew enjoy a cup of tea in a nearby café. The Sidney Herbert Memorial in the centre of the Market Place became the unofficial bus stop where people queued for the bus to Salisbury – the official stop is just visible above the white car at the front of the bus.

while before being forced to give up under pressure from Wilts & Dorset. In February 1921 the Town Council terminated their agreement with the Wilts & Dorset and draw up an entirely new agreement whereby all buses running between Salisbury and Wilton and using the stand in the Market Place should pay an annual rent of £2 per bus.

Arthur Street, farmer, author and broadcaster, was born at Ditchampton Farm, Wilton, on 7 April 1892, the youngest of a family of six. Born with a deformity of both feet, he underwent several operations to correct them, leaving him unable to walk until he was seven years old, most of his childhood having been spent in leg irons. At Michaelmas in 1918 he took over the tenancy of the farm, which was successful until 1920. To stave off bankruptcy, he then stopped growing corn, grassed the farm over and started a milk round in Wilton and Salisbury, doing the deliveries himself, rising at 4.30a.m. seven days a week. Helped by one man, he milked a herd of 70 cows in an open-air milking outfit.

His flair for writing can be said to have started in November 1929 when, suffering from 'flu, he read an article in the *Daily Mail* which really provoked him. When his wife challenged him to write a better one, he did, showing it to her on completion. She remarked that if he crossed out all the swear words, she thought it was not bad. With the relevant adjustments made, it was published in the *Daily Mail* on 22 November, receipt of a cheque for three guineas giving him the writing bug. He was soon writing columns in the *Salisbury Times* and, on a regular basis until his death, for the *Farmers' Weekly*. Having seen one of his articles in the *Salisbury Times*, Miss Edith Olivier, herself an author, suggested that he write a book about the farm in his father's time. After thinking it over, he eventually looked out some old farm documents and started to scribble words in pencil on old grocery books from a shop he had once owned in Wilton. His book was published on 21 January 1932 under the name A.G. Street, which he used in his writing and broadcasting career. When

The Bell Inn, photographed in the early 1900s, stands in the Ditchampton area of the town at the junction of the main Shaftesbury Road on the A30 and the Wishford Road. The railings were removed during the Second World War, while the building and wall to the left of the inn were demolished to make way for a car park. The arched entrance to the inn and its general appearance remain much the same today.

the book became a best seller, his writing career was well and truly launched.

As a result of the book's success, he was invited to London by Lionel Fielding of the BBC to discuss the possibility of his broadcasting on country matters. His initial broadcast, in April 1932, was the first of many, perhaps those best remembered being his contributions to the popular programme 'Any Questions', first broadcast in 1949. He enjoyed this particular form of broadcasting, and his Wiltshire drawl, combined with a dry, ready wit, soon made him a household name. Although he did experience some difficulty in writing his second book, the novel *Strawberry Roan*, for which he had to invent characters, it also became an instant success, and in 1949 was made into a film starring William Hartnell and Carol Raye, parts of it being shot on location at Compton Chamberlayne.

In 1951 he relinquished the tenancy of Ditchampton Farm, taking up the tenancy of Mill Farm at South Newton on the opposite side of the valley. Although he wrote no further books, until his death on 21 July 1966 he did continue to write articles for the *Farmers' Weekly*.

Long gone are the days when West Street looked like this, completely free of traffic except for a horse and two-wheeled carriage and occupants. The stationer's shop on the left was owned by W. Boning, who sold postcards of Wilton on which his name was printed. The building at the far end of the street, just seen on the left, is the Church Room, built in commemoration of Queen Victoria's golden jubilee and which, in 2006, also houses the Parish Office.

This beamed house in North Street (right) is one of the oldest in Wilton and was once the home of the master of the Free School, the railings of which can be seen next to it. Opposite is the Six Bells, which in 2006 is an Indian restaurant. The postmark on the reverse of this postcard, sold by W. Boning of Wilton, reveals that it was posted in Salisbury on 18 August 1909. Taken at a time when street photography was something of a novelty, the passers-by have stopped to watch the photographer at work, ensuring themselves a place in posterity.

The Talbot and Wyvern Hall, commonly known as the Coffee Tavern, in Kingsbury Square. Its foundation-stone laid in 1873 by Sir Edmund Antrobus, MP for Wilton, it was the headquarters of the Wilton Total Abstinence Society, also being used by many other organisations, and becoming a popular venue for all ages. The building was demolished in 1965 to make way for a new Georgian-style house.

A completely traffic-free West Street in the early 1900s. The thatched cottages were replaced in the early 1990s with Pembroke Court Retirement Flats. The entrance to the National School is on the right, with the railings of the Parish Church visible on the left.

Bill Hewlett told me an interesting story concerning farms in the district, many of which had their own water supply, sourced from deep wells which required pumps to extract the water. Bill's father, a plumber, worked with Harry Mould, who lived in North Street at Weavers Terrace, both men being employed by Jack Marks, who owned a plumbing business in the town. His workshop was in North Street on a site which, in more recent years, was occupied by the Wilton Coach Works, and it was Jack who was called on when the pumps required maintaining or repairing. Bill's father and Harry were sent out on these jobs, which sometimes meant travelling long distances on their bicycles, their only means of transport. They would set off, their tool bags, known as 'Plumbers' Boats' strapped to the handlebars, in all weathers, travelling as far afield as Swallowcliffe to repair or service pumps.

On arrival they would open up the well and, before they descended, would light a candle and lower it down. If it stayed alight there was air and it was safe to descend into the well. Many wells were

Children pose against the railing surrounding the ruined Chuch of St Mary in the 1900s. The bell tower of the Parish Church can be seen above the rooftops of Brede Street. Note the ruins are completely covered in ivy.

The area of Wilton known as Bulbridge, at the top of South Street. During the Second World War this narrow bridge over the River Nadder was frequently damaged by tanks using the road and was later widened to accommodate traffic to the new housing estate.

so deep that one had to go down in stages, repeating the process before entering each stage and, if the candle went out, waiting for the fresh air to circulate. Once the job was completed, they would ascend, sealing off each section in turn until they got back to the top. The deepest of these wells, considered to have been at Wilton at the entrance to Grovely Woods in the Hollows, is claimed to have been as deep as Salisbury Cathedral is high, 404ft. This well, which once supplied water for the pumping station at the Wilton Waterworks in the Wishford Road, was sealed up when the waterworks closed, there remaining no trace of it.

When the Free School closed, in 1921, it was bought by the Prinn family from Cornwall, part of it being used as a Labour Exchange. During a period of depression, many Welshmen descended on the town looking for work. Poor and desperate, their clothing ragged, they had come after hearing that navvies were needed to lay new water mains in the town and on the Pembroke Estate. In those days there were no machines to do the work, it was all manual and back breaking, trenches being dug with a pick and shovel. Fortunately many did get taken on. Bill Hewlett's father was also involved with the work, and years later, when the Estate required assistance in tracing the mains on their land, Bill's father was the only person who could say exactly where they were laid.

Pictured in the late 1800s, this impressive grocery shop in North Street, at the junction with Crow Lane, was one of a chain of such shops owned by John White, a successful businessman who attracted much business through his unusual window displays and clever advertising, in which people, horses and carriages were made to appear disproportionately small, making the shop look huge in comparison.

119

Wilton Wednesday Football Club, 1911–12. The club reached the final of the Salisbury Wednesday Cup and the semi-final of the Shaftesbury tournament in 1911–12. Left to right, back row: F. Down, A. Chivers, A. Moore, R. Saunders, A. Hinton, A. Morris, Mr L. Hinton (Chairman); front row: C. Jenvy, A. Romain (Capt.), L. Parsons, F. Robinson, J. Underwood (Hon. Sec.).

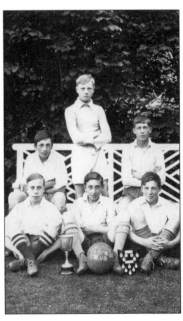

These three teams from the Wilton Boys Football Club entered a six-a-side tournament at Devizes in 1931, one team (centre row) winning the cup and another (front row) the shield. Left to right, back row: Mr Jeans, Chuck Cooper, Reg Wilton, Hubert James, Frank Weeks, Bill Humphries, Harry Noyce, Eric Blake; middle row: Sid Trim, Jumbo Binden, Chippy Scott, ?, Fred Ricketts, Jack Cope; front row: Ken Saunders, Charlie Furnell, Harry Ricketts, Jack Smith, Eddy Dimmer, Charlie Morris.

The boys who won the shield. Left to right, back row: Eddy Dimmer, Jack Smith, Harry Ricketts; front row: Ken Saunders, Charlie Furnell, Charlie Morris.

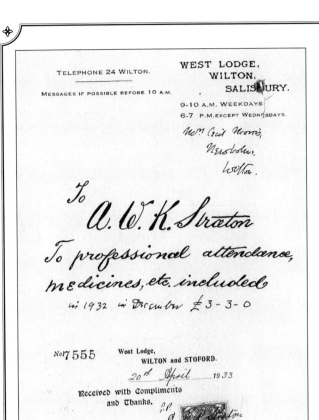

TELEPHONE 24 WILTON.

MESSAGES IF POSSIBLE BEFORE 10 A.M.

WEST LODGE,
WILTON,
SALISBURY.

9-10 A.M. WEEKDAYS
6-7 P.M. EXCEPT WEDNESDAYS.

Mrs Cecil Morris,
Newholme,
Wilton.

To A.W.K. Straton

To professional attendance,
medicines, etc. included
in 1932 in December £3-3-0

No 7555   West Lodge,
WILTON and STOFORD.

20th April 1933

Received with Compliments
and Thanks.

£ 3 : 3 : 0

A bill from Dr A.W.K. Straton for a home visit.

17, Fair View Road,
The Avenue,   WILTON.

March 10th 1934

Mrs C. Morris, "Newholme"

Dr. to F. BUDDEN,

WINDOW CLEANER, ETC.

For work done to Scullery.
Washing off & Distemp. ceiling
Washing down, Sizing walls
& Painting two coats.

1 Qt Gloss paint	6	6
1½ Pts Gloss "	4	9
4 lb Undercoating	3	0
Distemper & Size	1	0
	15	3
Labour	15	0
Received with many	1	10	3

thanks
F. Budden
29/5/34

*Invoice dated 10 March 1934 from Frank Budden, who
also offered a home decoration service.*

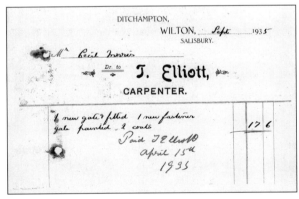

DITCHAMPTON,
WILTON, Sept 1935
SALISBURY.

Mr Cecil Morris

Dr. to J. ELLIOTT,
CARPENTER.

1 new gate & fitted 1 new fastener
gate painted 2 coats   17 6
Paid J Elliott
April 15th
1935

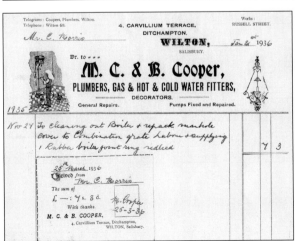

Telegrams: Coopers, Plumbers, Wilton.
Telephone: Wilton 69.

4, CARVILLIUM TERRACE,
DITCHAMPTON

Works:
RUSSELL STREET.

Mr. C. Morris

WILTON, Jan 31st 1936
SALISBURY.

Dr. to M. C. & B. Cooper,
PLUMBERS, GAS & HOT & COLD WATER FITTERS,
DECORATORS.
General Repairs.   Pumps Fixed and Repaired.

1935

Nov 21 To cleaning out Boiler & repack manhole
cover to Combination grate Labour & supplying
1 Rubber boiler joint ring nailed   7 3

25th March 1936
Received from Mr. C. Morris
The sum of
£ - : 7 s. 3 d.
With thanks.   M. Cooper
M. C. & B. COOPER,   26-3-36
4, Carvillium Terrace, Ditchampton,
WILTON, Salisbury.

LINOS AND
FLOORCLOTHS.

MILLINERY AND
MANTLES.

79, North Street,
WILTON, Mar 24 1936

Mr C Morris

BOUGHT
- OF - F. ROBINSON,
DRAPER ⁖ TAILOR ⁖ OUTFITTER.
Boot and Shoe Warehouseman.

Sports Coat 18/11

Paid
C. M. Robinson
March 24/36

Above left: *A bill from J. Elliott, carpenter, for making
and fitting a new gate, including a new fastener and
two coats of paint.*
Above: *A receipt from F. Robinson, for a sports coat
costing 18s.11d.*
Left: *Invoice from M.C. & B. Cooper for work carried
out on a boiler.*

Unfortunately, before his father could start the work, he died, and the Estate had to find other means to search for them.

When Bill himself was 12, together with two other boys of about the same age, he got a Saturday job on the Estate helping with the gardens, earning the princely sum of 6d. At that time the head gardener was Mr Davies, who was very strict. Every Saturday morning he would meet them at the gate and instruct them in how to conduct themselves should they chance to meet Lord and Lady Pembroke. Boys will be boys, however, and one Saturday, when Mr Davies was nowhere to be seen, they decided to give each other wheelbarrow rides along the narrow paths lined with ornate box hedges. One of the boys accidentally pushed the barrow into a hedge, tipping the other onto the greenery and splaying it out. Mr Davies went ballistic, dismissing the three boys on the spot for the trouble they had caused.

In the 1930s there were many shops in the town, between them supplying residents with all they required. In North Street there was Barrett & Brown, a successful grocery business which had survived since the 1920s, gaining a reputation for the quality of its service. The business had also cultivated regular customers over a wide area of the surrounding district, delivering orders, both retail and wholesale, in a Morris Commercial van. They remained in business in Wilton for just over two decades and in 1942 issued a handbill of prices of Scotch seed potatoes, as did Foyle's, the corn and seed merchants, who were in business a little further down the road on the opposite side. It is interesting to note that in the section for 'first earlies', the prices for different weights of the same brands are exactly the same, while on some of the other brands Foyles's prices are cheaper, on one particular brand by as much as 1s.6d. It is also interesting to note their telephone numbers, that for Foyles being Wilton 55 and for Barrett & Brown, Wilton 58. How times have changed.

Also in North Street was a large drapery store, Maffey & Lewry, which also did good business, and really went to town for Christmas 1933 by producing a catalogue of fancy goods and useful presents. Printed in colour, with green and red lettering on cream-coloured card, the catalogue ran to eight pages and included all sorts of Christmas gifts items, many of them in fancy boxes. Ladies' and gent's gloves, slippers, boxed or individual hankies, Yardley's gift cases of various perfumes, bath salts and soap, a special line in gent's braces with matching suspenders, men's tunic shirts, ladies' underwear sets in pastel boxes, dolls, rugs and children's books and, of course, boxes of twelve Christmas crackers were just some of the items listed.

Another large retail outlet doing good business at this time was the Wilton William Herbert Co-operative Industrial & Provident Society Ltd, situated in the Market Place on the site of the Wilton Health Centre. Throughout the early 1930s, posters in the town advertised increasing dividends, boasting one year in particular an increase to 1s.6d. in the pound. Another year, as a goodwill gesture, customers were invited to the Michael Herbert Hall for a social evening , a very successful event.

At a council meeting held in November 1938 another piece of Wilton's history was made, when Edith Olivier was elected Wilton's first lady mayor, quite an achievement for the daughter of former rector Canon Dacres Olivier. A popular choice, Edith had spent many hours of her busy life helping those less fortunate than herself, which endeared her to everyone. In her younger days she had written books containing her observations of life and of various personalities in the town. Being the first lady mayor, she announced in her acceptance speech that, although she would wear her mayoral gown at monthly council meetings, feeling it gave her presence, she did not expect other councillors to wear their gowns.

As it had once been the custom to distribute bread from the doorway of the old Church of St Mary on New Year's Day, Edith Olivier decided, because of her caring nature, to revive the custom, sending letters to recipients informing them of her intentions and describing how the custom had been started, about 100 years before, by those with compassion for others less fortunate than themselves.

She concluded by saying she felt it apt, as Wilton's first lady mayor, to revive this custom, the word 'lady' being derived from an ancient word meaning 'loaf giver'.

CHAPTER 9

Wilton at War

In September 1939 war clouds gathered over Wilton and the young men of the town were be called on to serve their country. There had been the threat of war for some months and the the council was fully engaged in drawing up plans to be implemented should hostilities take place.

Concerning the plan for the Talbot and Wyvern Hall to be used as an ARP (Air Raid Precautions) first-aid post, there was some confusion over who was to be responsible for the adaptation of the hall. The town clerk had written to the authorities asking for a straight 'yes' or 'no', but the reply was rather ambiguous. Many councillors, figuring the county to be responsible, suggested that they went ahead on those lines, informing the county ARP committee of their decision.

It was decided to ask for volunteer wardens but, with only 50 recruited, the council were unable to operate the scheme successfully unless at least double this number volunteered. While the scheme was discussed in great detail by the council and eventually passed to the county council for approval, the lack of recruits meant there were still delays in getting the scheme together. In an effort to rectify the situation and recruit more volunteers, notices were distributed headed 'No Air Raid Precautions in Wilton!' which continued by saying that this dreadful possibility would become fact unless another 100 inhabitants offer to lend a hand. It was also pointed out that, although the committee appointed by the borough council had the scheme ready, it could not work through lack of help. It also went on to say that should there be a raid when people were at work or away from home, when children were in school, or even in bed, a fully operational scheme, with everyone properly advised, would save lives and avoid confusion. The notices had the desired effect, though the delay meant that Wilton was the last local authority to send off its proposals.

With sufficient volunteers found, and with the

Wilton Volunteer Fire Brigade in the late 1930s. These highly trained civilians were in the front line along with Air Raid Wardens and Civil Defence Workers, never knowing what dangers may face them in the call of duty. Left to right, back row: Alan Newton, Arthur Collins, Phil Moore, Harry Dewland, Colin Tennant, Harold Rousell; second row: Reg Boon, Dick Best, Jim Saunders, Jumbo Binden, Bill Brent, Fred Rowe; front row: Ted Harding, ? Hobson, Gilbert Lever, Bert Cooper, Howard Cooke, Sam Carson, Bill Osborne.

No Air Raid Precautions in Wilton!

THAT DREADFUL THOUGHT becomes a **FACT** unless another hundred inhabitants offer to lend a hand. So far only fifty have offered their services. The Committee appointed by the Borough Council have the scheme ready — **BUT** it cannot work through **lack of help.**

Excuses are plentiful—

BUT when a Raid comes

You may be at work.
You may be away from home.
Your children may be in school.
You may be in bed.

☞The point is that IF THE A.R.P. SCHEME IS WORKING everyone will know

How to know when a raid is expected.
The best place to go and how to get there.
From whom to obtain a gas mask, and how to use it.
The best way to deal with mustard gas.
To whom to report fires, casualties, dangerous buildings, etc.

Come On!! Lend a Hand.

Tear off the attached slip and put in the box outside the Town Hall.
THIS IS URGENT, and may mean life or death to all you value most.

Issued by the Wilton A.R.P. Committee.

BOROUGH OF WILTON.

Air Raid Precautions.

I offer my services for the above scheme.

Name _____ Address _____

This notice was put through residents' doors in 1938 urging them to volunteer as air-raid wardens.

Some of the men of Wilton Volunteer Fire Brigade pose with their fire engine. Note the motorised water pump attached to the rear of the vehicle.

help of Percy Hare, the local wheelwright and under-taker, they soon got down to the business of getting organised. With the threat of war never far away, exercises in preparation continued in the town and surrounding areas. One of these involved the simulation of an air attack on the town, the imaginary targets being airfields and two aerodrome factories, Wilton House playing the role of one of the latter. The blackout was in force from 10p.m. until midnight, the exercise being designed to run in actual wartime conditions, as realistically as possible, simulating a situation in which heavy loses were inflicted. Everything went according to plan, even the Home Office representative being more than satisfied with the parts played by the people of Wilton. During the war they were to have plenty of warnings and, before there was a regular warden's post, patrolled the streets throughout the night. On top of this they served a large area around the town, covering around 20–30 miles each way, and the ARP committee, who had started to organise their services about a year before the war began, were fully prepared when it commenced. Such wardens as Cecil Morris, who owned a butcher's shop in West Street, were issued with a booklet outlining their duties in the event of war. The men were instructed to be of courage and presence of mind, and to proceed to the warden's post, at which time their public duties would begin. If bombs fell, it was the warden's duty to get his reports through to headquarters quickly and accurately and to give gas warnings immediately should a gas attack take place. Both the volunteer fire brigade and the ARP wardens were in the front line, which meant that both units could be in great danger, putting out fires and rescuing people from damaged buildings during air raids. Fortunately, no bombs fell on Wilton, but if they had, such people as Cecil were

fully trained to cope with any situation, as were the Women's Voluntary Service, the Civil Defence and the Volunteer Fire Brigade, all prepared to do their duty to protect the town and its residents. Luckily, when war was finally declared, there was a period which became known as the 'phoney war', when nothing much happened, allowing more time to train volunteers. Once the enemy commenced to bomb large towns and cities, these volunteers, never knowing when their services would be required, were ready to respond at a moment's notice. My father was a volunteer in the fire brigade, and I well remember him getting calls for duty soon after going to bed. His uniform was kept on a coat-hanger in the bedroom so that, when he received a call-out, he could quickly be dressed and on his way to the fire station. One night, during a serious raid on Bath, the Wilton brigade was called out to attend and it was not until they returned that anyone knew where they had been. With Southern Command at Wilton House, many residents wondered if it would be targeted by German bombers. Whether the German high command was unaware of its existence, or did not consider it of sufficient importance, Wilton House escaped attack. Had it not, then D-Day might well not have taken place.

In the days just before the commencement of the war, the mayor was deputed by the government to assist with a scheme to prepare for the evacuation of civilian populations from danger zones in times of war. The council engaged volunteer workers to make house-to-house calls in order to estimate the number of people it would be possible to accommodate in the borough in an emergency, first distributing a pamphlet explaining the scheme and expressing confidence that the people of Wilton would play their part. At the same time, the mayor made arrangements with the rector for a bell to be rung at the church daily at midday to remind all religious denominations to pray for peace. Also as part of the preparations, a blackout was imposed from 10p.m. until midnight in order to simulate air-raid conditions. It seems that all preparations went according to plan, a Home Office official being more than satisfied with the part played by the people of Wilton.

Soon after the declaration of war, the first evacuees arrived in the town, some of them from Court Lane School in Cosham, a suburb of Portsmouth. From Salisbury Railway Station they arrived by coach, scrambling off in good spirits, clutching emergency rations and gas masks, the latter being something of a novelty to the reception committee, as they had not yet been issued in Wilton. The children, aged between five and 11 years, were greeted by a crowd which included the mayor and mayoress, the Countess of Pembroke and the rector and his wife, after which they were quickly taken off to their billets by car. The next day another group arrived and soon settled into their new surroundings.

One can only imagine how these evacuees must

David Bowes and his sisters at their home in Cosham, Portsmouth, just before their evacuation to Wilton in September 1939. From left to right: Pat, David, Jean and Marie.

have felt, uprooted from their homes and parents and brought to a strange town to live with strangers. One of the first to arrive, David Bowes, liked Wilton so much that after the war he settled here and, at the time of writing, still lives in Wilton with his family. What prompted him to stay? Fortunately, he has written down his experiences, which now follow in his own words:

Evacuated To Wilton

September 1939 – Air-raid precautions in Portsmouth, where I was born. Evacuation, a new word for a six- year-old boy. 'You will be going away – but it will be only for six months, it will be a holiday, then you will be coming home.' Having never had a holiday, that was something new.

My older sisters and I were given a pillow-case each and gradually my parents started to put in three separate piles what we would possibly need. This done, we were ready for our holiday.

I cannot remember the exact day or date we left Portsmouth, but I can remember a big luggage label attached to the front of me, plus being given a bar of chocolate and an orange.

'You three children stay together,' were the last words I recall my mother saying as we boarded the train. The next thing I remember on that day, was standing in the school hall (now the Community Centre) with my sisters, being scrutinised by what I thought were very old ladies and gentlemen. All of a sudden my middle sister was taken by the arm and led away. With that I started to cry and, remembering mum's words later, I said I wanted my sister back. The tears worked, they must have, because the next thing she was back with me and my other sister again. I can only say that she was blonde and pretty, whereas Jean and my self were redheads – that spelt trouble.

From the school hall the three of us, along with others, were transferred to Bulbridge House in South Street, then the home of Lady Juliet Duff. There were 15 children and two lady helpers, a Mrs Gelding and her three daughters (Pauline, Barbara and Madeline) and a Mrs Lee with Viviene and Nicky. This house was totally different to what I was used to, with a butler, a cook, servants, etc., compared with a three-bedroom council-house.

I remember being allowed into the grounds the following morning, having never seen green fields, a tennis court or swimming pool. There was also an orchard, and myself and another boy decided that we would get all the green lumps off its branches, shaking the tree so vigorously that the lumps fell off. 'Don't do that!' shouted the voice of the butler (Harry Andrews), who took us aside and told us the green lumps were apples – to me apples were red and came in brown paper bags. Needless to say, we were banned from the orchard.

I stayed at Bulbridge House for nine months – the military requisitioned the house, the evacuees that stayed – many returned home – were dispersed around Wilton. My younger sister returned home, my elder sister went to live in Shaftesbury Road with Mrs and Mrs Ken Foyle.

I made the long journey of about 100 yards to live with Mr Sidney Coles and his wife Nellie, at the Sawmill, the rear entrance to the estate of Wilton Park. My word, what a difference, no butler, no maids or cook, but what a smashing couple they were. There was a lot of love in that house, as well as strictness, and I was made one of the family straight away, with a lot more aunts and uncles.

There was another boy evacuated there, and he turned out to have lived in the next road to me in Portsmouth. Between us, we thought we had arrived in heaven, as we began to explore inside of Wilton Park wall. Soon workmen arrived and began building Army huts inside the wall, running from the Sawmills Gate, up to opposite Burcombe Lane. The soldiers began to occupy the huts and we were in our element watching them parade and drill.

The Home Guard was formed and familiar Wilton faces began to appear in khaki. Col. Chrichton Maitland, Major Parker, Mr Foyle the grain merchant was RSM and they used to assemble and parade on the Sawmill road inside the gate. There was a wooden stand made by the Estate, which used to stand in the back yard overlooking South Street bridge. This was to be used to defend the bridge if the Germans came, three men, three old Endfield rifles and five rounds of ammunition apiece, not much against a Tiger Tank!

Excitement one particular day, when the word went round that a German aircraft that was shot down was going to be displayed in the market square. We were down there like a shot to see this aeroplane, but we couldn't get near it as a fence had been erected around it to keep souvenir hunters at bay. Nevertheless, it was a good feeling to see it, as it brought the war a little bit nearer for us boys. I often wondered if it dropped the bombs on my house, or the one my grandmother lived in at Portsmouth.

Living in Wilton Park, I soon began to lose my 'townie' approach and gradually began to take on a country feel for everything. When my mother used to visit, she said I spoke like a farmer. 'Nothing wrong in that,' I used to reply. There were trees and woods, a river where we used to fish, and all manner of things to do with nature.

The soldiers in the camp were good to us, and I remember all through those years we never locked our front doors, not much chance of that happening today. A guard was posted on the gate, and as a boy interested in the war and the Army, it was something to be able to sit in his hut and talk. One actually showed me how to take a sten gun apart and rebuild it, along with its magazine clip. With this knowledge, a boy ten years old, and a 40-year old soldier, we were ready for any invasion that would come.

What's this? A different uniform appeared, English speaking, but a different accent. It was the 'Yanks', American soldiers, who appeared, and started to build a camp alongside the Avenue (now the HQ of the Army Land Forces). Generous to a fault, it was chewing-gum and candy every time without saying those immortal words, 'Any gum chum?'. I remember one Christmas we went carol singing and the Americans had taken over the building that is now the Municipal Offices. They took our hats inside and when they returned them, they were full of English coins, chocolate bars and oranges, among other things.

The build up to D-Day was beginning and train-loads of tanks and armaments were arriving at Wilton Rail Station. A Matilda tank without the gun turret was used to tow half a dozen bren gun carriers. It ran from the station to Bishopstone Hill, turning right at the Wheatsheaf Inn, roaring up North Street, not stopping at the crossroads at the market, then up South Street and on up the hill. This convoy was driven at breakneck speed, and several times the parapet of the bridge in South Street was hit. On one occasion part of the masonry broke the water pipe which supplied our house, which meant we had water delivered in a milk churn every two days for about twelve months.

The war finally ended, what was going to happen to me? Mr and Mrs Coles were worried that I would go home and forget them. My parents obviously wanted me home. They compromised, saying I should finish my schooling here first.

I attended local schools, the primary school in West Street and the Secondary Modern at the Hollows. Miss Drake was headmistress at West Street, and neither she nor I could see eye-to-eye with one another. Whether she saw me as an infiltrator in her school, I don't know, but I always appeared to be on her wrong side. But I got my own back, I did pass my 11-plus exam.

Leaving school at 15 years old, my parents asked if I was going to come home to Portsmouth. My reply was, that 'Wilton was my home and I was going to stay here.' They took it extremely well and we never had bad words about it. From the age of six to 15 is a long time in a boy's life, and many events, things and people mould a person in those years. So I stayed on, apprenticed at F.W. Marks' garage. I got married to a Salisbury girl, Doreen, did my National Service and returned to Wilton, where we have lived ever since.

I did return to Portsmouth for a flying visit when I was 18 years old, 12 years after I left, but I was back in Wilton the same evening.

The mayor of Portsmouth wrote a letter which I still have, in 1940, saying he hoped that we would all return home soon. I suppose I couldn't read, because it's now 60 years since I left.

PS. I was talking to my mother about three months before she died at the age of 95, and at one point she said, 'I had four children in my house in the morning, in the evening, I didn't have any'. War is a terrible thing, it hurts everybody. Evacuation wasn't everybody's cup of tea.

With many men called up for active service, women played an important role in keeping the country running, especially those in munitions factories. Here a group of workers at Churchfields, Salisbury, engaged in the production of two-pound practice bombs for the Royal Navy, find time to pose for the camera.

No information exists about these men, other than the caption on the back of this photograph, which reads: 'The Rogues Gallery! Auxiliary Fire Brigade at the Works.' The building in the background is Fugglestone House, used by the Town Council during the Second World War, at the same time being requistioned by the Red Cross and the Auxiliary Fire Service. The house has long since been demolished, the site being used as the officers' mess for UK Land Forces.

When the fateful announcement was made, on Sunday, 3 September, that war had been declared, the town was well prepared, it did not take long for signs of war to become evident; Wilton being a main assembly point for troops, the town was overwhelmed with them. At night they were forced to sleep in the felt mill, the wool stores and anywhere else that could be provided at short notice. Even the Fairfield was utilised as a giant car park for the storage of masses of military vehicles, and it was not long before the streets echoed to the sound of marching feet as soldiers passed through for guard duties. The Greydawn Café in the Market Place did a roaring trade feeding the off-duty soldiers, and there were certainly plenty of them to be fed. However, with the government aware of the possibility of food shortages caused by a breakdown in distribution, Wilton housewives, along with others all over the country, experienced the start of rationing as early as January 1940, shopping with a ration book full of coupons. At first it was restricted to just a few items – four ounces per head per week of bacon and ham, 12oz of sugar and 4oz of butter. Rationing of meat followed in March and in July was extended to tea. It was not long before many other essentials were rationed, including clothing. A 'Dig for Victory' campaign was launched by the Ministry of Food, asking people with gardens or allotments to plant vegetables to grow for their own use, an initiative which eventually resulted in many front gardens being dug up – carefully tended lawns and flowerbeds were not a necessity in war; home-grown vegetables were. Although at this very early stage of the war many people were preoccupied with their own affairs, when the Germans dropped parachutists into Belgium in May 1940, attitudes changed and, as is common in such situations, rumours started to be spread, one of which was that parachutists disguised as clergymen and nuns had been dropped in this country. In case there was any truth in these rumours, people collected hefty objects and even old guns which might be useful in the event of an invasion. This in turn led to the formation of the Local Defence Volunteers, later known officially as the Home Guard, who spent all their spare time training to defend the town, led by Platoon Commander, William Moore. These invasion scares, all false, continued for quite a time and, after yet another false alarm, with typical Wiltshire wit, a local man was heard to remark, 'They Germans, they're not dependable – you can't rely on them for anything.'

With the lack of amenities really beginning to bite, various directives from a specially formed invasion committee informed residents of the actions that would be taken in the event of an emergency. The main priority being the water supply, to ensure that sufficient supplies would be available in the reservoir, mains water would be supplied only from 7a.m. to 8a.m. and from 5p.m. to 6p.m, during which times householders were instructed to fill jugs, kettles, basins and baths. When mains water was available, its use was restricted to drinking, cooking and the preparation of food. Baths were curtailed completely, and for washing and flushing WCs only the use of rainwater or river water was permitted. Should the main supply become exhausted or cut by the enemy, it was thought that river water would be safe to drink if boiled for three minutes. For those not close to a river, supplies would be delivered in water carts, while those living near rivers would have to obtain all their supplies from this source.

The Municipal Offices were moved from the Town Hall to Fugglestone House, in secluded grounds just off the Salisbury Road near the Crossroads, which also became the local administrative centre for the issue of ration books and gas masks. For greater security Southern Command requisitioned Wilton House in June 1940 as its operational HQ for the duration of the war. Although the Earl and Countess of Pembroke were allowed to stay in residence, their accommodation was limited to just two rooms. Mayor Edith Olivier, who lived in Daye House on the Wilton Estate, was worried that, in its new role, Wilton House would become a legitimate target for Hitler. Officers were billeted in houses on the Estate or around the town, while people of Wilton played their part by billeting service personnel in their homes. The Pembroke Arms Hotel, directly opposite Wilton House, was also requisitioned by the military and used as an officers' mess, while Lady Pembroke ran a canteen with a number of helpers in what, in 2006, is the Estate Office. The eighteenth-century riding school found a new use as a vehicle repair shop and Nissen huts were erected in the grounds under trees which acted as camouflage, so that they were invisible from the air. At this time, should the military require your premises or land, they took it, no matter who you were. Unable to complain and with no form of redress, you quite simply did as you were told without question; if you did not, you could find yourself in serious trouble with the authorities, in court or even prison if the situation was really serious.

Residents soon adapted to wartime conditions, to the shortages, the rationing and the many other restrictions that prevailed. Despite all these changes to their daily lives, they made every effort to carry on as normal, helping each other where possible and invoking that most valuable commodity, community spirit. It was not all doom and gloom, however, and many special entertainments were put on. One in particular, at New Year in 1941, was a spoof production of the pantomime *Cinderella* entitled *Heil Cinderella*, written by celebrated society photographer Cecil Beaton in collaboration with a colleague, John Sutro. Beaton, a personal friend of the mayor, Edith Olivier, persuaded her to take part in the production, which was staged by the Wilton House

Company at the Michael Herbert Hall in Wilton for four nights commencing 1 January. Edith played the part of the Fairy Godmother (for the purposes of this production changed to a witch) so well that she received many accolades, as did the entire production. Unfortunately for Edith, as mayor, the publicity proved rather embarrassing at council meetings. Due to its popularity the production toured many of the military camps in Wiltshire, although mayoral duties prevented Edith from taking part in any of these performances.

With factories in need of raw materials for the manufacture of tanks, aircraft and weapons, residents were once again asked to make sacrifices. Iron railings were removed from many properties, including St Mary's Church in the Market Place. As These donations of materials, money was also required, and in conjunction with Salisbury and the surrounding district, Wilton took part in a special War Weapons Week. Such was the importance of this fund-raising that the following leaflet was distributed to every home in Wilton and surrounding districts in order to get the message across:

BOROUGH OF WILTON
WAR WEAPONS WEEK

Most Wilton people will already know that we are joining with our neighbours in the city of Salisbury and the Rural District in an effort to raise the sum of £300,000 during a War Weapons Week. This week will begin on Saturday May 10, and will last until May 17; and I urgently call on everyone in Wilton,

men, women and children, to make their contributions to this goal.

I know that it is possible to feel discouraged by the comparison of one's own resources with the immense sum of money required, but I beg everyone to banish that feeling. The many millions that have been raised during the past eighteen months by the National Savings Committee have been contributed by small investors. This is the pride of a democratic country. Our strength comes from the fact that we are all pulling together, and I believe when the 17th May arrives we shall be surprised at the amount which will have been raised in Wilton.

Although our work is the serious business of raising money, a good many events have been arranged in connection with the week in which I hope as many as possible will take part. Details of these will be issued through public notices, but I will now call attention to a few which especially affect the town of Wilton.

Friday and Saturday, May 9th and 10th. A loan exhibition in the Town Hall, consisting of ancient and modern war weapons, and with a special children's section of original posters and models. This will be open each evening from 6 till 9, under the supervision of Mr A. Elliott. Admission on buying one or more 6d. War Savings Stamps.

Saturday May 10th. The Mayors of Salisbury and Wilton will open the week broadcasting to each other from their respective Town Halls, and this will be relayed on loudspeakers. The time will be announced later. A flight of bombers will pass over the town during the afternoon.

Members of the Auxiliary Fire Service, formed for the duration of the war, resplendent in their brass helmets.

Edith Olivier, who had been mayor since 1938, was asked to stay in office, many of the male councillors being unable to hold office due to wartime work commitments. This all changed in 1941, when Sam Shergold took on the role for the next 12 months. A driver on the railways, he was allowed to work special night shifts, from midnight to 8a.m., enabling him to perform his mayoral duties which, because of the war, were many more than in peacetime.

During September 1942, with invasion still a possibility, residents were given an experience of just what would be required of them should this occur. This took the form of a special exercise, over one weekend, from midday on Saturday until midday Sunday. Not only was Wilton involved, the people of Salisbury, Downton, Netherhampton and Quidhampton were included in this very realistic exercise, in which the civilian population was asked to co-operate fully, performing the tasks asked of them by the military, civil defence, police and other organisations. A special notice, sent by mayor Sam Shergold to all inhabitants of the town, gave the full facts of the invasion exercise. He commenced by saying that, although many had believed the country would never go to war, a view held until 3 September 1939, they had been proved to be wrong. These people, he continued were now expressing similar views, wrongly held, on the possibility of an invasion, and as a result were in great danger. It was the duty of everyone, he continued, to hinder any invader of our shores, to stand firm and do their duty. The mayor then outlined the particulars of the exercise. Military, Air Force, Home Guard and Civil Defence would combine in a full-scale exercise on 25, 26 and 27 September involving an attack on and

defence of the borough which would be made as realistic as possible. While large incidents would be dealt with by the Civil Defence Services, there would be incidents in every street which the inhabitants would have to deal with unaided. Places of entertainment, licensed premises and shops were to be closed from 4p.m. to midnight on Saturday 26, and all transport facilities were to be curtailed. Tear gas was also to be used, so gas masks had to be carried at all times; much to the relief of residents, despite rumours to the contrary, real bullets would not be used. As the exercise began, places of entertainment were closed and transport facilities ceased. Various problematic situations, created in nearly every street, were solved by the inhabitants, very few of them getting any sleep. The exercise over, several high-ranking officers of the American Army, together with the chief adjudicator, expressed admiration at the efficiency of the Home Guard.

So realistic was the exercise that in Salisbury there was some damage to business premises in the city, while Wilton remained unscathed. The knowledge gained from the exercise was fortunately never put to the test and there was never an invasion. In all, more than 10,000 troops and civil defence workers took part, along with cars, tanks and lorries, with several Guards battalions posing as enemy infantry and a Mustang aircraft supplying the aerial bombardment.

Life in Wilton under wartime conditions was put in the spotlight when the BBC, in conjunction with the Columbia Broadcasting System (CBS) in America, broadcast live from the town to both countries on Sunday, 21 February 1943. This programme was the third in a series, broadcast every week from Britain and the United States alternately, entitled 'Transatlantic Call – People to People', the Wilton edition being 'Country Town'. The American presenter of the programme was Bob Trout, and co-hosting the programme from Wilton, introducing people, was local broadcaster, author and farmer A.G. Street. As the programme was carefully scripted because of censorship, in an effort to make it sound more natural there was a two-hour rehearsal before the broadcast. All those taking part in the programme, interestingly, were paid a fee of two guineas, £2.10 in today's money. Although only transmitted on the Forces Network by the BBC, the broadcast went out on the general CBS network.

Bob Trout opened the programme with his obser-vations of Wilton on his arrival a few days before. After arriving by train at the Southern Station, he had turned into North Street to walk into town and heard children singing, the sound coming from a small school with a thatched roof and white-painted walls. This tranquil scene was shattered when several British tanks roared round the corner, drowning out the singing, and a few minutes later the hills echoed with the boom of gunfire as troops practised on Salisbury Plain. From out of nowhere, two planes

Crown Copyright Reserved

AIR RAID PRECAUTIONS
HANDBOOK No. 8
(2nd Edition)

THE DUTIES OF AIR RAID WARDENS

Issued by the Home Office
(Air Raid Precautions Department)

LONDON
PRINTED AND PUBLISHED BY HIS MAJESTY'S STATIONERY OFFICE
To be purchased directly from H.M. STATIONERY OFFICE at
the following addresses:
York House, Kingsway, London, W.C.2; 120 George Street, Edinburgh 2,
26 York Street, Manchester 1; 1 St. Andrew's Crescent, Cardiff;
80 Chichester Street, Belfast;
or through any bookseller
1938
Price 2d. net

The cover of an instruction handbook, published in 1938, concerning air-raid precautions to be carried out in the event of war.

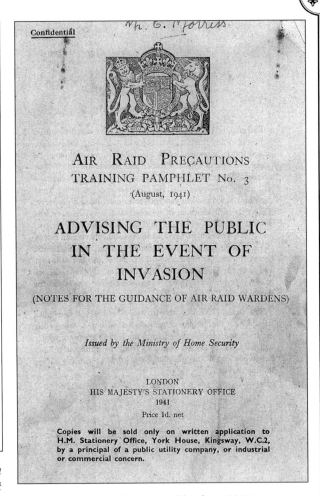

An air-raid precautions pamphlet from 1941.

WILTSHIRE CONSTABULARY   CIVILIAN WAR DEATHS.

Name and Address
of deceased.

Place where injury sustained.

Cause of death, *e.g.*, bomb, fire,
splinter, falling masonry.

Name, address and relationship
of nearest relative (or friend).

If relative aware of death.   Yes or No.

Date   194

Signature................................

Official capacity.........................

For instructions see back.

A form issued by the Wiltshire Constabulary for registering civilian war deaths.

BOROUGH OF WILTON.

AIR RAIDS PRECAUTIONS.

LECTURES AT THE TOWN HALL.

The COUNTESS of RADNOR

(an accredited Instructress in Gas and Chemical Warfare under the British Red Cross Society),

has kindly consented to give a Course of LECTURES in WILTON during the coming Autumn and Winter.

The course will begin on Tuesday, NOV. 16th, at 7 p.m., and will continue on the following Tuesday evenings. Five lectures will be given before Christmas, and four more will begin about the middle of January.

The course of Lectures will be open to men and women, and a Red Cross Examination on the subject will be held at its close. Those passing this Examination will receive a Certificate qualifying them to assist in Air Defence in case of a Raid.

Those attending the Lectures will require two handbooks :

Air Raid Precautions Handbook No I. (1st edition) Price 6d.
and Air Raid Precautions Handbook No. II. (2nd edition) Price 4d.
The Town Clerk will have a supply of these for sale.

A Register of Attendances will be kept, and it is hoped that a good number of people in Wilton and the district will come forward to receive this training which will enable them to be of real help to their country and their homes in time of need.

Names of those willing to join the classes should be sent, as soon as possible, to any of the following :

Mrs. Sykes, Ditchampton House, Wilton.
C. Eyers, Esq., 16 Kingsbury Square, Wilton.
or The Town Clerk, Municipal Offices, Wilton.

EDITH OLIVIER,
(For the Wilton Borough A.R.P. Committee).

A 1942 handbill concerning lectures on air-raid precautions.

roared over the ruined church in the Market Place. Trout described these events as 'the noise of war breaking up the song of peace,' and followed with a touching narrative which seemed to sum up the situation of the town at that time:

Little Eluzay Barford rests in that chancel, she died in 1733 at the age of 14. I hope she's not disturbed as the children of wartime Wilton are, by the roar of the planes and the rattle of the tanks. But their song goes on, painstakingly.

Bob found the people of Wilton friendly, and had spent the day before the broadcast meeting some of them. He had gone into Pike's newsagents, which he described as small and rather dark, with a glass counter inside which were displayed ink, pens, pencils and various other oddments. There were a few papers and magazines, while on shelves at the back were tobacco and cigarettes, boxes of notepaper and packets of envelopes, combs and hair slides and a jar of candies. When he tried to buy a paper, he was told that they were for regular customers only, to save on paper. Candles, too, could only be bought with a ration book. He also visited a number of people in their homes, finding them all different but homely and remembering such details as curtains, different wallpapers, linoleum on the floor, a narrow front hall with a coatstand, narrow stairs and a small, spotlessly clean parlour, with a thick green woollen tablecloth over the centre table. He recalled a polished silver teapot on the sideboard, framed photographs of children, some sewing on a chair, other small pictures in deep frames and large coloured Victorian pictures of cows, kittens or battles.

In the programme Bob spoke to Lord and Lady Pembroke about their contribution to the war effort, and of how the military had taken over the house for the duration. He then spoke to the mayor, Sam Shergold, who explained how the town was run, by a corporation of four aldermen and 12 councillors, all elected, as in other boroughs. Bob considered this to be political, but Sam assured him that there were no politics on this council, and that those who had put politics before public interest 'were now where they ought to be, under the daisies.'

Next was the turn of Sidney Lawrence, who had worked at the carpet factory for over 40 years, starting as a schoolboy, running about and helping where he could. Asked if he had made any famous carpets, Sidney replied that he had helped make one for Queen Mary, and had laid carpets all over the country, in royal palaces and workmen's cottages. Although brief mention was made of the wartime cessation of carpet making in Wilton, there was no discussion of what the factory was making instead. The programme concentrated on peacetime pursuits, with only brief references to the war.

Although prepared for an invasion, the only one that actually came was of the American troops camped in the Avenue, their arrival certainly livening up the town. Jeeps seemed to be everywhere, darting about all over town, nearly every soldier seeming to have one of his own. I remember being given a ride by an American billeted with us – quite an experience, as he drove very fast indeed. They were friendly, though, and were welcomed by most, although some took exception to their 'brash, gum-chewing manner'. With no experience of the shortages suffered in Britain, they soon won the hearts of children with candy and packets of American chewing-gum, which had a flavour all its own.

The Americans also requisitioned part of Grovely Woods, on the downs above the town, where they established an ammunition store, the trees providing ideal camouflage. The wide road was tarmacked and the area heavily guarded, the public being denied any access. This proved an irresistible temptation to a couple of small boys, aged 11 and 12, who would go to the ammunition dump and help themselves to useful bits and pieces, having gained access by going up 'the Green Drive' until they were opposite the site. When the patrolling jeep had passed, they would dart across the wide road to the other side where, hidden from view, they could pick up what they fancied and load their trolley at their leisure. The dangerous part of their operation was crossing the road on the return journey with the heavily loaded trolley. One day, when they had almost made it, the the trolley proved too heavy to get up the grassy bank and their booty began to slip off just as the jeep turned at the end of the road. The soldiers spotted them, turned on the siren, flashed their lights and sped back towards them. The boys grabbed what they could and dashed into the cover of the woods where, knowing the area like the backs of their hands, they managed to shake off the pursuing soldiers. After this escapade, the boys decided not to make any more visits.

Though Wilton was surviving the war, there were many reminders of it, Southampton being only 20 miles away. During night-time raids it seemed much closer, a huge orange glow in the sky over Southampton being visible from many Wilton bedroom windows, frightening even at that distance. Many remembered the spring of 1942, when Wilton experienced two air-raid alerts in one night, with waves of bombers flying near the town. We really thought it was our turn, especially when several bombs fell not far away in fields just outside Wilton Park wall, near Netherhampton, fortunately causing no damage. That was the night that the Wilton fire brigade was called out to Bath. These men, all volunteers and on constant call day and night, could be ready at a moment's notice. Some nights they even slept at the fire station so that they could attend calls more quickly. Like the Home Guard and ARP, they worked at other jobs during the day.

Another part of Wilton useful to the military was Bishopstone Hill at the top of South Street, where there is a long avenue of trees. Here Army vehicles, including tanks, were stored and maintained in complete safety, invisible from the air and safe from attack. Inspection pits were dug here, one of which, at the time of writing, still survives.

Wilton House, where the D-Day landings were planned, fortunately remained unscathed. Much of the careful planning took place in the Double Cube Room, the valuable paintings being carefully protected and covered with maps of the French beaches, while in the grounds, behind the walls surrounding the house, there were secret exercises in further preparation for the landings. To ensure good communications at headquarters, around 750 miles of telephone wire were laid in and around Wilton and on Salisbury Plain, all the equipment putting the upmost strain on the building. In the State Rooms, the valuable furniture was replaced with trestle tables and desks. Many papers and documents relating to these operations will remain under wraps until 2017.

Everything was done by the military to ensure that the D-Day plans remained a secret, especially with the arrival at the house of the occasional high-profile visitor. Such visitors, including Prime Minister Winston Churchill, General Eisenhower, General Montgomery and King George VI, all entered the grounds in unmarked cars by way of the Sawmills entrance in South Street to protect their identity. Staff at Wilton House had the job of managing the training, feeding, accommodation and transport of the troops massing for D-Day and, as the plans gained momentum and the whole area became one huge camp, people began to suspect that something important was going on.

And so dusk fell on the evening of 5 June 1944, a remarkable night for Wilton, the like of which will never be seen again. The events are graphically described by then Wilton resident, Reg Lewry, of North Street, who wrote to a close friend, serving in France, telling him of the night the aerial armada passed over the town:

Dear Jimmy – We wondered if you were still mixed up with D-Day or were still in the lovely garden you described so well in your last letter from England's countryside.

We had a marvellous thrill here, though, and because I want to tell you about it I have left our address out.

From the back of our house, just as it was getting dark, came such a drone of aero engines that I, who was writing downstairs, went out to see, and oh what a sight!

Oh boy, what a sight, and it could have been laid on specially for us, it could not have been better.

I got excited, of course, and raced back to Win and the children and our billetee, who by the way in his excitement leapt out of bed and shouted, 'My God, this is it then, it was to have been yesterday'.

The scene outside was amazing, hundreds upon hundreds of troop-carrying planes, each with all lights on, passing from left to right above the meadows at the bottom.

As far as the eye could see they were in sight each way, and many miles to the left two stationary search-lights made an enormous V in the sky; it was the most thrilling touch imaginable.

The stream seemed never ending for we could see them coming from the left head on, and as their height appeared to vary with distance it had the effect of an enormous Christmas tree roaring towards us.

I shook old Derek awake [his son] *and all he had to do was sit up in bed to see the stream passing by.*

At last the end came and we all retired but, before we had properly got to sleep, the roar started again, and the gliders began, the whole show being repeated.

It was blowing half a gale and we feared for those gliders and paratroopers, for although there was such a 'Hell for leather and here we go go' sound about those full-out engines, we knew that thousands of men would have to land somewhere without means of propulsion.

The next morning at the factory somebody came rushing through to say, 'We've landed in Normandy', to which one man said, 'Well I'm blowed, that's a funny place to go'. Another replied, 'Well that's better than France, wherever it is'.

With all the very best of luck to you and the grand job you've started so magnificently. – Reg.

Looking back on the events of that June night, one cannot help but wonder how many of the men who flew over Wilton that night, looking down on their homeland from their aircraft, ever set their feet back on English soil, and how many were buried as heroes in foreign ground.

Owing to the success of D-Day, the war with Germany ended early in May 1945. When the news was announced, Wiltonians, as did every village, town and city, celebrated the end of hostilities in Europe with thankful hearts and great relief. Every flag residents could muster was quickly found and hung from windows; pennants of red, white and blue fluttered in the streets and a huge Union Jack was hung from the Parish Church. Despite pouring rain, crowds of people made their way to the Market Place to hear the prime minister's speech relayed by loud-speaker. Then the crowd, made up mostly of American soldiers and civilians, including many young children, watched while buglers of the Scots Guards sounded the ceasefire. At that very moment, as if on cue, the rain clouds parted and the Market Place was bathed in brilliant sunshine. The clouds of war had finally lifted and the sunshine of peace was shining down.

Crowds flocked to the Market Place again that

evening to hear the king's speech, after which the people of Wilton indulged their love of torchlight processions. Led by 50 torch-bearers, 2,000 revellers made their way to Grovely Down, where German prisoners of war from the small camp at the top of Shaftesbury Road, opposite the cemetery, had erected a huge bonfire – unwillingly taking part in this celebration of the defeat of their country. The actual lighting of the bonfire was jointly performed by the Countess of Pembroke and an American officer. Such was the size of the blaze, it could easily be seen at Harnham, just outside Salisbury. A radio van relayed music while people danced and rejoiced until well past midnight.

After their relief at the war being over and with celebrations of the victory behind them, people slowly began to concentrate their energies on more peaceful pursuits. They knew that the long weary years of war could not be wiped away overnight, but once again community spirit prevailed, helping them through the difficult times that lay ahead.

Little Eluzay Barford's rest in the chancel of St Mary's Church was not disturbed by the war, and she still rests there today in peace.

MOORE BROS.,
West End,
WILTON,

HAVE pleasure in announcing that they will receive the broadcast of

H.M. The King's
SPEECH

at their premises

On Wednesday Morning

Commencing at 10.30.

Do not miss this unique
opportunity of Listening in.

There will be NO CHARGE.

Wilton Printing Works,

A notice advertising the broadcast of a speech by the king. It was not uncommon for such services to be offered, enabling people to hear important news without having to go home to do so.

CHAPTER 10

The Aftermath of War

With the war in Europe now over, the town slowly started to make a recovery. There were still shortages, particularly of everyday items, and rationing was still very much in force. With the German prisoners of war repatriated, the camp was used to house displaced persons from Europe, mainly from Poland, Hungary, Yugoslavia and the Ukraine. In return for their accommodation, many of them worked locally on a voluntary basis; one of them married a local girl and settled here. After a few months the American forces began to leave, some taking Wilton girls as GI Brides, one of these being Grace Croome, who lived in West Street.

When the war ended, I was only seven years old and, like many other children at that time, took war for granted. Having known nothing else, rationing, shortages and the many other limitations were a normal part of our everyday lives, and we took the sound of guns booming on Salisbury Plain, the soldiers and Army vehicles, the blackout and the unlit streets in our stride. We had heard our parents talk of peace and of the years before the war began but, having never experienced this for ourselves, we could not fully understand the concept. Carrying gas masks was normal for us, and we knew that when a warden shouted 'Gas!', then we must quickly put them on. I well remember looking out of our front-room window during an exercise and seeing a warden place a canister in the gutter on the opposite side of the road, pulling at the end to release a great deal of smoke. I found out later that these were tests to see how gas would behave should canisters be dropped from enemy aircraft.

Due to shortages of accommodation at the Army camps, officers were billeted with us, as they were at many homes in the town. With food rationed, many of the billeted officers ate their meals in the mess at camp, only sleeping at the house. The billetees would quite frequently leave, having been posted elsewhere and, later in the war, the American officers also billeted out would often bring a few luxuries as a goodwill gesture, knowing the hardships we were going through. Sweets, or candies, were favoured by youngsters like myself; although sweets were available, like everything else they were on ration, and were a real treat when sufficient coupons had been saved up. Even after the war, rationing continued for quite some time.

One of the most frightening sounds was the wail of air-raid sirens, which went right through you. It usually meant enemy aircraft were approaching, on their way to bombing raids further up country, or even targeting our area. Despite a large military presence in the area, Wilton remained free of raids, the few bombs that did fall widely were thought to have been jettisoned to decrease weight, ensuring a safe return to base in Germany.

With clothes also rationed, this was an era of make do and mend, and it was quite usual for a school blazer to be bought in a larger in size, to allow for growth and make it last longer. This meant the sleeves were too long, but tucking them up inside with a few stitches to hold them in place solved that problem. Careful wearing ensured the blazer lasted as long as possible, and if the elbows got badly rubbed, a thin patch was sewn over the area – quite the height of wartime fashion. After school, blazers were to be taken off and hung in the wardrobe.

With the war over, we children enjoyed much more freedom, playing football and cricket with friends in the meadows behind the terraced houses opposite my home. If it was too wet in the meadows, then the Bell Inn car park, just a few yards down the road, made a good football pitch. With few cars on the roads in those days, it was empty for most of the day. If the game got a bit out of hand, with too many near misses of windows, the landlord would come out and tell us off. As often as not the ball would end up in the road, but was quickly retrieved before any cars came along.

Comics soon became more plentiful, although paper shortages meant copies of such comics as *Radio Fun*, *Film Fun*, *Wizard*, *Knockout* and *Eagle* had to be ordered from the newsagent, possibly from Winter's in West Street, near the Market Place, where two very prim sisters, Beatrice, who was tall, and the much shorter May, sold many different items of stationery, as well as postcards, newspapers and magazines. They had once sold books and were most particular about what they sold, refusing to stock anything they considered unsuitable, even saucy postcards. I was told the following true story by Ron Cutler, who died many years ago. He and a friend had been to Salisbury and, for a bit of fun, had purchased some saucy postcards. Back in Wilton, they went into Winter's and placed some of the saucy cards in the postcard rack, then took one each to the counter. They handed the postcards to Beatrice face down, so she got the shock of her life when she turned them over. Recovering her composure, she asked where they had come from, Ron's reply being that he had got them from the rack. Beatrice asked May to have

Wilton children in the Michael Herbert Hall, at what is thought to have been a special tea in celebration of the wedding of Princess Elizabeth and the Duke of Edinburgh in November 1947.

A gathering of town worthies, possibly connected with the opening of a youth club in the town. The presence of the mayor, Cllr Caroline Stokes, helps date the picture to 1947. Sitting to her right is Mrs Drury, wife of the rector, William Drury, and Rosemary Corbin (in the wheelchair), with Eileen Hooker kneeling beside her (in the white skirt). Miss Drake, the headmistress of the the Junior School in West Street is seated next to the two gentlemen on the right in the front row.

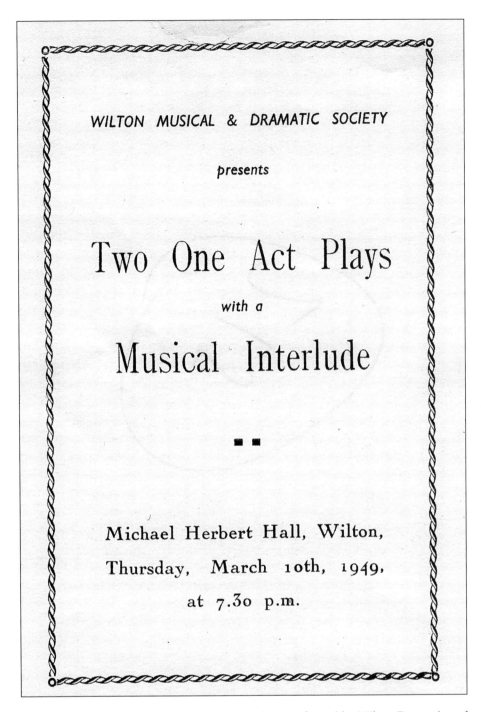

WILTON MUSICAL & DRAMATIC SOCIETY

presents

Two One Act Plays

with a

Musical Interlude

■ ■

Michael Herbert Hall, Wilton,
Thursday, March 10th, 1949,
at 7.30 p.m.

The cover of the programme for two one-act plays performed by Wilton Dramatic and Musical Society.

a look, and her sister returned a few minutes later clutching the offending postcards and muttering that she did not know how they had got there. She then took the others from Beatrice and tore them all up. Ron and his friend were never suspected of planting the offending postcards.

Naturally, we youngsters got up to mischief, our main 'crime' being scrumping apples, when we would nip into gardens and pick what we called the 'fallers'. Most people never seemed to mind, but one had to watch out for Ben Newman, the local bobby. The only policeman in the town, he certainly knew how to keep law and order and was in the habit of

turning up and catching those making mischief, delivering a light tap to the back of the head, behind the ear. For more serious matters he would hand out the same instant justice and then take you back home, telling your parents what you had done. We all had respect for him, and vandalism was unheard of in those days. Ben could often be seen late in the evening trying the doors of shops and other commercial premises. If they were not secure he would get someone to come out and lock up.

The names of the men and women who failed to return home after the war were carved on the war memorial, along with the names of those who had given their lives in the First World War.

Although there had been some celebrations on VE Day, while the war still continued in the Far East, the council decided to delay official celebrations until it was over. These celebrations finally took place in June 1946, on a day during which heavy rain persisted throughout the morning and afternoon, giving the organisers some anxious moments. As a result of the rain, the sports event arranged for the afternoon was reluctantly postponed, though by the evening it had cleared sufficiently for a carnival procession through the town, which proved a huge success. Later, as darkness fell, a second procession through the streets eventually made its way to the top of the Avenue, where a huge bonfire and firework display rounded off the day's festivities

Clubs and societies flourished once again, including the Wilton Dramatic and Musical Society, which had a membership of 90, the chairman being the local rector, the Revd W.E. Drury. Their ambition was to perform at least two productions a year, one outdoors in the summer, possibly something by Shakespeare, and in the winter, just before Christmas, something suitable for the festive season. The earliest record I have of any of their productions is of their third, performed in January 1946. This was an ambitious venture to say the least, a double bill comprising a one-act comedy, *The Lady From Abroad* and a two-act version of Charles Dickens's *A Christmas Carol*. Many well-known Wiltonians appeared in the casts, especially in the latter production, some playing more than one part. Some of those involved were: Richard Marks as Ebeneezer Scrooge, Eric Ruffle as Marley's Ghost, Michael Croome as Scrooge as a boy, with Bridget Moore as his sister, Ellen, Evelyn Blandford as Mrs Cratchit and Eileen Bryant, Dawn Waters, Jean Moore, Michael Croome and Marcia Holley as the Cratchit children, with Hugh Moore as Tiny Tim. There were seven scenes and music for the production was selected and arranged by Eric Cooke.

The society flourished until the 1960s, putting on such popular productions as *The Bishop's Candlesticks* and *One Wedding, Two Brides*, which featured two of Wilton's carnival queens, Mary Shergold as Helen (the bride) with Phyllis Turner as her sister, Rosalie. During the 1955 carnival the players put on the farce *Important People*. That this production required an orchestra presented no problem to the society, as Mr Charles S. Hart, who lived in North Street, had an orchestra which, popular and well known, had played at many Saturday night dances at the Michael Herbert Hall in South Street. The demise of the Dramatic and Musical Society was brought about by falling attendance, many people preferring to watch television in the comfort of their own homes.

A spell of severe weather, with heavy falls of snow and arctic conditions, marked the beginning of 1947. To add to the misery, shortages of vital supplies,

including coal, led to power cuts, drastically affecting public transport. The resolve of Wilton's residents was not broken, however, and they made the best of the situation, helping each where they could.

Southern Command announced that they would soon be vacating Wilton House, returning it fully to the Earl of Pembroke. Their aim was to hand it back at the end of the year, or early in the new year at the latest. By this time only the ground floor was being used, chiefly by the GOC-in-Chief, the Chief of Staff and other officers.

By now shops were doing well, patronised not only by residents of the town, but also by those from villages in the Wylye and Nadder Valleys. There were plenty of shops to choose from, including three butchers, eight grocers and two newsagents, as well as bakers, confectioners and fishmongers. There was the Co-operative store in the Market Place, while a draper's shop in North Street sold everything from haberdashery to ladieswear, menswear being available from separate premises further down the street.

The carpet factory was back in full production, the weavers being fully employed on a special order from the Empire Theatre in London's Leicester Square for a carpet, made in one piece, measuring 23ft 4ins by 39ft 6 ins for the lower foyer of the theatre. This order was completed in 1948. The felt mills were also back in full production, as was Brewer's. The town was getting back on its feet.

The Wilton Scout Group, which had been officially formed and recognised on 23 November 1911, and the Cub Pack, officially formed in September 1914, were still going strong. During the war, a Wilton section of the First Bemerton Group was formed, meetings initially taking place in the Church Room at Wilton and later, thanks to the kindness of the rector, Revd W.E. Drury, in the attic of the rectory. In November 1946, the group was re-registered from Bemerton and meetings were held in the Talbot and Wyvern Hall, thanks to an arrangement made by the GSM of Bemerton and Wilton Estate. This arrangement lasted until the building was sold and subsequently demolished in 1962.

The many changes of leadership in the group eventually led to its lapse in 1948. Although they re-formed in January 1950, it was not until November of that year, when John Naish became leader, that the formation of a new group committee put the movement back on its feet. One Wilton Scout in particular, Bob Blandford, remained loyal to the troop in the 1940s, and at the 1950 re-formation became a Scouter himself, beginning a long and successful career with the movement.

Bob, who always put others first, was a highly respected member of the community, a quiet, unassuming man with no pretentious airs and graces despite his many different achievements in the town, particularly in the Scout movement.

He spent his working life on the railways,

On 10 March 1949, the Wilton Musical and Dramatic Society performed two one-act plays, the first of which was The Boy Comes Home, *set at the end of the First World War.* From left to right: *Nancy Moore, O. Davis, M.R. Moore, Brian Foster and David Redway.*

The second play performed was The Playgoers, *a one-act farce.* From left to right: *Philip W. Moore, Margaret Ledsham, Mary Shergold, H. Aubrey, Molly Bowden, Eve Blandford, Dorothy Foyle and Jean Moore.*

A Christmas party for Carpet Factory workers in the late 1940s, an annual event held at the Michael Herbert Hall.

Wilton Scout Troop in the late 1940s.

Members of the First Bemerton and Wilton Boy Scout Troop soon after its formation, c.1945. The eight adults are (from left to right): *Revd 'Skipp' White, Mr E. King (ADC), Cllr H.E. Randall, Cllr A. Courtney (Mayor of Salisbury), Mr E. F. Jay (Group Scout Master), the Mayoress of Salisbury, Mr H.M. Lotchworth (District Commissioner) and Major S. Collett (Hon. Adviser Physical Education and Scouting, First Bemerton Boy Scout Group). At this time this was Wiltshire's Largest Scout group, with around 150 members.*

eventually retiring at Christmas in 1977 after 48 years of faithful service. The following January, for services to the industry, he was awarded the MBE, which he fully deserved, wearing it with dignified pride on special occasions. He had worked as a signalman at Salisbury, where he remained until his retirement, praised by his bosses for never being late or absent during his career.

He began his scouting activities as a Wolf Cub, joining the combined Bemerton and Wilton Scout Troop during the Second World War. Gradually he worked his way up the scouting ladder, eventually becoming ADC Venture Scouts, a key figure in the district. His activities were not confined to Wilton. At Woodlarks Camp, in Farnham, he spent much time and effort helping the handicapped enjoy a summer camp. He travelled abroad, attending jamborees and international camps in America, Turkey, Sweden, Holland and Australia. For his long and loyal services, he was presented with the prestigious Silver Acorn. In whatever he did, Bob always gave of his best, ever faithful to the Scout promise of doing one's duty to God and the Queen and keeping the Scout Law

A regular communicant, he was a sidesman and a member of the Parish Church; a member of the Wilton branch of the Royal British Legion; gave 25 years' service to the Wilton Riding for the Disabled Association as a side-walker beside the ponies and as a general factotum, as he called himself. As if this

was not enough, he stood for the Town Council, was duly elected and served for nine years, becoming mayor in 1995 and again in 2001, his many civic duties increasing his workload. Illness curtailed his activities in 2003 and, sadly, he died in November of that year. He is still remembered and very much missed in the town today.

One prime concern after the war was council-housing, plans being put in hand to build new homes. By November 1944 the council had already made tentative plans to purchase ten acres of land from the Wilton Estate in the Wishford Road, aiming to build 25 houses in the first year after the war, and a further 25 the following year.

Eventually an agreement was reached with Wilton Estate, and land in the middle of Ditchampton Farm was purchased. The tenant farmer, Arthur Street, protested that this would render the farm unworkable, not only causing harm to farming, but with few benefits to the town. Though the Ministry of Agriculture backed him, they were forced eventually to give way. Although the council had managed to find two alternative sites, nearer to the town, with all the main services already laid on, they were turned down by government departments, leaving them with no alternative but to build on the Ditchampton Farm site. The development included a number of Reema-type houses, built in sections which locked together, which were not only quicker to build, but also cut down on repair costs.

The farmhouse at Ditchampton Farm, where A.G. Street lived, c.1946.

Emergency accommodation was also provided at Fugglestone with the erection of prefabricated buildings. Although only intended as a temporary measure, they remained occupied for many years.

Later, more housing was built in the Bulbridge area, in a development consisting of both council and private houses and later including, at the higher end of the site, housing for officers serving at Southern Command Headquarters, then at the former American camp in the Avenue.

By 1949 the council offices had been moved from the Town Hall to a former masonic hall in Kingsbury Square, where a special exhibition of the town's archives attracted a large number of visitors. The exhibition included documents discovered in an old chest after the move from the Town Hall. A tailor's dummy was put to good use, displaying the uniform of the former Free School, while a corner of the mayor's parlour was devoted to items belonging to the late Edith Olivier, including a chair cover she had made, an antique needlework table and some books.

Edith Olivier, after suffering three strokes, had died in May 1948. The daughter of Canon Dacres Olivier, she was born in 1872, one of eight children in what appears to have been a very close family. Although a parson's daughter, it was said of her that she never fitted any preconceived pattern, being gifted with a rare quality of wit.

A great deal of her childhood is revealed in her writings, especially of the games she played with her sister Mildred, of whom she was extremely fond. She and Mildred would sometimes climb out onto the roof in the evenings, sitting astride the ridge and watching the people go by. From this lofty position, they would watch their own parents in the garden, who never suspected that they were not safely tucked up in bed. When Edith became a writer, one of her books described life in the town, her stories of the inhabitants revealing many aspects of those late Victorian and early Edwardian days.

At her funeral in the Parish Church, attended by a congregation which included the mayor and corporation, glowing tributes to her life and work in the community were paid by the rector. During her life she had made many friends, many of them staying at her home, Daye House, in Wilton Park. Many of these friends were well-known personalities of the day, including the war poet Siegfried Sassoon, Cecil Beaton, Lord David Cecil and the composer William Walton. There can be no doubt that one of her best and closest friends was the artist Rex Whistler, who had illustrated some of her books. When he was killed on active service during the war, Edith was completely devastated. On the Ditchampton housing estate, one of the roads was named Olivier Road in memory of her services to the town.

✦ CHAPTER 11 ✦

The Later Years

Changes were now taking place in Wilton. Fancy Row in North Street was demolished in the early 1950s to make way for a new development of council-housing, the building to be carried out by the Town Council. The area was ripe for demolition, many of the small houses having become run down and no longer habitable. In fact the area had become a real eyesore, practically a slum, the houses cramped and poorly lit. With the residents rehoused, the properties were demolished. During late October 1955 the Under Secretary to the Ministry of Housing and Local Government, Mr S.W.C. Philips, officially opened the new development, named Churchill Court after Sir Winston Churchill, which would eventually contain 29 flats, of which 11 had already been completed.

The council received praise from the Under Secretary, who said that Wilton had made a useful contribution to housing, comparing favourably with other councils. He also thought it enterprising of the council to have built flats, this being rare in small towns, stating that the external appearnce of the flats was far superior to those he had seen on a recent visit to Russia.

The name Fancy Row derives from the eighteenth century, when the inhabitants worked at home, making fancy waistcoats and elegant linings for the gentlemen's dress of the period. One can safely assume that these workers were poorly paid for the hours they worked in such cramped, poorly lit conditions. In consolation, their meagre earnings may have allowed them to claim assistance from the Poor Relief Fund. Records of the period show that in 1821 the business was run by a leading clothier, James Hayward, and by 1860 involved 26 small cottages arranged in an L-shaped terrace.

One hardy annual in the Wilton social calendar was the Wilton church fête held every Whit Monday on the rectory lawn, an ideal time and setting for this typically English pastime. The lawn was lined with tall hedges and trees stretching down to the river, where rowing-boat trips were available. A variety of items was carefully arranged on lines of trestle tables, from mouth-watering home-made cakes, toys, tinned foods, baby clothes and bric-a-brac, to old magazines and comics. The latter were a great attraction, all neatly rolled into bundles tied with string at only 2d. a bundle. Other attractions included bowling for a

Children from Fancy Row, just off North Street, 1924. Left to right, back row: D. Waters, ? Waters (sisters), ?, F. Blake, Ken Saunders, Reg Saunders, Mrs Saunders; second row: Ethel Baker, ?, Edie Wilton, Reg Wilton, Claire ?; front row: Arthur Baker, Lilly Bundy, Josie Turner, Molly Waterman, Charles Furnell, Flossie Waterman.

Fancy Row just before demolition. The photograph was taken by Howard Cook, then a member of the Town Council.

The construction of the first block of flats with, in the background, the back of Pembroke Terrace in North Street. In later years Wylye Lodge was opened on the site, offering sheltered accommodation for the elderly and handicapped.

pig, donkey rides, a fortune teller, gymnastic displays and country dancing. The baby show was always popular and attracted numerous entries, all dressed in their finery, each being carefully weighed by the town's nurse. The music for the afternoon was often by way of rather scratched 78r.p.m. records of popular tunes of the day, amplified through loudspeakers, interrupted occasionally by the announcement of events and forthcoming features. Another occasional attraction was the ascent of the church tower, the long climb up various ladders to the top offering breathtaking views across the town, nestled comfortably in tree-lined rolling downland.

Although the church fête is still a popular event, at the time of writing it is held in the meadow behind the Parish Church on the second Saturday in June. Many people travel in from the surrounding villages and from Salisbury, hunting for bargains and spending a few hours in this idyllic setting.

In March 1963 Alderman Vincent Hugh Moore was invested as Honorary Freeman of the Borough of Wilton, having served on the Borough Council for 50 years. This honour, the highest that a council can bestow, is awarded only on rare occasions to someone who has made an outstanding contribution to the community. According to the late Grahame Moody, a councillor at the time and a keen local historian, Alderman Moore was the first ever Honorary Freeman of this ancient borough. He was born in the town and his family had lived here for many years, in 1898 his grandfather, father and uncle all being on the council at the same time. During his 50 years on the council, Alderman Moore had been mayor on five occasions, 1928/29, 1929/30, 1946/47, 1952/53 and 1953/54.

Little did anyone realise that the local town government of Wilton would change dramatically in 1974, new legislation brought in by the government sweeping away overnight the self-governing borough system and handing the majority of its power to the new governing body, Salisbury District Council. Wilton would be represented by only two councillors on this new body and the town would no longer have the final say in its own affairs. One concession made was that the town could keep its mayor, the last of the old borough mayors being Albert Belk, at the time a teacher at the Senior School. The following year the first mayor under the new regime of local government in Wilton, was Tim Morland, also a teacher at the Senior School.

These changes in local government were not the

The year 1952 saw the revival of the Beating of the Bounds ceremony, which dates back to very early times, when parish boundaries were regularly defined in this manner. Here the party assembles at the Market Cross before setting off led by the mayor, Mr Grahame Moody (holding the boundary maps). To his right, wearing plus fours, is the rector, Revd William Drury, the tall man behind him being Revd John James Haynes, minister of the Congregational Church in Crow Lane. The two boys holding sticks (far right) are Douglas Morris and, wearing the dark blazer, Philip Boon.

After opening the Wilton church fête in 1994, actress Elizabeth Counsell, who played the role of Veronica in the popular TV series Brush Strokes, *poses with the rector, Canon Bede Cooper, who always wears a red rose for the occasion. They later toured the stalls, chatting with stallholders.*

only ones to affect the town. In 1975 the County Council decided that the two-tier system of education in State schools would be upgraded to a three-tier system. Under this system the Primary School in West Street would become a First School, and the Senior School in the Hollows would become a Middle School, Wilton children finishing their education at Westwood St Thomas School at the western end of the city. When a new purpose-built First School was built on the Bulbridge Estate, the West Street school closed.

This system had been under discussion for many years in Wilton, many people being against the idea. The two existing schools were regarded with pride by the community; teaching standards were good, as was the discipline. In 1972 the prospect of the proposed changes caused head teacher Tom Feather to retire, his place being taken by Rex Sawyer, who thus had the ideal opportunity to become involved in meaningful consultations, shaping the way for the new system, which came into play at Michaelmass term in 1975.

John Boulter, head teacher since 1959 at the Primary School, now to become the First School, was able to draw on his past experience to plan for the changeover, during which there would be not only a new curriculum to contend with, the school would also be moving to a completely new building.

147

Early members of Wilton Rifle Club in the grounds of Wilton House, having been presented with tankards by Lord Pembroke (seated centre with the shield). Immediately behind Lord Pembroke, is Jack Cope, who maintained the cemetery in Shaftesbury Road where, as soon as mourners had left the cemetery and once the grave was filled in, he would dig another ready for the next burial. As a result of this practice, he was to eventually dig his own grave.

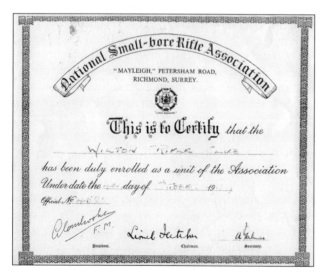

Wilton Rifle Club, formed in 1949, was enrolled with the National Association on 4 October that year. The official membership number of the Wilton Club was No. 452.

The changeover went well, and at the end of the summer term in 1978, John Boulter retired, having seen the new system settle in satisfactorily.

This system remained in place for 30 years until, in July 2005, the County Council, after discussing a return to the two-tier system over the previous three to four years, decided to close the Middle School in Wilton and build a new Senior School next to Westwood St Thomas School to accommodate children from the Wilton area. Despite protests at the closure of the Middle School, the scheme took effect from July 2005, the school building closing its doors for the last time after 70 years' service to the community. The First School reverted to being a Primary School.

The summer of 1978 saw the passing, at the age of 86, of one of Wilton's most active and popular octogenarians, Mrs Bessie Partridge. In 1899 she had come from Hampworth to Wilton with her parents, who took over the Six Bells in North Street. After the death of her father, Mr Pike, the family moved next door into Albany Cottage, at the time of writing a dental surgery In 1913 a shop opposite became vacant and was taken over by Mrs Pike, eventually becoming a newsagent's selling sweets, tobacco, cigarettes and stationery items – the same shop is mentioned in Chapter 9 in connection with the wartime broadcast from Fugglestone House.

After the death of Mrs Pike in 1945 Bessie, by now Mrs Partridge, took over the running of the shop, staying in business until her retirement in 1974 at the age of 81. She retired not because of her age, but because of the introduction of VAT. Trying to remember what carried tax and what didn't, she said,

Members of Wilton Rifle Club at their club room in Bell Lane, 1959. Left to right, back row: *John Scott, Sam Shergold, Cecil White, George White, Brian Braybrook, Henry Jay, Ted Lench, George Dodge, Col Boardley, Basil Hayter, Mike Morris, Jack Kiddle, Des Sutton, Roy Orchard, John Lench;* second row: *May Kiddle, Mrs Turner, Molly Clarke, Mrs Boardley;* front row: *Mike Lloyd, Ray Partridge, Eric Carter, Wheatsheaf landlord (name not known), Dick Turner, Jim Clarke, Michael Oakley, Doug Morris.*

made her head spin. The shop was taken over by her grandson, who later took over the larger vacant shop of Robinson's a little further down North Street, selling toys in the original shop, which closed a few years later. The second shop, reputed to be the town's oldest family business, closed late in 2004 and, towards the end of 2005, work began on converting the shop into three townhouses.

Although Bessie had retired, she found plenty to do to keep herself active, and during the first four years made 18 tapestries, many with birds, flowers and rural scenes. Exhibited at an arts and craft show in the town, one of them won a special merit. Her other love was knitting, and early in her retirement she knitted 150 pairs of socks, keeping her entire large family supplied.

In July 1981, under mounting pressure from the public, Salisbury Council gave its consent to the revival of the town market.

Although it had been 120 years since stalls had been pitched in the Market Place, the original charter of 1121 granting the town a market had never been revoked and was still valid. Why the market origi-

nally ceased in about 1860 is not known, but it is possible that the number and variety of shops in the town at that time affected the market traders, who left to make a better living in Salisbury. The original market would not have been on the same site as today, but would have been in the area between the the old church and the Health Centre, where the Market Cross which still stands today. In earlier times a Market Cross was a sign that the traders at that market were honest. Almost 25 years later after the market was reinstated, it is still going strong, bringing much welcome business to the town.

It was around this same period that changes were taking place in the town's shops, many of the old familiar names disappearing from the scene, mainly due to the retirement of the proprietors. Since 1974 ten shops had closed in North Street alone and only two grocers were still in business, as opposed to seven previously. These changes were due to a revolution in shopping habits, supermarkets now taking over the role of the traditional grocer by supplying a huge range of goods under one roof at very competitive prices – prices which could not be matched by

Some of the regulars enjoy a pint at the Victoria Arms in West Street in the 1950s. A note scribbled on the back of the photograph reads: 'beer about 1s.3d.–1s.6d. a pint' (7½p). Foreground, from left to right: Landlord Fred Payne, Herbie Godwin, Dick Dickinson, Gertie Bryce, Bert Pavey, Toby Hinton, Harold Trim, Olive Trim (with her back to camera). In the background are Tom Bryce, Joan Roberts, Happy Cannings, Dave Roberts and Joe Lickman. The pub closed down in the late 1990s.

Mine hosts at the Victoria Arms, Doris and Fred Payne, with some of their regulars.

small businesses. The increase in car ownership also made it easier to shop for groceries in Salisbury.

With the demise of the old-style grocer came the end of the delivery service which, for many years in Wilton, had been offered by many shopkeepers, especially by grocers and butchers, of which there were four in the town. In Wilton's heyday, early on a Friday evening, Wilton traders would load up their vans with orders for delivery to customers in the surrounding villages. In the early years some of the drivers would arrive back in Wilton late and a little the worse for wear, having been offered more than one drink on their rounds. Deliveries around the town, and later to the new housing estates, were

usually made on Saturday mornings. Many of these deliveries had originally been made by errand boys on bikes, even out to the country areas. On the special trade bikes used by some grocers and butchers, and by Winter's the newsagent's, the wicker basket attached to the handlebars was so large that the front wheel of the bike was very much smaller than the rear one. Often, in the space made by the frame, a black metal plate bore the name and details of the shop.

In December 1977 the Town Hall, which had been used by various clubs and societies for meetings, was closed to public functions. At the same time it was also announced that, with the conversion of the former Primary School in West Street now complete, it would be opening in January the following year as a venue for those organisations and societies now using the Town Hall. It was planned to convert the Town Hall into flats, but this scheme never came to fruition and it was eventually bought by the Baptists and converted into a chapel.

Around this time, organisations and societies were flourishing, and there was something to suit most tastes. There was the Floral Arrangement Society, which attracted a large membership led by chairperson Mrs May Kiddle. Not only did they have talks and demonstrations on the art of flower arranging, they also arranged special exhibitions, and were very much to the fore when the Parish

A mayoral procession in 1974, thought to be Wilton's last year as a borough council. Behind the mace-bearer, are (from left to right), Revd Denton White (the rector), Geopold Lush (town clerk), and the mayor, Cllr Albert Belk. The procession is leaving West Street and about to enter the Market Place for the inspection of youth organisations, which preceded the mayoral party.

The mayor, Cllr Albert Belk, inspecting the parade in the Market Place.

Partridge's original shop in North Street, during the celebrations for the coronation of Queen Elizabeth II in 1953.

Church held a Flower Festival to celebrate its 150th anniversary in October 1955. Unfortunately, the society later ceased its activities, due to falling numbers.

Another organisation which had been in the town for many years was the St John Ambulance Brigade, a strong, vibrant organisation attracting a large membership of young people, a familiar sight at many events in and around the town and in the mayor's annual civic service and Remembrance Sunday parades. The membership was once so strong that there had been plans to start a Badger group for six-to-ten-year olds. Later, however, due to difficulties in recruiting new members, the brigade was disbanded.

The Army Cadet Force, once a strong presence in the community, suffered the same fate. At one time unable to take on any more members due to a high complement of girl cadets, numbers gradually fell off and they closed down.

It was the same for the Women's Institute. They too were once strong in the town, with regular meetings every month. At their last meeting, in March 1994, it was announced that the Wilton Branch would close, committee members feeling that the years were catching up with them. Many had served for a number of years and, with no recruits to take on the roles of officers or committee members, the sad decision was made to suspend the Wilton Branch, leaving the door open for it to be reinstated if the situation arose. The branch had started in 1919, holding meetings at Netherhampton before moving to Wilton.

It is not all doom and gloom on the social activities front, however, and some organisations are flourishing. The Wilton Cancer Committee are very successful and annually raise huge amounts of money for their cause through such events as a summer party, at which a silent auction raises a high proportion of their revenue, as does their annual sale, both events being well supported with the donation of gifts by local traders and members of the public. In 2005 they organised a charity walk in the grounds of Wilton House which is to become an annual event, known as the 'Wilton Walk'.

Other organisations include the Mothers' Union, which runs monthly morning and evening groups in addition to their traditional afternoon monthly meetings. The Royal National Lifeboat Institution is also very active, as is the Over Sixties' Club and the Wilton Day Centre for the Elderly. For budding musicians, there is the popular Wilton and District Youth Band, which plays at such local events as the annual Parish Church fête, the carnival and the annual lighting of the Christmas tree in the Market Place, and also gives a free annual Christmas concert at the Michael Herbert Hall. The Scout and Girl Guide movements are also very active, each having a strong membership and taking part in many activities. The Wilton Historical Society, formed in 1977, is also successful, with a large membership.

West Street in the 1950s looking towards the former gatehouse and the Priory Church, with some of the houses in St John's Square clearly visible. Above their rooftops can be seen the downs leading to Grovely Woods, from which there is a wonderful view of the town.

Although undated, this picture shows a view of the Town Hall from West Street. The Handiman Shop on the left once belonged to Francis Preety, an ironmonger who used to sell bags of nails by weight. Next door is the Post Office, moved from its previous location in South Street, with Oakshot's the grocer's on the corner. The shop on the right advertising Lyons Maid ice-cream, is Snoad's, a confectioner and tobacconist. The off-licence was formerly a public house, the New Inn.

Morris's, the family butcher in West Street, although only a small shop, catered for many customers. Pictured here soon after its closure, it was demolished to so that an arcade could be made through to the gardening department of the Handiman Shop.

Besides regular meetings, it also organises an annual summer party and an annual outing to places of interest. Until the autumn of 2004, it also operated a town museum at the carpet factory, the expenses for which were generously covered by the factory owners. Unfortunately, due to rising costs, the factory was forced to cease its contribution, leading to the closure of the museum.

Another organisation is the Royal British Legion,

the Wilton Branch having been founded in 1921. In December 2001 they celebrated their 80th anniversary with a special service at the Parish Church, the original branch standard being carried to the altar by war veteran Jim Clarke, to a rendition of 'Take Me Back to Dear Old Blighty' by the Wilton Royal British Legion Band.

Throughout its long history, the branch has raised large sums of money by selling poppies in the town

Remembrance Day, 1980, with members of the Wilton Royal British Legion marching to the Parish Church for the annual Remembrance Service from the Market Place. Leading the contingent is Jim Hammersley, at the time landlord of the Greyhound Inn, with Jim Spencer carrying the Legion standard.

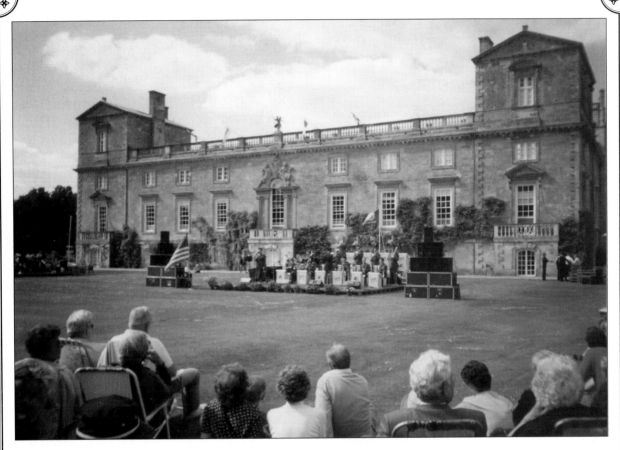

Wilton House makes the ideal backdrop for the US Army field band The Jazz Ambassadors, playing wartime music in the Glenn Miller style for a garden party celebrating the 50th anniversary of the D-Day landings.

The director/conductor of The Jazz Ambassadors at Wilton House.

Two members of the Central Band of the Royal Air Force flanked by members of The Jazz Ambassadors on the lawns of Wilton House. The man second from the right told the author that he would always remember the occasion as being typically British.

Wilton Carnival, 1994. Wilton Over Sixties' Club evoke the spirit of D-Day on its 50th anniversary with their float entitled 'Wartime Memories'.

Wilton Guides celebrate the Guiding movement with their float 'From Small Beginings to A Worldwide Family', in the 1994 Carnival.

The lighting of Wilton's Christmas tree, now very much an annual event, was started back in the 1950s. The lighting was organised by Jack Kiddle, who in the early days had to physically climb the tree to arrange the lights. Here he puts the finishing touches to the star at the top.

and district for Remembrance. Although the years have taken their toll on the membership, today the branch still has between 30 and 40 members.

Since the end of the war, Wilton House has continued to be involved in many events, which have been well supported both by locals and by people coming in from other districts. In 1978 a record crowd approaching 30,000 was attracted to a huge spectacular organised by the United Nations Children's Fund. This included military displays of the Army 'White Helmets' acrobatic motorcycle display team, a flypast of Spitfires and Hurricane fighters, plus a Lancaster bomber and a Royal Navy Air Sea Rescue Demonstration. Radio One disk-jockeys Tony Blackburn and Ed 'Stewpot' Stewart hosted a two-hour live radio show, and an unannounced attraction became the focus of attention. Jeff Lynne, leader of the Electric Light Orchestra, dropped in on the event by helicopter with his girlfriend, Sandy Kappleson.

Another special event with a military theme took place in late May 1994, with a D-Day garden party, to commemorate the 50th anniversary of the D-Day landings, much of which had been planned at Wilton House. Huge crowds turned up to see performances by the US Army field band The Jazz Ambassadors, who played wartime music in the style of Glenn Miller. Also attending was the Central Band of the Royal Air Force, who played an entirely different, though equally appreciated, repertoire. I chatted with a member of the American band, who summed up the event, remarking that he would always remember this engagement on their tour as a typically British occasion, and unlike anything in America. I wonder if he still remembers that engagement today?

Wilton House continues to host a variety of special occasions, including antiques fairs, equestrian events, the annual music and firework event every July and, more recently, a country day.

September 1992 saw the revival of Wilton carnival which, with the exception of that held in 1977 in celebration of the Queen's silver jubilee, had not been held since 1960. Despite a few hiccoughs beforehand, all went well with the procession and events held in the Castle Meadow. A donkey derby was one of the highlights of the afternoon, the commentator being the rector, Canon Bede Cooper. Dressed as he was in a Flash Harry pork-pie hat and sporting a burnt-cork moustache, he went unrecognised by many of his parishioners. The jockeys for the races, volunteers from the Grovely Riding School, had great difficulty staying mounted but, like everyone else, enjoyed the event, which was raising money for charity. Subsequent carnivals which, at the time of writing, total 14, have also proved successful and, although at times it seems the carnival may not go on, it continues to survive.

November 1997 saw the opening of the first phase of the Wilton Shopping Village, which utilised many of the buildings of the former carpet factory in the King Street area. Included in this first phase was the largest store on the site, the Edinburgh Woollen Mill, in effect a large deparment store with ten different shops under one roof. The Wilton Carpet Factory shop was also included in the first phase of the scheme, relocating to a new position not far from the original factory site. In the second phase the historic courtyard area was developed, the 300-year-old buildings having to be specially converted. When this phase opened the following Easter, there were 24 different retail outlets trading on the site. It was hoped that a pathway linking the site with the town would be included, but in 2006 this has still not come to fruition. Some of the original shops have since been replaced by others, ensuring a good variety for those on a shopping spree.

What lies ahead for Wilton, as in the previous century, is uncertain. What happens towards the end of this century many of us will never know, but I think it can safely be said that the ancient town of Wilton will survive, its history enriched by a further 100 years of time.

Subscribers

Elvin R. Adams, Wilton, Wiltshire

Penny Adams (née Sutton), Lytchett Matravers, Dorset

Mr Peter W. Aldridge, Wilton, Wiltshire

Mrs Wendy Alford, Wilton, Wiltshire

Evelyn Arber, Wilton

John Aston, born 1936 Wilton, William Aston, Wilton Royal Carpet Factory, 1926–53

David M. Baldwin, South Newton, Wiltshire

John Baxter, Wilton, Wiltshire

Rex Baxter, Wilton

Mrs Karen D. Blackman (née Newman), Wilton, Wiltshire

Colin C. Blake, Chandlers Ford, Hampshire

Mary Blake, Wilton

Rev Derek W.F. Brice, Cheam, Surrey

Gillian Brown

Pat Brown, Allington

Eric H. Carter, Wilton, Wiltshire

Mary I. Clarke (Spencer)

Angela Compton, Wilton, Wiltshire

Martin Coombes, Wilton, Wiltshire

Barbara Couch (née Evans), Ontario, Canada

C.A. Davis, Wilton, Wiltshire

Mr Richard G. Dibble, Wilton, Wiltshire

David and Diana Dixey, Wilton 2006

Martin James Drewett, Wilton

Michael Peter Drewett, Wilton

Paul James Drewett, Wilton

Peter James Drewett, Wilton

Peter Edge, North Street, Wilton, Wiltshire

Mr David A. Elliott, Wilton, Wiltshire

C.A.J. Fitzherbert-Green, Wilton

Brian Ford, Wilton, Wiltshire

David Fraser, Wilton

Mark and Sandy Groves, Wilton, Salisbury, Wiltshire

Mr and Mrs P.D.B. Groves, Loudwater, Hertfordshire

Mr David Ellery Hann, Wilton, Wiltshire

C.F. Hardy and Family, Wilton, Wiltshire

Vivien Hardy, Great Ashby, Stevenage

Barbara Hare, Wilton

Gordon E. Harper, Bridport, Dorset – former resident of Wilton

Mrs M. Hatcher, worked for the Ellison family at Pit Folly 1936–39

Basil Hayter, Wilton, Wiltshire

A.G. and P.M. Henderson, Wilton

Ann and Richard Hindley, Wilton, Wiltshire

Susan and David Hindley, Corbridge, Northumberland

Sylvia M. Holloway

HQ Land Command, Officer's Mess

Stephen Gregory James, Wilton, Wiltshire. 24.04.06.

May Kiddle, Wilton, Wiltshire

Kevin Lench, Wilton, Wiltshire

Rachel Maidment (née Drewett), Wilton

Jenny A. Main

Tim and Jane Mayhew, Ugford Farmhouse, Wilton

Mr Douglas A. Morris, Andover, Hampshire

Mr Michael G. Morris, Wilton, Wiltshire

Rosslyn O'Connor, Wilton, Salisbury

Colin Stuart Partridge, Wilton, Wiltshire

B. Penny, Wilton, Wiltshire

Mrs Mary A. Read, Winterslow, Wiltshire

Priscilla Reed, Wilton, Wiltshire

John and Wendy Rees

The Rees Family, Victoria Road, Wilton

David J. Rhodes, Wilton, Wiltshire

Kayley and Alexander Rousell, Gillingham, Dorset

Marilyn, Justin, Jeremy, Terry Sainsbury, Wilton, Wiltshire

Mavis Sainsbury, Salisbury, Wiltshire

Rex Sawyer, Tisbury, Wiltshire

Jennie and Alistair Shearing, Wilton

Mr K. Shearing, Salisbury

P. Shergold, Wilton, Wiltshire

Michael E.J. Stokes

Norma Stone, Wilton, Wiltshire

H.J. Stout, Wilton, Wiltshire

Cecil and Cecilia Targett, Wilton, Wiltshire

Mrs W. Trethowan (née Evans), Tregaron, Wales

Roger W. Vercoe, Westbury, Wiltshire

John F.W. Walling, Newton Abbot, Devon

Mrs Carol Walter

Douglas Albert Watts, Kingsway, Wilton

Martyn E. White, Great Wishford

Wilton Town Council

Dennis Young, Little Dunham, Norfolk

Community Histories: Further Reading

The Book of Addiscombe • Canning and Clyde Road Residents Association and Friends

The Book of Addiscombe, Vol. II • Canning and Clyde Road Residents Association and Friends

The Book of Ashburton • Stuart Hands and Pete Webb

The Book of Axminster with Kilmington • Les Berry and Gerald Gosling

* The Book of Axmouth & the Undercliff • Ted Gosling and Mike Clement

The Book of Bakewell • Trevor Brighton

The Book of Bampton • Caroline Seward

The Book of Barnstaple • Avril Stone

The Book of Barnstaple, Vol. II • Avril Stone

The Book of The Bedwyns • Bedwyn History Society

* The Book of Bere Regis • Rodney Legg and John Pitfield

The Book of Bergh Apton • Geoffrey I. Kelly

The Book of Bickington • Stuart Hands

The Book of Bideford • Peter Christie and Alison Grant

Blandford Forum: A Millennium Portrait • Blandford Forum Town Council

* The Book of Blofield • Barbara Pilch

The Book of Boscastle • Rod and Anne Knight

The Book of Bourton-on-the-Hill, Batsford and Sezincote • Allen Firth

The Book of Bramford • Bramford Local History Group

The Book of Breage & Germoe • Stephen Polglase

The Book of Bridestowe • D. Richard Cann

* The Book of Bridgwater • Roger Evans

The Book of Bridport • Rodney Legg

The Book of Brixham • Frank Pearce

The Book of Buckfastleigh • Sandra Coleman

The Book of Buckland Monachorum & Yelverton • Pauline Hamilton-Leggett

The Book of Budleigh Salterton • D. Richard Cann

The Book of Carharrack • Carharrack Old Cornwall Society

The Book of Carshalton • Stella Wilks and Gordon Rookledge

The Parish Book of Cerne Abbas • Vivian and Patricia Vale

The Book of Chagford • Iain Rice

The Book of Chapel-en-le-Frith • Mike Smith

The Book of Chittlehamholt with Warkleigh & Satterleigh • Richard Lethbridge

The Book of Chittlehampton • Various

The Book of Codford • Romy Wyeth

The Book of Colney Heath • Bryan Lilley

The Book of Constantine • Moore and Trethowan

The Book of Cornwood and Lutton • Compiled by the People of the Parish

The Book of Crediton • John Heal

The Book of Creech St Michael • June Small

The Book of Crowcombe, Bicknoller and Sampford Brett • Maurice and Joyce Chidgey

The Book of Crudwell • Tony Pain

The Book of Cullompton • Compiled by the People of the Parish

The Book of Dawlish • Frank Pearce

The Book of Dulverton, Brushford, Bury & Exebridge • Dulverton and District Civic Society

The Book of Dunster • Hilary Binding

The Book of Easton • Easton Village History Project

The Book of Edale • Gordon Miller

The Ellacombe Book • Sydney R. Langmead

* The Book of Elmsett • Elmsett Local History Group

The Book of Exmouth • W.H. Pascoe

* The Book of Fareham • Lesley Burton and Brian Musselwhite

The Book of Grampound with Creed • Bane and Oliver

The Book of Gosport • Lesley Burton and Brian Musselwhite

The Book of Haughley • Howard Stephens

The Book of Hayle • Harry Pascoe

The Book of Hayling Island & Langstone • Peter Rogers

The Book of Helston • Jenkin with Carter

The Book of Hemyock • Clist and Dracott

The Book of Herne Hill • Patricia Jenkyns

The Book of Hethersett • Hethersett Society Research Group

The Book of High Bickington • Avril Stone

The Book of Honiton • Gerald Gosling

The Book of Ilsington • Dick Wills

* The Book of Kessingland • Maureen and Eric Long

The Book of Kingskerswell • Carsewella Local History Group

The Book of Lamerton • Ann Cole and Friends

Lanner, A Cornish Mining Parish • Sharron Schwartz and Roger Parker

The Book of Leigh & Bransford • Malcolm Scott

The Second Book of Leigh & Bransford • Malcolm Scott

The Book of Litcham with Lexham & Mileham • Litcham Historical and Amenity Society

The Book of Loddiswell • Loddiswell Parish History Group

The New Book of Lostwithiel • Barbara Fraser

The Book of Lulworth • Rodney Legg

The Book of Lustleigh • Joe Crowdy

The Book of Lydford • Compiled by Barbara Weeks

The Book of Lyme Regis • Rodney Legg

The Book of Manaton • Compiled by the People of the Parish

The Book of Markyate • Markyate Local History Society

The Book of Mawnan • Mawnan Local History Group

The Book of Meavy • Pauline Hemery

The Book of Mere • Dr David Longbourne

The Book of Minehead with Alcombe • Binding and Stevens

The Book of Monks Orchard and Eden Park • Ian Muir and Pat Manning